AN ANALYSIS

OF

PALEY'S

MORAL AND POLITICAL

PHILOSOPHY,

IN THE WAY OF QUESTION AND ANSWER,

FOR THE USE OF STUDENTS.

Cambridge:

PRINTED FOR R. NEWBY, TRINITY STREET;

AND

G. AND W. B. WHITTAKER, AVE MARIA LANE,

LONDON.

1824.

Printed by T. C. Newby, Angel-Hill, Bury.

ADVERTISEMENT.

THE favourable reception given to their "Analysis of Paley's Evidences," has encouraged the publishers to proceed with his "*Moral and Political Philosophy*" upon the same plan, comprehending all the arguments, together with all the necessary illustration used by the author. At the same time, every endeavour has been made, consistently with this view of general utility, to reduce the bulk of the original work, and, by dividing it into questions and answers, to direct the mind of the student to the particular aim and scope of the several arguments.

ALOGY OF THE ENGLISH TONGUE. *See I*

HEBREW, the Language of Adam and Noa

SHEM, or Asia.

JAPHETH, or Europe.

Persians or Elamites, and Dacians.

Magogites, or Scythians.

Thobelites or Iberians and Etruscans.

aracens, and Tartars.

Titans, Teutons, or German Goths.

Huns, Vandals, Scots, and Irish.

Normans.

Saxons.

Italians.

Spaniar and Portug

s.

ENGLISH.

MORAL PHILOSOPHY.

BOOK I.

PRELIMINARY CONSIDERATIONS.

CHAP. I.

DEFINITION AND USE OF THE SCIENCE.

Q. What is meant by Moral Philosophy, Morality, Ethics, &c.?

A. That science which teaches men their duty and the reasons of it.

Q. What is the use of such a study?

A. Without it the rules of life, by which men are ordinarily governed, often mislead them, through a defect either in the rule, or the application.

Q. What are these rules?

A. The Law of Honour, the Law of the Land, and the Scriptures.

CHAP. II.

THE LAW OF HONOUR.

Q. What is the Law of Honour?

A. A system of rules constructed by people of fashion, solely to facilitate their intercourse with each other.

Q. What then is adverted to by this Law?

A. Only what tends to incommode this intercourse: wherefore it only prescribes and regulates duties betwixt *equals*, omitting the Supreme Being, and our inferiors.

Q. Why are profaneness, neglect of public or private devotion, want of charity, cruelty, &c. accounted no breaches of honour?

A. Because a man is not the less agreeable as a companion for these vices, nor unqualified for those concerns which are usually transacted between gentlemen.

Q. Why is the law of honour favourable to licentiousness?

A. Because it is constituted for the conveniency of men occupied in the pursuit of pleasure. Thus it allows of fornication, prodigality, drunkenness, duelling, &c. and lays no stress upon the opposite virtues.

CHAP. III.

THE LAW OF THE LAND.

Q. By what part of mankind is the Law of the Land often made the rule of life?

A. By those who are beneath the Laws of Honour: and these are satisfied whilst they do, or omit nothing for which the law can punish them.

Q. Now under what two defects does every system of human laws, considered as a rule of life, labour?

A. 1. They omit many duties as not objects of compulsion; *viz.* piety to God, bounty to the poor, &c. &c. those duties which by their nature must be voluntary, being considered out of the reach of their authority.—2dly, they suffer to go unpunished, those crimes which cannot be previously defined, as luxury, prodigality, disrespect to parents, &c.

Q. What is the alternative?

A. Either the law must precisely define the offence it punishes, or the discretion of the magistrate must determine wether the offence be that which the law designed to punish; which is just so much tyranny. Where, therefore, the distinction between right and wrong is too subtile to be ascertained by preconcerted language, the law generally leaves men to themselves.

CHAP. IV.

THE SCRIPTURES.

Q. Are we to expect in the SS. specific directions for every moral doubt that can arise?

A. No. Such a detail of particular precepts would have rendered the sacred volume too bulky to be either read or circulated.

Q. How is morality taught in Scripture?

A. General rules are laid down of piety, justice, benevolence, and purity; such as worshipping God in spirit and in truth; doing as we would be done by, &c. &c.

Q. How are these rules illustrated?

A. Occasionally either by *fictitious examples*, as in the parable of the good Samaritan; or by *instances which actually presented themselves*, as in Christ's reproof of his disciples at the Samaritan village; or, *lastly*, in the *resolution of questions which those about our Saviour proposed to him*; as his answer to the young man who asked him, "What lack I yet?" &c.

Q. In what point alone does this method differ from that in which Grammar, Navigation, and other practical sciences are taught?

A. The examples in the SS. are not annexed to the rules with didactic regularity, but delivered as occasion suggested them; a method which gave them a peculiar energy and persuasion, especially to those who were present.

Q. Beside this, what do the SS. presuppose in the persons to whom they speak?

A. A knowledge of the principles of natural justice.

Q. And how are they employed?

A. Not so much to teach new rules, as to add *new sanctions* and *greater certainty*, which seems to be the proper business of a revelation, and most wanted.

CHAP. V.

THE MORAL SENSE.

Q. How does Paley state this question?

A. He relates from Valerius Maximus the story of Caius Toranius, whose father being proscribed by the Triumvirate, was basely betrayed by his son, for whose safety and honour he was principally anxious. He then asks, if the story were related to a savage without experience or instruction, who had been quite cut off from any intercourse with his species, and was therefore under no influence of example, authority, sympathy, or habit, whether such an one would feel, upon the relation, any degree of that sentiment of disapprobation concerning Toranius's conduct which we feel?

Q. How does he proceed in his statement?

A. He observes that they who maintain the existence of a *moral sense*, of an *instinctive* love of virtue and hatred of vice, or an intuitive perception of right and wrong, affirm that he would; whilst those who deny such an existence, affirm the contrary—and upon this issue is joined.

Q. Now as the experiment never has nor can be made, how can the event be judged of?

A. By probable reasons only.

Q. What do they, who contend for the affirmative, declare?

A. That we approve examples of generosity, gratitude, &c., and condemn the contrary, instantly, without deliberation, and disinterestedly, often without being conscious of, or able to give a reason for this approbation; which is also uniform and universal, the same sorts of conduct being approved or disapproved in all ages and countries of the world.

Q. What answer do the opponents of the system give to these assertions?

A. 1. They contradict the fact of the alleged uniformity; and show from the accounts of historians and travellers that there scarcely exists a vice which in some countries and in some ages has not been countenanced and approved by public opinion: that theft, for instance, which is severely punished in most countries, was not unfrequently rewarded by the laws of Sparta; that though a polished European is delighted when he meets with the appearance of comfort and happiness in social life; a wild American is equally so when he beholds his victim writhing in torture at the stake; that among ourselves some call the forgiveness of injuries, magnanimity, and others meanness; all which looks little like the indelible characters of Nature.

Q. Since it cannot be denied, although this uniformity does not exist, that some sorts of actions do command and receive the esteem of mankind *more* than others, and that the approbation of them is general though not universal, they account for this general approbation of virtue as follows:

"Having experienced, in some instance, a particular conduct to be beneficial to ourselves, or observed that it would be so, a sentiment of approbation rises up in our minds; which sentiment afterwards accompanies the idea or mention of the same conduct, although the private advantage which first excited it no longer exist."

And this continuance of the passion, after the reason of it has ceased, is no more than what happens in other cases, especially in the love of money. Thus the custom of approving certain actions commenced; and it is not difficult to explain how it is transmitted and continued, viz. from authority, and imitation, from habits gained in early youth and strengthened by age, from censure and encouragement, from looks, conversation, and the general turn of language, &c.

Q. With regard to imitation, which has been

mentioned among the existing classes of similar moral sentiments, where is the efficacy of this principle most observable?

A. In children; in whom if there be any thing which deserves the name of an *instinct*, it is their *propensity to imitation*.

Q. Now what do children imitate or apply most readily?

A. Expressions of affection and aversion, of approbation, hatred, resentment, and the like; and when these passions and expressions are once connected by the association which unites words with their ideas, the passion will follow the expression, and attach upon the object to which the child has been accustomed to apply the epithet.

Q. What is another considerable objection to the system of moral instincts?

A. No maxims are *innate*, since none are absolutely and universally *true*. Thus, veracity itself is *excused* in many cases towards an enemy, a thief, or a madman: the like may be observed concerning the obligation of promises; and so of most other general rules when they come to be actually applied.

Q. What other argument has been also proposed on this side of the question?

A. It is said, that together with the instinct there must have been implanted a clear and precise idea of the object upon which it was to attach; these being inseparable, even in imagination; or, in plainer terms, if we be urged by nature to the approbation of particular actions, we must have received also from nature a distinct conception of those actions; which is not the fact.

Q. Why will this argument, though difficult to answer, fail to convince?

A. Because it bears alike against all instincts, those of brutes as well as of men.

Q. Upon the whole what does Paley conclude?

A. Either that there are no such instincts as compose what is called the moral sense; or that they are not distinguishable from prejudices or habits, and therefore not to be depended upon in moral reasoning. It is not safe to assume certain principles as so many dictates of nature, and draw from them conclusions as to right and wrong actions independently of their tendency.

Q. By what example does he illustrate this?

A. By that of Aristotle, who lays it down as a self-evident maxim that nature intended barbarians to be slaves, and from that maxim proceeds to justify the then prevailing policy.

Q. As nothing is so soon made as a maxim, and the laws of custom are very apt to be mistaken for the order of nature, what will be the tendency of a system of morality built upon instinct?

A. To find out reasons and excuses for opinions and practices already established; but it will seldom correct or reform either.

Q. If we admit the existence of these instincts, and ask what is their authority, how has it been replied?

A. That no man can act in deliberate opposition

to them without a secret remorse of conscience.

Q. How may this answer be withstood?

A. This may be borne with if the sinner finds the pleasure of the sin to exceed the remorse of conscience, of which he alone is the judge, and concerning which, when he feels them both together, he can hardly be mistaken; the moral-instinct man has then nothing more to offer.

For if he allege that these instincts are so many indications of the will of God, and presages of what we are to look for hereafter; this is to resort to a rule and motive ulterior to the instincts themselves, and at which we shall arrive by a surer road.

Q. In Paley's system, therefore, what does this celebrated question become?

A. One of mere curiosity.

CHAP. VI.

HUMAN HAPPINESS.

Q. What is meant by the word Happy?

A. It is a relative term: *i. e.* when we call a man happy, we mean that he is happier than others with whom we compare him, or than he himself was in some other situation.

Q. In what does happiness consist?

A. Any condition may be called happy in which

the aggregate of pleasure exceeds that of pain; the degree of happiness depends upon the quantity of this excess; and the greatest quantity of it attainable in human life, is what we mean by happiness.

Q. In this enquiry what does Paley omit?

A. Much usual declamation upon the dignity and capacity of our nature; the superiority of the rational over the animal part of our constitution; the refinement of some satisfactions, or the grossness of others.

Q. Why does he omit this?

A. Because he holds that pleasures differ only in continuance and intensity.

Q. What then does he make it his business to shew?

A. First, in what Human Happiness does consist. Secondly, in what it does not.

Q. In what, then, does it *not* consist?

A. It does *not* consist in the pleasures of sense, by which are meant the animal gratifications of eating, drinking, &c., nor in the more refined pleasures, such as music, painting, &c., nor in the pleasures of active sports, as hunting, shooting, &c.

Q. Why do not these pleasures constitute Happiness?

A. Because—First, they occupy a very short portion of our time: Secondly, they lose their relish by repetition; for, who knows not the difference between a new and a familiar gratification?

Thirdly, The eagerness for intense delights

takes away the relish from all others; and as such delights fall rarely in our way, the greater part of our time becomes, from this cause, empty and uneasy.

Q. By what delusion are men great sufferers in their happiness?

A. They expect too much from what is called pleasure, *i. e.* from those intense delights which vulgarly engross that name, and thus render themselves unfit for those gently soothing engagements, the due variety and succession of which are the only things that supply a continued stream of happiness.

Q. What may be observed of those whose professed pursuit is pleasure, unrestrained by fortune or conscience?

A. That with whatever eagerness and expectation they set out, they become by degrees fastidious in their choice of pleasure, languid in the enjoyment, yet miserable under the want of it?

Q. Why so?

A. These pleasures soon arrive at a limit from which they ever afterwards decline; there being an imperfection of the organs, for which if you try to compensate by repetition, you suffer still more by satiety, and the diminution of sensibility—to say nothing of the loss of opportunities or the decay of faculties, which leave the voluptuary destitute and desperate.—It is also allowed that pleasures purchased by the incumbrance of fortune do not compensate for the perpetual irritation of embarrassed circumstances.

Q. Does happiness consist in an exemption from pain, labour, care, &c. &c.?

A. No: such a state is usually attended, not with ease, but with depression of spirits, imaginary anxieties, and hypochondriacal affections; hence the expectations of those who retire from business to enjoy the remainder of their days in leisure, seldom answer; much less theirs, who quit the world for cloisters and hermitages.

Q. What may be said of those imaginary distresses which men feel for want of real ones?

A. As they depend upon no assignable subject of uneasiness, they often admit of no relief.

Q. Upon this principle how may even a moderate pain be useful?

A. It acts as a refreshment upon which the attention may fasten and spend itself; the same may be observed of a literary controversy or law-suit, and particularly of gaming, the passion for which in men of fortune and liberal minds, is only to be accounted for on this principle.

Q. Does happiness consist in greatness, rank, or elevated station?

A. Were it true that all superiority afforded pleasure, it would follow that the more persons we were superior to, in the same proportion we should be the happier: but no superiority yields any satisfaction, save that over our equals. The Shepherd perceives no pleasure in his superiority over his dog; the farmer over the shepherd; the lord over the farmer; or the king over the lord—But if the same shepherd can run or wrestle better than all the peasants of his village; if the farmer be superior to any in the hundred, the lord to any nobleman in the county, and the king to any prince in Europe; in all these cases the parties feel an actual satisfaction in their superiority.

Q. What conclusion follows from this?

A. That the pleasures of ambition, supposed to be peculiar to high stations, are common to all. The farrier who is in greater request for shoeing a horse than any other in his neighbourhood, may possess the delight of distinction as truly as the statesman, scholar, and soldier, who have filled Europe with their fame. No superiority except that over a rival is of any account, and rivalships fall out amongst men of all degrees. Thus, it is not what either possesses that constitutes the pleasure, but what one possesses more than the other.

Q. We have shown that happiness does not consist in greatness: since its pleasures are common to all conditions, is it doubtful whether the pursuits of ambition be productive of more happiness or misery to the pursuers?

A. Yes: for as the pleasure of success is exquisite, so also is the pain of disappointment. The pleasure is short; we soon cease to look back upon those we have left behind, and engage in a succession of struggles whilst there is a rival left within the compass of our views; and when there is none, the pleasure with the pursuit is at an end.

Q. Having seen what happiness does not consist in, what does Paley next propose to consider?

A. In what it does consist.

Q. What is our great business in the conduct of life?

A. To know beforehand what will please us, and what pleasures will hold out. This knowledge is more difficult than it may appear at first sight, for sometimes pleasures which are alluring in the prospect prove insipid in the possession, or do not last; others also arise which we have missed by not foreseeing; and after the experiment has been made change is commonly impracticable; besides shifting and changing would generate a habit of restlessness most destructive to happiness.

Q. Is it possible to propose any plan of happiness which would succeed with all?

A. The diversity of taste, capacity, and constitution in the human species, and the variety which habit and fashion have introduced in these particulars would render this impracticable.

Q. What then is all that can be said?

A. That there is a presumption in favour of those conditions of life in which men appear most cheerful and contented; for though the apparent happiness of mankind be not always a true measure of their real happiness, it is the best we have.

Q. Taking this for a guide, in what does Paley believe happiness to consist?

A. First, in the exercise of the social affections; since those commonly have good spirits who have about them many objects of endearment, as wife, children, &c.; to the want of which may be imputed the peevishness of Monks. Of the same nature is the pleasure which results from acts of bounty and beneficence.

Q. What does happiness, secondly, consist in ?

A. The exercise of our faculties in pursuit of some engaging end : for it seems as if no plenitude of present gratifications can make the possessor happy for a continuance, unless he have something to hope for and to look forward to. We may conclude this to be the case from comparing the spirits of men engaged in any interesting pursuit with the dejection of those who want nothing more, or who have too soon drained the sources of their satisfaction. It is this vacuity of mind which carries the rich to the horse-course and gaming-table, and engages them in pursuits of which the success bears no proportion to the solicitude and expense with which it is sought.

Q. What does Paley say of Hope, which thus appears to be of so much importance to our happiness ?

A. It is of two kinds ;—that where there is something to be done towards obtaining the object of our hope, and that where there is nothing to be done ; the first alone being of any value ; the latter apt to corrupt into impatience.

Q. What is required for enabling us to provide a succession of pleasurable engagements ?

A. Judgment in the choice of *ends*, and a command of imagination by which we may transfer a pleasure to the *means;* after which, the end may be forgotten as soon as we please. Hence those pleasures are most valuable which are most productive of activity in the pursuit.

Q. Why has a man who is earnest in his endeavours after happiness in a future state, in this respect an advantage over all the world?

A. Because he has constantly before his eyes an object of supreme importance, productive of perpetual activity, the pursuit of which (and it can be said of no other,) lasts during his life. Yet even he has many ends besides the *far end*, but then they are all capable of being referred to it.

Q. What does Paley remark upon the importance of engagement?

A. As it is of the greatest importance in itself, so the more significant our engagements are, the better: yet *any* which are innocent, are better than none; as the building a house or the raising a tulip, &c., for whilst our minds are occupied with the business before us, we are commonly happy, but when the mind is *absent* and the thoughts wandering, we are often miserable.

Q. Thirdly, upon what does happiness depend?

A. Upon the prudent constitution of the habits. An art in which the secret of human happiness in a great measure consists, is to form the habits in such a manner that a change may be for the better. The habits themselves are much the same; for whatever is made habitual becomes easy and indifferent.

Q. What follows from this?

A. The advantage is with those habits which

allow of an indulgence in the deviation from them. The luxurious receive not more pleasure from their dainties, than the peasant from his bread and cheese; but the peasant whenever he goes abroad finds a feast, whereas the epicure scarcely escapes disgust. The card-player and the peasant pass their time much alike except that a suspension of employment distresses the one but is a refreshment to the other; and this appears in the different effects that Sunday produces upon the two, being to one a burthen and to the other a day of recreation. Similar observations may be made upon one who has learnt to live alone, and another who has accustomed himself to constant society, when both are obliged to be in solitude.

A reader, who has inured himself to books of science and argumentation, if a novel, a well-written pamphlet, a narrative of a curious voyage, or a journal of a traveller, fall in his way, enjoys the entertainment whilst it lasts, and can return to his graver reading, without distaste. Another, with whom nothing will go down but works of humour, pleasantry and novelty, will consume a bookseller's window in a forenoon: but he is rather in search of diversion than diverted; and as books to his taste are few, and rapidly read, he is soon left without resource from this principal supply of harmless amusement.

Q. What may be said concerning circumstances of fortune?

A. So far as they conduce to happiness, it is not the income, but the increase of income, that affords the pleasure. One who begins with a hundred, and advances his income to a thousand pounds a year, and an other who sets off with a thousand, and dwindles down to a hundred, may, in the course of their time, have the receipt and spending of the same sum of money: yet their satisfaction will be very different.

Q. Fourthly, what does happiness consist in?

A. In health; by which is understood, as well freedom from bodily distempers, as that tranquillity and alacrity of mind, which we call good spirits; depending commonly upon the same causes and management, as our bodily constitution.

Health, in this sense, is the one thing needful; therefore no pains or restraint for its sake is too much: whatever difficulties it lays us under, a man, who pursues his happiness rationally and resolutely, will submit.

When we are in perfect health and spirits, we feel a happiness independent of any outward gratification, and of which we can give no account. This is an enjoyment which the Deity has annexed to life; and it probably constitutes, in a great measure, the happiness of infants and brutes, especially of the lower and sedentary orders of animals, for which it is difficult to find out any amusement.

Q. What two conclusions will the above account of human happiness justify?

A. First, that happiness is pretty equally distributed amongst the different orders of civil society.

Secondly, that vice has no advantage over virtue, even with respect to this world's happiness.

CHAP. VII.

VIRTUE.

Q. What is virtue?

A. *The doing good to mankind, in obedience to the will of God, and for the sake of everlasting happiness*—according to which definition, "the good of mankind" is the subject; "the will of God" the rule; and everlasting happiness the motive of human virtue.

Q. How has virtue been divided by some moralists?

A. Into *benevolence*, which proposes good ends; *prudence*, which suggests the best means of attaining them; *fortitude*, which enables us to encounter opposing difficulties; and *temperance*, which overcomes the passions that obstruct our pursuit.

Q. How can you illustrate this by example?

A. *Benevolence* prompts us to defend an oppressed orphan; *prudence* suggests the best method of so doing; *fortitude* enables us to bear up against any danger, loss, or repulse, attending our undertakings, and *temperance* keeps under the love of ease or amusement which might divert us from it.

Q. In what other manner has virtue been divided?

A. Into *prudence* and *benevolence* only; prudence attentive to our own interest; benevolence to that of others; both directed to the increase of happiness; and taking equal concern in the present and future.

Q. What are the four Cardinal Virtues?

A. *Prudence, Fortitude, Temperance,* and *Justice.*

Q. What is the division of Virtue, to which we are now most accustomed?

A. That into duties—towards *God*; as piety, reverence, &c.; towards *others*, as justice, charity, &c.; towards *ourselves*, as sobriety, temperance, &c.

Q. What does Paley proceed to state?

A. Some observations relating to the general regulation of human conduct; unconnected, indeed but very worthy of attention.

I. Q. How is it proved that mankind act more from habit than reflection?

A. It is only on few and great occasions that men deliberate at all; on fewer still that they inquire regularly into the rectitude or depravity of what they are about to do, or wait for the result of it. We are generally determined by an impulse which is the effect of pre-established habits.

Q. How is this constitution well adapted to the

exigencies of human life, and to the imbecility of our moral principle ?

A. In the current and rapid opportunities of life, there is little leisure for reflection ; and even were there more, a man who has to reason about his duty, when tempted to transgress it, is almost sure to reason himself into an error.

Q. If we are thus passive under our habits, what becomes of *virtue* and *vice*, and what is the use of any moral or religious knowledge ?

A. In the *forming and contracting* of these habits.

Q. What important rule of life results from hence ?

A. That many things are to be done, and abstained from, solely for the sake of habit.

Q. Can you explain this by example ?

A. A beggar in great apparent distress, asks our charity. If we argue whether the distress be real, whether its relief might not encourage idleness, invite impostors, &c., it may seem doubtful whether we ought to give him any thing ; but when we reflect that this misery excites our pity, and that it is of great consequence to us to cherish this quality, which is soon stifled by opposition, we shall yield to compassion rather than offer violence to a habit of so much use. A man of confirmed good habits will act so without consideration.

Again ; a man brought up with a dread of lying, even if an occasion present itself, where at the expence of a little veracity, he may display his wit, divert his company, and, at the same time, injure no one by this liberty, when he reflects that his scruples about lying have hitherto preserved him from it, and that these scruples will soon wear away, and leave him subject to this most pernicious of all bad habits, such an one will forego present pleasure, rather than lay the foundation of so contemptible a character.

Q. From what has been said, what may be explained?

A. The nature of *habitual* virtue.

Q. Notwithstanding the previous definition of virtue, *it appears that* a man may perform many a virtuous act, without having either the good of mankind, the will of God, or everlasting happiness in his thoughts. How is this to be understood?

A. In the same manner that a man may be a very good servant, without being conscious at every turn, of an express attention to his master's interest; but to do this, he must have long served under the direction of such a motive.

Q. Does Paley agree to the saying that man is a bundle of habits?

A. Yes; he asserts that there is not a quality or function of body or mind, which does not feel the influence of this great law of animated nature.

II. Q. What answer may be given to the objection that the Christian religion has not ascertained the precise quantity of virtue neccessary to salvation?

A. It is impossible for any form of words to be devised which might express this *quantity*, and it is also impossible to constitute a standard of moral attainments, suited to the diversity, which subsists in the capacities and opportunities of different men.

Q. What seems most agreeable to our ideas of justice and consonant to the SS. to suppose?

A. That there are rewards and punishments of all degrees, from the greatest happiness to extreme misery.

Q. What follows from this?

A. That whatever advancement we make in virtue, we procure a proportionable accession of future happiness, whilst every accumulation of vice is an accumulation of misery.

Q. How may we answer what has been said, "that providence would never admit one part of mankind into heaven and condemn others to hell," since there must be little to choose between the worst man who is admitted and the best who is excluded?

A. That there may be as little to choose in their conditions.

Q. What general positions does Paley think may be safely advanced on this subject?

A. 1. That a state of happiness is not to be expected by those who are conscious of no moral or religious rule, who have been prompted to or withheld from no action by any regard to virtue or religion; for a brute would be as proper an object of reward as such a man, and religion itself would cease to have either use or authority.

2. That a state of happiness is not to be expected by those who reserve to themselves the habitual practice of any one sin, or the neglect of one known duty; because no obedience can proceed from proper motives, which is not universal; because such an allowance [illegible] to [illegible] of all sins; and because when our *duties* are recited in the SS. they are put *collectively*, *i. e.* they are all of them required in the Christian character, (See 2 Peter i. 5, 6, 7.) and when *vices* are enumerated they are put *disjunctively*, as separately and severally excluding the sinner from heaven. (See 1 Peter iv. 8.) Those texts which seem to lean a contrary way, as that "charity shall cover a multitude of sins," &c., cannot, for the above reasons, apply to sins deliberately and obstinately persisted in.

3. That a state of mere unprofitableness will not go unpunished. This is clearly shewn by the parable of the talents, (Matt. xxv. 24.) &c., which supersedes all further reasoning upon the subject.

III. Q. How is the rule, that in every question of conduct where one side is doubtful and the other safe, *we are bound to take the safe side*, best explained?

A. By the example of suicide. A reasoner upon the subject may *doubt* whether he can lawfully destroy himself: he can have no doubt but that it is lawful to let it alone. By virtue of this rule, he is bound to pursue the safe side whilst a doubt remains upon his mind.

Q. Allowing that it is required to take the safe side, what more does this observation require?

A. That the action or omission concerning which we hesitate, whatever it may be, would then be sinful while this doubt remains on our minds. This is expressly told by St. Paul, Rom. xiv. 23.

and because when our duties are recited in the SS. they are put collectively, i. e. they are all of them required in the Christian character, (See 2 Peter i. 5, 6, 7.) and when vices are enumerated they are put distributively, as separately and severally excluding the sinner from heaven. (See 1 Cor. vi. 9.) Those texts which seem to lean a contrary way, as that "charity shall cover a multitude of sins," &c. cannot, for the above reasons, apply to sins deliberately and obstinately persisted in.

3. That a state of such uncertainties will not go unpunished. This is clearly shewn by the parable of the talents, (Matt. xxv. 24.) &c., which supersedes all further reasoning upon the subject.

III. Q. How is the rule, that in every question of conduct where one side is doubtful and the other safe, we are bound to take the safe side, best explained?

A. By the example of suicide. A man upon the subject may doubt whether he can lawfully destroy himself, he can have no doubt but that it is lawful to let it alone. By virtue of this rule, he is bound to pursue the safe side whilst a doubt remains upon his mind.

neral happiness, is required by the will of God; and what has all these properties, must needs be right; for right means conformity to the rule we go by, whatever that rule be.

SECONDLY, it is to be observed, that these answers all leave the matter short; for the inquirer may turn round and ask his teacher, Why am I obliged to do what is right; to act agreeably to the fitness of things; &c. or to obey the will of God?

Q. What is the proper method of conducting the inquiry?

BOOK II.

MORAL OBLIGATION.

CHAP. I.

THE QUESTION, *WHY AM I OBLIGED TO KEEP MY WORD?* CONSIDERED.

Q. Why am I obliged to keep my word?

A. Because it is right, say some persons; because it is agreeable to the fitness of things; or, it is conformable to reason and nature; or, it is conformable to truth; or, it promotes the public good; or, because it is required by the will of God.

Q. Upon which different accounts, what two things are observable?

A. FIRST, that they all ultimately coincide.

The fitness of things, means their fitness to produce happiness: the nature of things, means that constitution of the world by which some actions produce happiness, and others misery; reason, is the principle by which we discover or judge of this constitution; truth, is this judgment expressed or drawn out into propositions. So it necessarily follows, that what promotes the happiness of the whole, is agreeable to the fitness of things, to nature, to reason, and to truth: and what promotes the general happiness, is required by the will of God; and what has all the above properties, must needs be *right*; for, right means conformity to the rule we go by, whatever that rule be.

SECONDLY, it is to be observed, that these answers all leave the matter *short*; for, the inquirer may turn round and ask his teacher, *Why* am I obliged to do what is right; to act agreeably to the fitness of things; &c. or to obey the will of God?

Q. What is the proper method of conducting the inquiry?

A. FIRST, to examine what we mean when we say a man is *obliged* to do any thing; and THEN, to show, *why* he is obliged to do the thing which we have proposed as an example, namely, "to keep his word."

CHAP. II.

WHAT WE MEAN WHEN WE SAY A MAN IS OBLIGED TO DO A THING.

Q. When is a man said to be *obliged?*

A. "*When he is urged by a violent motive, resulting from the command of another.*"

Q. 1. Why must the motive be violent?

A. If a person, who has done me some little service, or has a small place in his disposal, ask me for my vote, I may give it him, from gratitude

[illegible]
[illegible]
great benefactor, [illegible] de-
pends, require it, I give it him of course; and say
as an answer, that my father or my master *obliged*
me to do it; that I had received so many favours
from, or had so great a dependence upon, such a
one, that I was *obliged* to vote as he directed me.

Q. II. Why must it result from the *command* of another?

A. Let a man be offered a gratuity for doing any thing, he is not *obliged* by that offer to do it; though he may be [illegible] [illegible] considers himself as *obliged* to comply, though he might lose less by a refusal in this case, than the former.

Q. Though it may be too much to say, that the words *obligation* and *obliged* are uniformly used in this sense, yet in what cases may we always reckon ourselves to be obliged?

A. Whenever the motive is violent enough, and coupled with the idea of command, authority, law, or the will of a superior.

Q. And from this account of obligation, what follows?

A. That we can be obliged to nothing, but what we are to gain or lose something by; for nothing else can be a violent motive to us. As we should not be obliged to obey the laws, or the magistrate, unless rewards or punishments, pleasure or pain, depended upon our obedience;

[illegible] without the question [illegible] right, [illegible] or to obey the commands of God.

CHAP. III.

THE QUESTION, WHY AM I OBLIGED TO KEEP MY WORD?

Q. The preceding definition of obliged being kept in mind, if it be asked Why am I obliged to keep my word; what will be the answer?

A. Because I am urged by a violent motive (namely, the expectation of being after this life rewarded, if I do, or punished for it, if I do not,) resulting from the command of another (namely, of God); which solution goes to the bottom of the subject, as no further question can reasonably be asked.

Q. What, therefore, is our motive, and what our rule?

A. Private happiness, and the will of God.

Q. Whence does Paley say that an air of mystery arose, which seemed to hang over this subject, when he first turned his thoughts to it?

A. He supposed, with many authors, that to be obliged to do a thing, was very different from being induced only to do it; and that the obligation to practise virtue, &c., was quite different, [illegible].

Q. [illegible] to what appears?

A. That moral obligation is like all others; and is nothing more than an inducement of sufficient strength, and resulting, in some way, from the command of another.

Q. How do you exemplify the difference between an act of *prudence*, and an act of *duty*?

A. If I distrusted a man who owed me a sum of money, it would be an act of prudence to get another bound with him; but I should hardly call it an act of duty. On the other hand, it would be a very unusual kind of language, to say, that, as my friend, when he went abroad, placed a box of jewels in my hands, it would be prudent in me to preserve it for him till he returned.

Q. In what, then, is the difference, since in both cases we consider solely what we shall gain or lose by the act?

A. The only difference is this, that in the one case we consider what we shall gain or lose in the present world; in the other case, we consider also what we shall gain or lose in the world to come.

Q. [illegible]

A. [illegible].

Q. [illegible]

A. That virtue conducts [illegible] happiness [illegible] of it than he could attain by a different [illegible].

[illegible]

[illegible] tion of rewards and punishments at his pleasure [illegible]

[illegible] foundation upon which the whole [illegible]

[illegible]

CHAP. IV.

[illegible]

Q. This being our rule, what will be included in inquiring what is our duty, in any instance, or, what we are obliged to do?

A. To inquire what is the will of God in that instance; which consequently becomes the whole business of morality.

Q. Now what are the two methods of coming at the will of God on any point?

A. I. By his express declarations, where they are to be had, and which must be sought for in Scripture.

II. By what we can discover of his designs and disposition from his works; or, as we usually call it, the light of nature.

Q. What observations has Paley here subjoined?

[illegible]

or explain them, by what he [illegible] had from other quarters of his master's general inclination or intentions.

Mr. Hume, in the fourth Appendix to his Principles of Morals, has been pleased to complain of the modern scheme of uniting Ethics with the Christian Theology. But what has Mr. Hume [illegible] union? But any one read the 2nd part of the [illegible]

[illegible]

The method of coming at the will of [illegible]

[illegible] Mr. [illegible]

[illegible] only [illegible] that God [illegible] happiness of his creatures, and, consequently, [illegible] [illegible] or explain them, by what [illegible] left from other [illegible] of his master's general inclinations or intentions.

Mr. Hume, in the fourth Appendix to his Principles of Morals, has been pleased to complain of the modern scheme of [illegible] Ethics with the Christian Theology. But what has Mr. Hume himself [illegible] this union? Let any one read the 2nd part of the 9th section of [illegible] any motives there proposed [illegible] But the [illegible] If they be in fact [illegible] [illegible] thing [illegible]

The method of coming at the will of [illegible]

[illegible]

can be attributed to accident? [illegible]

[illegible] in different terms?

A. Contrivance proves design; and the tendency of the contrivance shows the disposition of the designer. The world abounds with contrivances; and all which we are acquainted with, are directed to beneficial purposes. Evil, no doubt, exists; but is never, that we can perceive, the object of contrivance. Thus, teeth are contrived to eat, not to ache; their aching now and then is incidental to the contrivance, not the object of it. In describing implements of husbandry, you would hardly say of the sickle, that it is made to cut the reaper's fingers, though this accident often happens: but if you had occasion to [illegible] to extend [illegible] the very objects of contrivance. [illegible] in the works of nature. [illegible] pose; and no anatomist ever discovered [illegible] of organization calculated to produce pain and disease. Since, then, God hath provided for our happiness, and the world appears constituted with this design at first, so long as this constitution is upholden by him, we must in reason suppose the same design to continue.

Q. Paley observes, that many persons are sooner convinced of a truth by a single example than by the contemplation of universal nature. What example does he give, in which he himself particularly recognises the benevolence of the Deity?

A. The pleasures of very young children. The pleasures of adults may be reckoned partly of their own procuring; especially if there has been any industry or contrivance to come at them; or if they are founded upon any qualification of their own acquiring. But the pleasures of a healthy infant are so manifestly provided for it by another, that every child at its sport affords a kind of sensible evidence of the finger of God, and of the disposition which directs it.

Q. What do we conclude therefore?

A. That God wills and wishes the happiness of his creatures.

Q. And this conclusion being once established, what are we at liberty to proceed with?

A. The rule built upon it, namely, "that the method of coming at the will of God, concerning any action, by the light of nature, is to inquire into its tendency to promote or diminish the general happiness."

A. That the bad consequences of actions are twofold, particular and general.

Q. What are the particular bad consequences of an action?

A. The mischief which that single action directly and immediately occasions.

Q. [illegible] ? [illegible] Whatever is expedient, is right. It is the utility of any moral rule alone, which constitutes the obligation of it.

[illegible]

Q. But to all this [illegible]

A. The fright and pain which the deceased [illegible]

A. That many actions are useful, which no man in his senses will allow to be right. There are occasions in which the hand of the assassin would be very useful. As when the possessor of some great estate employs his influence and fortune to annoy, corrupt, or oppress, all about him. When his estate would devolve, by his death, to a successor of an opposite character. It might be useful to rob a miser and give the money to the poor, as this money would then produce more happiness?

Q. Must we then admit such actions to be right, which would be to justify assassination, plunder, and perjury; or must we give up our principle, that the criterion of right is utility?

A. It is not necessary to do either.

Q. What, then, is the true answer?

A. That these actions, after all, are not useful, and for that reason alone, are not right.

Q. To see this point clearly, what must be remarked?

A. That the bad consequences of actions are twofold, *particular* and *general*.

Q. What are the particular bad consequences of an action?

A. The mischief which that single action directly and immediately occasions.

Q. [illegible]

[illegible]

Q. [illegible]

A. The fright and pain which the deceased [illegible]

[illegible]

Q. [illegible]

[illegible]

Q. [illegible]

A. [illegible]

Q. [illegible]

A. [illegible]

Q. To see this point clearly, what must be remarked? [illegible]

A. He returns to the [illegible] thought him better out of the way [illegible] allow it; to all who so act, [illegible] be [illegible] commit [illegible] world [illegible]

Q. The necessity of general [illegible] government is [illegible] Paley [illegible] government: i. e. of any dispensation whose object is to influence the conduct of reasonable creatures.

Q. How is this manifest?

A. If, of two actions perfectly similar, one be punished, and the other be rewarded or forgiven, the subjects of such a dispensation would no longer know what to expect or how to act. Rewards and punishments would become accidents, occasioning pain or pleasure when they happened, but having no previous influence on the will upon the conduct. General rules, therefore, are included in the very idea of reward and punishment. Consequently, whatever reason there is to expect future reward and punishment at the hand of God, there is the same reason to believe that the dispensation of it will be by general rules.

Q. What reflection does Paley think proper to anticipate here?

A. It has been said that as so much of the guilt of a bad action consists in the *example*; if the action be done with perfect secrecy, that part of the guilt drops off. In the case of suicide, if a man can take away his life without being suspected to have done so, he is not chargeable with any mischief from the example; nor does its punishment seem necessary to save the authority of any general rule.

Q. How does Paley answer this?

A. 1. Those who reason so do not observe, that they are setting up a general rule, of all others the least to be endured; namely, that secrecy, whenever secrecy is practicable, will justify any action. Were such a rule

[illegible]

[illegible] would [illegible]

(1.) Whether the SS. do not [illegible] will be brought to light? [illegible]

[illegible]

God will deal with [illegible]

They will then [illegible] the same [illegible] world, as if they had [illegible] disproportionate to that severity of the laws which is founded almost entirely upon the general consequence [illegible]?

A. The particular consequence of coining is, perhaps, the loss of [illegible] him who receive the counterfeit: the general consequence, if [illegible] abolish the use of money [illegible].

The particular consequence of forgery is [illegible]

A. By asking what would be the [illegible] if the same [illegible]

[illegible]

a single action with the [illegible] whole?

A. The [illegible] of punishing the [illegible] action ([illegible]) will always be in proportion to the [illegible] that would [illegible] from the [illegible] of the [illegible].

Q. "Whatever is expedient is right." How does Paley explain this?

A. It must be expedient on the whole, in all its effects collateral and remote, as well as in [illegible] and direct; [illegible] consequences it [illegible] what way or at what distance they ensue.

Q. What are some of the instances by which Paley illustrates this doctrine, where the particular consequence and malignity of the crime is very disproportionate to that severity of the laws which is founded almost entirely upon the general consequence?

A. The particular consequence of coining is, perhaps, the loss of a guinea to him who receives the counterfeit: the general consequence, if the same practice were generally permitted, is, to abolish the use of money.

The particular consequence of forgery is, a damage of [illegible] pounds to him who accepts the bill: the general one is the stoppage of paper-currency.

The particular consequence of breaking into a house empty of inhabitants, is, the loss of a pair of [illegible] or a few spoons: the general [illegible] nobody could leave their house empty: &c. &c.

Q. [illegible]
importance of [illegible]

A. [illegible]
same manner, though the particular consequence
be very different. The [illegible] of the
house-breaker is the same, whether [illegible] be
five pounds or fifty. For the general consequence
is the same.

Q. [illegible] want of distinction between
particular and general consequences [illegible] the ancient moralists into [illegible]?

A. They saw the [illegible] ac-
tions good or evil, without regard to the good
or evil they produced; but were startled at the
conclusions to which a steady adherence to the
consequences seemed sometimes to conduct them.

Q. How did they relieve this difficulty?

A. They contrived the τὸ πρέπον, or the *ho-
nestum*, as a measure of right, distinct from utility.
Whilst the *utile* corresponded with their habitual
notions of the rectitude of actions, they went by
it. When they fell in with such cases as those in
the sixth chapter, they [illegible]:
they could only say, the [illegible]
useful, but [illegible],
they [illegible] it to be [illegible].

Q. From the foregoing principles, how [illegible]
explain [illegible]
understood, viz.—" [illegible]
[illegible]

A. [illegible]

for the sake of any particular good consequence we may expect [illegible]; since the advantage which compensates for the violation of the rule [illegible]

Q. What is Paley's concluding reflection upon the subject of consequences?

A. We need only [illegible], that any action of life with respect to the public, must be inconsiderable as affecting the agent. It has [illegible] but a small effect upon the [illegible]; punishment or destruction bears a small proportion to the sum of happiness and misery in the creation.

CHAP. IX.

Of Rights.

Q. Right and obligation are reciprocal. How is this explained?

A. Wherever there is a right in one person, there is a corresponding obligation upon others. If one man has a "right" to an estate, others are "obliged" to abstain from it. If parents have a "right" to reverence from their children; children are "obliged" to reverence their parents; and so in all other instances.

Q. Now, since moral obligation depends upon the will of God; right, which is correlative to it,

[illegible]
does right signify? [illegible]

A[illegible]

Q. But if the Divine [illegible]
tion of [illegible]
proposition [illegible]
h[illegible]
How then are these [illegible]
sig[illegible]

[illegible]
will [illegible]
will in the [illegible]
at certain conclusions; which [illegible]
we soon learn to pronounce actions right or wrong, as they agree or disagree with them: but when the habit is once established of stopping at the rules, we can go back and compare with them even the Divine conduct itself; and yet it may be true (only not observed by us at the time) that the rules themselves are deduced from the Divine will.

Q. What is Right?

It is a quality of persons or of actions.

Of persons, as when we say [illegible] has a "right" to [illegible] "right" to reverence from their children [illegible] has not a "right" [illegible]

Of actions, [illegible] "To punish murder with death [illegible] who gave up his place, [illegible] his judgment [illegible]

Q. [illegible] stitution may be made?

A. [illegible]

Q. How may this be done in the for[illegible]

[illegible]

Q. How are Rights distinguished, when applied to persons?

[illegible] 1. Natural or adventitious. 2. Alienable or unalienable. 3. Perfect or imperfect.

Q. How do you explain the first division?

A. [illegible]

Adventitious rights are such as would [illegible]

[illegible] or a right, in [illegible] of men, [illegible]

Q. It may be asked, [illegible] rights depend upon the will of God, and civil society [illegible]

Q. [illegible]

A. [illegible] to [illegible] God will the happiness of mankind, and the [illegible] civil society [illegible] to that happiness. Many things [illegible] the support of civil society [illegible] the conservation of particular societies already established, [illegible] with the will of God [illegible] "rights" [illegible] without that [illegible] civil society [illegible]

Q. [illegible]

A. [illegible] ly derived from human [illegible] respect them [illegible] upon the [illegible] the will of God. A man claims a right to a particular estate [illegible]

[illegible] same sin in dispossessing him of his estate by [illegible] over his subjects [illegible]

Q. What do you remark concerning the [illegible] division of rights [illegible]

[illegible] explain themselves.

The right we have to [illegible] [illegible]

The right of a prince over his people, of a master over his servants, [illegible]

Q. Upon what does the distinction depend?

A. Upon the mode of acquiring the right. If the right originate from a contract, and be limited to the person by the express terms or [illegible] interpretation of such contract, or by a personal condition annexed to the right, then it is unalienable. In all other cases it is alienable.

Q. Which is the right to civil liberty?

A. It is alienable; though in the [illegible] zeal, it has often been pronounced unalienable. The reason why we detest the [illegible] of those who have sold their liberty is, that, with their own, they sold [illegible] the liberty of others, which they had no right to dispose of.

Q. What do you remark concerning the [illegible] division of rights, perfect and imperfect?

A. Perfect rights may be asserted by force, or, what is the same thing, by course of law.

perfect rights by law.

Q. What examples can you give of perfect rights?

A. A man's right to his life, person, house; for he may repel an attack upon these by instant violence, or punish the aggressor by law; a man's right to his estate, furniture, money, &c.; for, if they be injuriously taken from him, he may compel restitution or satisfaction.

Q. What of imperfect rights?

A. In elections, &c. where the qualifications are prescribed, the best qualified candidate has a right to success; yet, if he be rejected, he has no remedy, either by force or law; his right therefore is imperfect. Children have a right to affection and education from their parents; and parents to duty from their children: yet, if these rights be on either side withholden, there is no compulsion.

Q. It may be difficult to apprehend how one should have a right to a thing, and yet have no right to use means to obtain it. Into what is this difficulty, like most others in morality, resolvable?

A. Into the necessity of general rules.

Q. How is it consistent with the will of God that a person should possess a thing, and not that he should use force to obtain it?

A. By reason of the indeterminateness of the object, or of the right, the permission of force, in this case, would lead to the same permission in other cases, where there existed no right. To allow the candidate abovementioned to demand success by force, is to make him the judge of his own qualifications. You cannot do this but give equal make all other candidates the same; which would open the door to demands without number or reason. So, a poor man has a right to relief from the rich; but the mode, season, and quantum of that relief, or who shall contribute to it, are not ascertained. Yet these points must be ascertained, before a claim to relief can be prosecuted by force; or else the very nature of property would cease. In the instances of gratitude, affection, &c. force is excluded by the very idea of the duty, which must be voluntary or cannot exist.

Q. Wherever the right is imperfect, what else is so?

A. The corresponding obligation. I am obliged to prefer the best candidate, to relieve the poor, &c. but in these cases, my obligation, like their right, is imperfect.

Q. Why does the term *imperfect* obligation seem ill-chosen?

A. Because it leads many to imagine, that there is less guilt in its violation, than of a perfect one: which is a groundless notion. For an obligation being perfect or imperfect, determines only whether violence may or may not be employed to enforce it. The degree of guilt is determined by circumstances, independent of this distinction. A man who, by a partial or corrupt vote, disappoints a worthy candidate of a station upon which, possibly, his livelihood depended, and who thereby grievously discourages merit and emulation, commits a greater crime, than if he filched a book out of a library, or picked a pocket of a handkerchief

Q. As the indeterminateness of an obligation renders it imperfect, by what kind of precepts is it commonly produced?

A. By positive ones, which are often indeterminate in their extent; as in the instance of the Fifth Commandment.

Q. What constitutes perfect obligations?

A. Negative precepts or prohibitions, which are generally precise; as in the instance of the Sixth Commandment.

Q. In what do Religion and Virtue find their principal exercise?

A. In the imperfect obligations; the laws taking care of the rest.

CHAP. XI.

THE GENERAL RIGHTS OF MANKIND.

Q. What is meant by these?

A. The rights which belong to the species collectively; the original stock, which they have since distributed among themselves.

Q. What are these?

A. I. A right to the fruits or vegetable produce of the earth.

As God had created us with a want and desire of food, and provided things suited to sustain and satisfy us, we may fairly presume, that he intended we should apply these things to that purpose.

2. A right to the flesh of animals;

Which is a very different claim from the former. Some excuse seems necessary for the pain and loss we occasion to brutes, by restraining them of their liberty, and putting an end to their lives, for our pleasure or conveniency.

Q. What are the reasons alleged in vindication of this practise?

A. That the several species of brutes preying upon one another, affords an analogy to prove that the human species were intended to feed upon them; that, if let alone, they would overrun the earth, to the exclusion of mankind; and that they are requited for what they suffer, by our care and protection.

Q. Upon which reasons what does Paley observe?

A. That *the analogy* is extremely lame; since brutes have no power to support life by other means; but we have, by fruit, herbs, and roots, like many tribes of Hindoos. The two other reasons may be valid, as far as they go; for, if man had been supported by vegetable food, many animals which die to furnish his table, would never have lived: but they do not justify our right to the extent in which we exercise it. What danger is there, for instance, of fish interfering with us? or what do *we* contribute to their support or preservation?

Q. As it is difficult to defend this right by

any arguments, to what are we really indebted for it?

A. To the permission recorded in Scripture, Gen. ix. 1, 2, 3.

Q. Since it appears from Reason or Revelation, or both, to be God's intention, that the productions of the earth should be applied for the support of man, what follows?

A. That all waste and misapplication of them is contrary to his intention; and therefore wrong, for the same reason that any other crime is so. Such is the converting of manors into a forest for hunting; or suffering them to continue in that state; or destroying, or suffering to perish, great part of an article of human provision, to enhance the price of the remainder; or diminishing the breed of animals, by a wanton consumption of the young: the same evil in a smaller way, is the expending of human food on superfluous dogs or horses; and the reducing of the quantity, in order to alter the quality.

Q. Who seems to inculcate this lesson?

A. Our Saviour, when he bids his disciples "gather up the fragments, that nothing be lost." And it opens indeed a new field of duty. Schemes of profit, prompt the active to convert their property to the most advantage; and their own advantage, and that of the public, commonly concur. But it has scarcely entered into the minds of mankind, to reflect that it is a *duty*, to add what we can to the common stock of provision, by extracting out of our estates the most they will yield; or that it is any sin to neglect this.

Q. From the same intention of God, what other conclusion do we draw?

A. "That nothing ought to be made exclusive property, which can be conveniently enjoyed in common.

Q. How do you exemplify this?

A. It is the general intention of God, that the produce of the earth be applied to the use of man. Under this general donation, one man has the same right as another. You pluck an apple from a tree, or take a lamb from a flock, for your immediate use, and I do the same; and we both plead the general intention of the Supreme Proprietor. So far all is right: but you cannot claim the whole tree, or flock, and exclude me from any share, and plead this general intention; you must show something more. You must show by probable arguments at least, that it is God's intention, that these things should be parcelled out to individuals: until this be shown, the general intention, which is all that appears, must prevail; and, under that, my title is as good as yours. Now there is but one argument to induce such a presumption; that the thing cannot be enjoyed at all, or with nearly the same advantage, while it continues in common, as when appropriated. This is true, where there is not enough for all, or where the article in question requires care or labour: but where the thing is in its nature capable of being enjoyed by as many as

still, it seems an arbitrary usurpation upon the rights of mankind, to confine the use of it to one, for instance.

If there be fisheries, which are inexhaustible, as the cod-fishery upon the Banks of Newfoundland, and the herring-fishery in the British seas are said to be, then all those conventions, by which one or two nations claim to themselves, and guaranty to each other, the exclusive enjoyment of these fisheries, are so many encroachments upon the general rights of mankind.

Q. Upon this principle, what great question in Natural Law may be determined?

A. *Utrum mare sit liberum?* that is, whether the exclusive right of navigating, or a control over the navigation of particular seas, can be claimed, consistently with the law of nature, by any nation? What is necessary for each nation's safety, we allow; as their own bays, creeks, harbours, and the sea contiguous to their coast; and upon this principle of safety must be defended the claim of the Venetian State to the Adriatic, &c. But, when Spain asserts a right to the Pacific Ocean, or Portugal to the Indian Seas, &c., they erect a claim which interferes with the benevolent designs of Providence, and which no human authority can justify.

Q. What other may be called a general right, as being incidental to every one who is in a situation to claim it?

A. The right of extreme necessity; viz. to use or destroy another's property, when necessary for our own preservation; as a right to throw goods over-board, to save a ship; or to pull down a house, in order to stop the progress of a fire; &c. Of which the foundation seems to be this: that when property was first instituted, the institution was not intended to operate to the destruction of any. Or rather, perhaps, these are the few cases, where the particular exceeds the general consequence; where the remote mischief from the violation of the general rule, is over-balanced by the immediate advantage.

Q. What however is due?

A. Restitution, when in our power: because the laws of property are to be adhered to, so far as consists with safety; and because restitution, which is one of those laws, supposes the danger to be over.

Q. But what is to be restored?

A. Not the full value of the property destroyed, but what it was worth at the time of destroying it; which, considering the danger it was in of perishing, might be very little.

BOOK III.

RELATIVE DUTIES.

PART I.

OF RELATIVE DUTIES WHICH ARE DETERMINATE.

CHAP I.

OF PROPERTY.

Q. How does Paley illustrate this title?

A. By a flock of pigeons in a field of corn. If you should see ninety-nine of these gathering all they got, into a heap; reserving nothing for themselves but the refuse; keeping this heap for the weakest, and perhaps worst, pigeon of the flock; sitting round, and looking on, all the winter, whilst this one was devouring and wasting it; and if a pigeon more hardy or hungry than the rest touched a grain, all the others tearing it to pieces; you would see what is every day practised among men. Among men, you see the ninety-nine scraping together superfluities for one (oftentimes the feeblest and worst of the whole set); getting nothing for themselves but a little of the coarsest provision; looking quietly on, seeing the fruits of their labour spent or spoiled; and if one of the number take a particle of the hoard, the others joining against him, and hanging him for the theft.

CHAP. II.

THE USE OF THE INSTITUTION OF PROPERTY.

Q. What are the advantages which account for an institution, the view of which, as above given, is so paradoxical?

A. I. It increases the produce of the earth.

The earth requires cultivation: and none would be willing to cultivate it, if others were admitted to an equal share of the produce. So of flocks and herds of tame animals.

A nation of North-American savages, consisting of two or three hundred, will be half-starved upon a tract of land, which with European management, would maintain as many thousands.

In some fertile soils, with abundance of fish upon the coasts, a considerable population may subsist without property in land; as in Otaheite: but in less favoured situations, as New Zealand, the inhabitants for want of a more secure establishment of it, are often driven by the scarcity of provision to devour one another.

II. It preserves the produce of the earth to maturity.

We may judge what would be the effects of a community of right to its productions, from observing, that the cherry tree in a hedge row, or nuts in a wood, which are seldom of much advantage to any body. Corn, if any were sown, would never ripen; lambs and calves would never grow up; for the first person that met them had better take them as they are, than leave them for another.

III. It prevents war, waste, and tumults, which must be eternal, where there is not enough for all, and there are no rules to adjust the division.

IV. It improves the conveniency of living two ways. It enables mankind to divide themselves into distinct professions, on which much of the advantage of civilised over savage life, depends. When a man is from necessity his own tailor, carpenter, cook, and fisherman, he will not be expert at any of his callings. Hence the rude habitations and implements of savages; and the length of time their operations require.

It likewise improves the accommodations by which human life is supplied, by appropriating to the artist the benefit of his discoveries and improvements; without which, ingenuity will never be exerted with effect.

Q. Upon these accounts what may we, with a few exceptions, pronounce?

A. Even the poorest and worst provided, in countries where property and its consequences prevail, are better off, with respect to food, raiment, houses, and the necessaries of life, than any are in places where most things are in common.

The balance, therefore, preponderates in favour of property with a great excess.

Great inequality of property, abstractedly considered, is an evil; but it is the evil which flows from those rules by which men are incited to industry, and by which the object of their industry is rendered secure and valuable. If any great inequality be unconnected with this origin, it ought to be corrected.

CHAP. III.

THE HISTORY OF PROPERTY.

Q. What does Paley say upon this subject?

A. The first objects of property were the fruits a man gathered, and the wild animals he caught; next to these, the tents or houses he built, the tools he made use of to catch or prepare his food; and afterwards weapons of war and offence. Many savage tribes have advanced no farther than this, who return the produce of their exchanges with foreigners into the common treasury. [illegible]

[illegible] of cheese, [illegible] wealth of the Patriarchs, as they do still of the modern Arabs. As in the East there existed a great scarcity of water, wells probably were soon made property; which we learn from the contentions and treaties about them in the O.T.; and from its being recorded, among the most memorable acts of eminent men, that they dug or discovered a well. Land, which is now so important a part of property, was probably not made so till long after the institution of many other species, that is, till the country became populous, and tillage thought of. The first partition of an estate which we read of, took place between Abram and Lot; and was one of the simplest imaginable: "If thou wilt take the left hand, then I will go to the right; or if thou depart to the right hand, then I will go to the left." There are no traces of property in land in Cæsar's account of Britain; none amongst the nations of N. America; the Scythians are said to have appropriated their cattle and houses, but to have left their land in common.

Property in immoveables continued at first no longer than the occupation; that is, as long as a man's family continued upon it, or his cattle pastured upon it, [illegible] or drive them out; but when he [illegible] or changed his pasture, another, if he found them unoccupied, entered upon them, by the same title, and made way in turn for his successor. There

permanent property in land was probably posterior to civil government, and to have been, therefore, settled by lot, or the will of the reigning chief.

CHAP. IV.

IN WHAT THE RIGHT OF PROPERTY IS FOUNDED.

Q. What difficulty exists in explaining the origin of Property in Land, consistently with the Law of Nature?

A. The land was once, no doubt, common; and the question is, how any part could justly be taken, and so appropriated to the first owner as to give him an exclusive right to it.

Q. What does the diversity of accounts given by moralists of this matter indicate?

A. That none of them are satisfactory.

Q. What is the first account given?

A. That mankind, when they suffered a particular person to occupy a piece of ground, by tacit consent relinquished their right to it; it thenceforward became his property, and no one afterwards had a right to molest him in it.

Q. What is the objection to this?

A. That consent can never be presumed from

silence, and ignorance of the matter, which must have been the case with all mankind, excepting at the place where the appropriation was made. And to suppose that the ground previously belonged to the neighbourhood, and that they could confer it upon whom they pleased, is to suppose the question resolved, and a partition of land to have already taken place.

Q. What is the next account?

A. That each man's limbs and labour are his own exclusively; now, by occupying a piece of ground, he so mixes his labour with it that the ground becomes thenceforward his own, and you cannot take it from him without taking away also something which is indisputably his.

Q. When does this solution, which is Mr. Locke's, appear a fair one?

A. When the value of the labour bears a considerable proportion to the value of the thing; or where the thing derives its chief use and value from the labour. Thus, game and fish, when caught, become much more valuable; and this increase of value is strictly the property of the fowler or fisherman. So, also, wood or iron, manufactured into utensils, becomes the property of the manufacturer; because the value of the workmanship far exceeds that of the materials. Upon this principle, a parcel of unappropriated ground, which a man should pare, burn, plough, harrow, and sow, would justly enough be thereby made his own.

Q. When does this solution fail?

[illegible] the thing [illegible] of a tract of land by erecting a standard, or publishing a proclamation to the birds and beasts, or of turning your cattle into a piece of ground, or planting a hedge round it. Nor will even the clearing, manuring, and ploughing of a field, give the first occupier a right to it in perpetuity, and after this cultivation and all effects of it are ceased.

Q. What other, and in Paley's opinion better, account is given?

A. As God has provided these things for the use of all, he has given each leave to take of them what he wants; by this leave, a man may appropriate what he stands in need of, without asking the consent of others; as, when an entertainment is provided for the freeholders of a county, each guest goes, and eats and drinks what he wants, without having or waiting for the consent of the other guests.

Q. But how far only does this reason justify property?

A. As far as necessaries, or, at most, a competent provision for our natural exigencies. For, in the entertainment we speak of, you would hardly permit any one to fill his pockets, or to carry away a quantity of provision to be hoarded up, or wasted; especially if, by so doing, he pinched the guests at the lower end of the table.

Q. What is required for these accounts to avail us in vindicating our present claims of property in land?

A. That our estates were actually acquired at first, in some of the ways which these accounts supposed; and that a regular regard should have been paid to justice, in every successive transmission of these estates; for, if one link in the chain fail, every title posterior to it falls to the ground.

Q. What is the real foundation of our right?

A. THE LAW OF THE LAND.

Q. How do you shew this?

A. It is the intention of God, that the produce of the earth be applied to the use of man: this intention cannot be fulfilled without establishing property; it is consistent therefore with his will, that it be established. The land cannot be divided into separate property, without leaving it to the law of the country to regulate that division: it is consistent therefore with the same will, that the law should regulate the division; and, consequently, "consistent with the will of God," or "right" that I should possess that share which these regulations assign me.

All reasoning upon this right must terminate in the will of God; therefore the shortest way of arriving at this will, is the best.

Q. What then does the right to an estate not depend upon?

A. Neither the manner or justice of the original acquisition; nor the justice of each subsequent change. It is not the less, because the estate was taken first possession of by a family of aboriginal Britons; nor because they were turned out by a Roman, or the Roman by a Saxon invader, or the Saxon by a Norman adventurer; from whom, after many interruptions of fraud and violence, it has devolved to me.

Q. What else does it not depend upon?

A. The *expediency* of the law which gives it to him. On one side of a brook, an estate descends to the eldest son; on the other side, to all the children alike. The right of the claimants under both laws is equal; though the expediency of such opposite rules must necessarily be different.

Q. What bad use is apt to be made of the conclusion to which these principles apparently lead?

A. It seems to follow, that a man has a right to keep and take all the law will allow him; which in many cases will authorise the most flagitious chicanery. Thus a debtor might refuse to pay a simple contract debt, which has been not demanded for six years, though conscious of the justice of the debt. A minor might contract a just bargain (other than for necessaries), and yet avoid it by pleading his minority.

Q. What is the distinction to be taken in such cases?

A. With the law resides the disposal of property: so long, therefore, as we keep within the *design* and *intention* of a law, it will justify us, whatever be the equity or expediency of the law itself. But when we convert to one purpose, an expression of law, intended for another, we plead, not the intention of the law, but the words; that is, a dead letter; for words *without* meaning or intention, have no effect in justice; much less, words taken *contrary* to the intention of the speaker or writer.

Q. How do you apply this distinction to the above-mentioned examples?

A. If a man be ignorant or dubious of the justice of the demand made upon him, for an antiquated debt, he may conscientiously plead the limitation; because *he applies the rule of law to the purpose for which it was intended.* But when he refuses to pay a debt, the reality of which he is conscious; he cannot plead the intention of the statute, unless he can show, that the law intended to interpose, to acquit men of debts, of the existence and justice of which they were themselves sensible. Again, if a young person perceive that he has been practised or imposed upon, he may honestly take the privilege of his nonage, to defeat the circumvention. But, if he thus avoid an equitable contract, he extends the privilege to a case in which it is not allowed by intention of law, and in which consequently it does not, in natural justice, exist.

As property is the principal subject of justice, or of "the determinate relative duties," it has been discussed in the first place; these duties are now stated.

CHAP. V.

PROMISES.

I. *From whence the obligation to perform promises arises.*

II. *In what sense promises are to be interpreted.*

III. *In what cases promises are not binding.*

I. Q. *From whence does the obligation to perform promises arise?*

A. Some suppose a sense of the obligation of promises to be an innate moral principle; but without assuming any thing without proof, this obligation may be deduced from its necessity to the well-being, or the existence of human society.

Q. How do you show this?

A. Men act from expectation; which is in most cases determined by the assurances we receive from others. If no dependence could be placed upon these, it would be impossible to form a judgment of many future events, or to regulate our conduct with respect to them. Confidence therefore in promises, is essential to the intercourse of human life; or the greatest part of our conduct would proceed upon chance. But there could be no confidence in promises, if men were not obliged to perform them; the obligation therefore is essential to the same ends, and in the same degree.

Q. What may be said of those who imagine, that if this obligation were suspended, a general caution and distrust would ensue, which might do as well?

A. They do not consider how, every hour, we trust to, and depend upon, others; and how impossible it is to stir a step, or to sit still a moment, without such trust and dependence. This holds of the most important as well as the most familiar occurrences in social life.

Q. In what sense are promises to be interpreted?

A. Where the terms of promise admit of more senses than one, the promise is to be performed "in that sense in which the promiser apprehended at the time, that the promisee received it."

It is not the sense in which the promiser actually intended it, that always governs the interpretation of an equivocal promise; because at that rate you might excite expectations which you never meant, nor would be obliged, to satisfy. Much less is it the sense in which the promisee actually received the promise; for then you might be drawn into engagements which you never designed to undertake. It *must*, therefore, be the sense in which the promiser believed that the promisee accepted his promise.

Nor will this differ from the actual intention of the promiser, where the promise is given without collusion or reserve: but the rule is so put, to exclude evasion whenever the popular meaning of a phrase, and the grammatical signification of the words differ; where the promiser attempts to make his escape through some ambiguity of his expressions.

Temures promised the garrison of Sebastia, that, if they would surrender, *no blood should be shed.* The garrison surrendered; and he buried them all alive. Thus, Temures fulfilled his promise in the sense in which he intended it at the time; but not in which the garrison received it, nor in which Temures knew that the garrison received it: in which last, according to our rule, he was bound to have performed it.

Q. From this account of the obligation of promises, upon what does it depend?

A. Upon the *expectations* which we knowingly and voluntarily excite. Consequently, any action or conduct which we are sensible excites expectations in another, is a promise, and creates as strict an obligation as the most express assurance. The taking, for instance, a kinsman's child, and educating him for a liberal profession, as much obliges us to place him in that profession, as if we had given him a promise to do so under our hands and seals. This is the foundation of *tacit promises.*

Q. What is the difference of obligation between simply declaring your present intention, or accompanying your declaration with an engagement to abide by it, which constitutes a complete promise?

A. In the first case, the duty is satisfied, if you entertained at the time the intention you expressed, however soon, or for whatever reason, you afterwards change it. In the latter case, you have parted with the liberty of changing.

Q. But since most of those forms of speech, which, strictly taken, amount only to declarations of present intention, do yet, in the usual way of understanding them, excite expectation; such as "I intend you this place"—"I design to leave you this estate," &c.; if you choose to make known your present intention, and yet reserve to yourself the liberty of changing it, how must you guard your expressions?

A. By an additional clause, as "I intend at *present*,"—"*if I do not alter*,"—or the like. And as there can be no reason for communicating an intention, but to excite some degree of expectation, a wanton change of an intention once disclosed, always disappoints, and is therefore wrong.

Q. *In what cases are promises not binding?*

A, 1. Where the performance is *impossible.*

But the promiser is guilty of a fraud, if he be secretly aware of the impossibility, at the time of making the promise. Instances of this sort are the following: A father, in settling marriage-articles, promises to leave his daughter an estate, which he knows to be entailed upon the heir male of his family:—A merchant promises a ship, or share of a ship, which he is privately advised is lost at sea. The promiser, in these cases, with knowledge of the impossibility, is justly answerable in an equivalent; but otherwise not.

When the promiser himself, occasions the impossibility, it is a direct breach of the promise; as [illegible] to get rid of the engagement.

2. Promises are not binding, where the performance is unlawful.

Of which there are two cases; one, where the unlawfulness is known to the parties, at the time of making the promise; as where an assassin promises his employer to dispatch his rival, or a servant to betray his master. The parties are not obliged to perform such a promise, because they were under *a prior obligation to the contrary*. From which what is there to discharge them? Their promise,—their own act and deed.—But an obligation, from which a man can discharge himself by his own act, is no obligation at all. The guilt therefore of such promises lies in the making, not in the breaking of them.

The other case is, where the unlawfulness did not exist, or was not known, at the time of making the promise; as where a woman gives a promise of marriage, and before the marriage, she discovers that her intended husband is too nearly related to her, or that he has a wife yet living. In all such cases, it is presumed that the parties supposed what they promised to be lawful, and that the promise proceeded upon this supposition. The lawfulness therefore becomes a condition of the promise; which failing, the obligation ceases. Of this nature was Herod's promise to his daughter-in-law; from the obligation of which he was discharged, for the reason now laid down, as well as for that given in the last paragraph.

Q. To what does this rule, "that promises are void, where the performance is unlawful," also extend?

A. To imperfect obligations. Thus, if you promise a man a place, or vote, and he renders himself unfit to receive either, you are absolved from the obligation; or, if a better candidate appears, and you are bound by oath, or otherwise, to govern yourself by the qualification, the promise must be broken.

Q. What caution does Paley here recommend, especially to young persons?

A. "Never to give a promise, which may interfere in the event with their duty;" for, if it do so interfere, their duty must be discharged, though at the expense of their promise, and not unusually of their good name.

Q. What species of obligation is the specific performance of promises reckoned?

A. A perfect obligation.

Q. Now, where a perfect and an imperfect obligation clash, some casuists have determined that the former is to be preferred. Is there any reason in this?

A. No: none but what arises from the terms perfect and imperfect; the impropriety of which has been already remarked.

Q. In truth, of two contradictory obligations, which ought to prevail?

A. That which is prior in point of time.

Q. Which destroys the validity of a promise?

unlawfulness in the subject, or motive, or in the performance?

A. In the *performance*; and, therefore, the reward of any crime, after it is committed, ought, if promised, to be paid; for the sin and mischief are over, and will be neither more nor less for the performance of the promise.

Q. Does a promise lose its obligation because it may have proceeded from an *unlawful motive*?

A. No.

Q. What error did Bishop Sanderson commit in this instance?

A. He acquitted a certain person of his obligation, who in the life-time of his wife, then sick, had paid his addresses, and promised marriage, to another woman;—the wife died; and the woman demanded performance of the promise; but he, it seems, had changed his mind, or pretended doubts concerning the obligation of such a promise. Now, however criminal the affection might be, which induced the promise, the performance, when it was demanded, was lawful; which is the only lawfulness required.

Q. On what occasion cannot a promise be deemed unlawful?

A. Where it produces, when performed, no effect beyond what would have taken place had it never been made; which is the only case where the obligation of a promise will justify a conduct, which otherwise would be unjust. A captive may lawfully recover his liberty, by a promise of neutrality; for his conqueror takes nothing by the promise, which he might not have secured by his death or confinement. Promises however, which come into the place of coercion can extend no further than to passive compliances; for coercion itself could compel no more. Upon this principle, promises of secresy ought not to be violated, although the public would derive advantage from the discovery: the public lose nothing by the promise which they would have gained without it.

Q. 3dly, When are promises not binding?

A. When they *contradict a former promise*. Because the performance is then unlawful; which resolves this case into the last.

Q. 4thly, When are they not binding?

A. *Before acceptance.* Until the promise be communicated to the promisee, it is the same only as a resolution in the mind of the promiser, which may be altered at pleasure. For no expectation has been excited, therefore none can be disappointed. Even if a third person, *without any authority from me*, conveys my declaration to the promisee, I have not then done what constitutes the essence of a promise;—*voluntarily* excited expectation.

Q. 5thly, What promises are not binding?

A. Those which are *released by the promisee.*

This is evident: but it may be sometimes doubted who the promisee is. If I give a promise *to A*, of a place or vote for B; then A is the promisee, whose consent I must obtain, to be released.

If I promise a place or vote to B *by* A, that is, if A be a messenger to convey the promise; or if A be employed to introduce B's request, and I answer in any terms which amount to a compliance with it; then B is the promisee.

Promises to one person for the benefit of another, are not released by the death of the promisee: for this neither makes the performance impracticable, nor implies any consent to release the promiser from it.

Q. 6thly, What promises are not binding?

A. *Erroneous* promises in certain cases; as,

1. Where the error proceeds from the mistake or misrepresentation of the promisee.

A promise supposes the truth of the account, which the promisee relates to obtain it. A beggar solicits charity by a story of the most pitiable distress; you promise to relieve him, if he will call again.—In the interval you discover it to be made up of lies;—this no doubt, releases you from your promise.

2. When the promise is understood by the promisee to proceed upon a certain supposition, or when the promiser apprehended it to be so understood, and that supposition turns out to be false.

This intricate rule will be best explained by an example. A Father receives an account from abroad, of the death of his only son;—he promises his fortune to his nephew.—The account turns out false.—The father is released from his promise; not merely because he never would have made it, had he known the truth of the case,—for that alone will not do;—but because the nephew himself understood the promise to proceed upon the supposition of his cousin's death: or, at least, his uncle thought he so understood it; and could not think otherwise.

Q. What is the foundation of this rule?

A. A man is bound only to satisfy the expectation which he intended to excite; whatever condition therefore he intended to subject that expectation to, becomes an essential condition of the promise.

Errors, which come not within this description, do not annul the obligation. I promise a candidate my vote;—another candidate appears, for whom I would have reserved it, had I known his design. Here, as before, my promise proceeded from an error; and I never should have given such a promise, had I been aware of the case, as it turned out.—But the *promisee* did not know this;—*he* did not receive the promise as proceeding from any such supposition;—nor did I at the time imagine he so received it. This error, therefore, must fall upon my own head, and the promise be observed.

Q. Upon what depends the question, whether promises extorted by violence or fear ought to be binding?

A. Upon this:—whether mankind, upon the whole, are benefited by the confidence placed on such promises?

Q. What example does Paley give?

A. A highwayman, disappointed of his booty, threatens to murder you;—you promise, that if he will spare your life, he shall find a purse of money at a place appointed; upon the faith of this promise, he forbears from violence: your life was saved by his confidence in a promise extorted by fear; and the lives of many may be so saved. This is a good consequence. On the other hand, confidence in promises like these greatly facilitates the perpetration of robberies, and almost unlimited extortion. This is a bad consequence: and in the importance of these opposite consequences, resides the doubt concerning the obligation of such promises.

There are other cases plainer; as where a prisoner of war promises, if set at liberty, to return within a certain time. Such promises, say moralists, are binding, because the violence or duress is just; but the truth is, because there is the same use of confidence in these promises, as in those of a person at liberty.

Q. Can the obligation of *Vows* (or promises to God) be made out upon the same principle as that of other promises?

A. No; but the violation of them implies a want of reverence to the Supreme Being, which makes it sinful.

Q. As the rules laid down for promises are applicable to vows, for what reason was Jephtha's vow (as commonly understood) not binding?

A. Because the performance, in that case, became unlawful.

CHAP. VI.

CONTRACTS.

Q. What is a contract?

A. A mutual promise.

Q. What, therefore, is the obligation of contracts, in the sense in which they are to be interpreted, and the cases in which they are not binding?

A. The same as of promises; *i.e. whatever is expected by one side, and known to be so expected by the other, is to be deemed a part or condition of the contract.*

Q. What are the several kinds of contracts, and the order in which Paley considers them, exhibited in one view.

A.

Contracts of
- **Sale.**
- **Hazard.**
- **Lending of**
  - **Inconsumable Property.**
  - **Money.**
- **Labour.**
  - **Service.**
  - **Commissions.**
  - **Partnership.**
  - **Offices.**

CHAP. VII.

CONTRACTS OF SALE.

Q. What rule of justice ought principally to be inculcated in bargains?

A. That the seller is bound in conscience to disclose the faults of what he offers to sale.

Q. Amongst other methods of proving this, what does Paley give?

A. It will be allowed, that to advance a falsehood, in recommendation of our wares, by ascribing to them some quality which we know that they have not, is dishonest. Now compare with this the concealment of some fault, which we know that they have. The motive in these two cases is the same, *viz.* to procure a higher price than we expect otherwise to obtain: the effect, that is, the prejudice to the buyer, is also the same; for he finds himself equally out of pocket, whether the commodity turn out worse by the want of some quality which he expected, or the discovery of some fault which he did not expect. If therefore actions be the same, as to all moral purposes, which proceed from the same motives, and produce the same effects; it is making a distinction without a difference, to esteem it a *cheat* to magnify beyond the truth the virtues of what we have to sell, but none to conceal its faults.

Q. What adds to the value of this kind of honesty?

A. That the faults of many things cannot be known by any, but by the persons who have used them; so that the buyer has no security but in the integrity of the seller.

Q. What exception is there to this rule?

A. Where the silence of the seller implies some fault in the thing to be sold, and the buyer has a compensation in the price for the risk; as where a horse is sold by public auction, without warranty: the want of this gives notice of some unsoundness, and produces an abatement in the price.

Q. What other kind of transaction may be referred to this practice of concealing the faults of what we want to put off?

A. That of passing bad money; which is much the same, as if one who had been robbed upon the highway should conceive that he had a right to reimburse himself out of the pocket of the first traveller he met.

Q. What does Paley observe concerning what is called the market price?

A. That where there exists no monopoly or combination, it is always a fair price; for it will always be proportionable to the use and scarcity of the article. Hence, all those expressions, "provisions are extravagantly dear," "corn bears an unreasonable price," and the like, import no unfairness or unreasonableness in the seller.

Q. If your tailor or drapor charge you, or even ask you, more than the market price for a suit of clothes, why do you pronounce him dishonest?

A. Whoever opens a shop, or in any manner exposes goods to sale, virtually engages to deal with his customers at a market-price. This is expected by the buyer; is known to be so expected by the seller; which, according to the rule delivered above, makes it a part of the contract, though not a syllable be said. The breach of this implied contract constitutes the fraud. If you disclaim any such engagement, you may set what value you please upon your property.

Q. If the thing sold be damaged, or perish, between the sale and the delivery, ought the buyer to bear the loss, or the seller?

A. This will depend upon the particular construction of the contract. If the seller, either expressly, or by implication, or by custom, engage to *deliver* the goods; and they be damaged in the conveyance, the seller must abide by the loss. If the thing sold remain with the seller, at the instance, or for the conveniency of the buyer, then the buyer undertakes the risk.

Q. By what are innumerable questions of this sort determined?

A. Solely by *custom*; because the contracting parties are presumed to include in their stipulation, all the conditions which custom has annexed to contracts of the same sort: and when the usage is notorious, and no exception made to it, this presumption is generally agreeable to the fact.

CHAP. VIII.

CONTRACTS OF HAZARD.

Q. What does Paley mean by contracts of hazard?

A. Gaming and insurance.

Q. What some say of this kind of contracts, "that one side ought not to have any advantage over the other," is neither practicable nor true. Why so?

A. It is not practicable; for that equality of skill and judgment, which this rule requires, is seldom to be met with. I might not have it in my power to play with fairness a game at cards, billiards, or tennis, once in a twelvemonth, if I must wait for a person, whose art, skill, and judgment, is neither greater nor less than my own. Nor is this requisite to the justice of the contract. One party may give to the other the whole stake, if he please, and the other may justly accept it; much more therefore may one give to the other a part; or, what is the same thing, an advantage in the chance of winning the whole.

Q. What is the proper restriction?

A. That neither side have an advantage by means of which the other is not aware; for this is an advantage taken, without being *given*. If I sit down to a game at whist, and have an advantage over the adversary, by means of a better memory, or knowledge of the game, the advantage is fair; it is obtained by means of which the adversary is aware, when he sits down with me. But if I gain an advantage by packing the cards, or by concerted signals with my partner, it is dishonest; because it depends upon means which the adversary never suspects that I make use of.

The same holds of all contracts into which chance enters. If I lay a wager at a horse-race, founded upon the appearance, character, and breed of the horses, I am entitled to any advantage my judgment gives me; but if I carry on a correspondence with the jockeys, and find out that a trial has been made, or that it is settled which horse shall win the race; such information is so much fraud, because derived from sources which the other did not suspect, when he proposed the wager.

In insurances, where the underwriter computes his risk entirely from the account given by the person insured, it is necessary to the justice and validity of the contract, that this account be exact and complete.

CHAP. IX.

CONTRACTS OF LENDING OF INCONSUMABLE PROPERTY.

Q. When the identical loan is to be returned, as a book, or a horse, &c. what is it called?

A. *Inconsumable*; in opposition to corn, wine, money, and those things which perish, or are parted with, in the use, and can therefore only be restored in kind.

Q. The questions under this head are few and simple:—what is the first?

A. If the thing lent be lost or damaged, who ought to bear the loss or damage?

Q. What answer may be given to this?

A. If it be so by the use, or by accident in the use for which it was lent, the lender ought to bear it; as, if I hire a job-coach, the wear and soiling of the coach belongs to the lender; or a horse, to go a particular journey, and in going it, the horse die, or be lamed, the loss must be the lender's: on the contrary, if the damage be occasioned by the fault of the borrower, or by accident in some use for which it was not lent, then the borrower must make it good.

Q. How are the two cases distinguished?

A. In one case, the owner foresees the damage or risk, and therefore consents to undertake it; in the other case, he does not.

Q. An estate or a house may, during a lease, be so increased or diminished in value as to become worth much more, or much less, than the rent agreed to be paid for it. In some such cases it may be doubted, to whom, of natural right, the advantage or disadvantage belongs. What does the rule of justice seem to be?

A. If the alteration might be *expected* by the

parties, the hirer must take the consequence; if it could not, the owner.

Q. Give an instance of this rule?

A. If an estate in the fens of Lincolnshire be overflowed with water, so as to be incapable of occupation, the tenant, notwithstanding, is bound by his lease; because he entered into it with a knowledge and foresight of the danger. On the other hand, if, by the irruption of the sea into a country where it was never known to have come before, by the change of the course of a river, the breaking out of a volcano, the incursions of an enemy, or by a mortal contagion amongst the cattle, if, by such means an estate lose its value, the loss shall fall upon the owner; that is, the tenant shall either be discharged from his agreement, or be entitled to an abatement of rent.

CHAP. X.

CONTRACTS CONCERNING THE LENDING OF MONEY.

Q. Since there exists no reason in the law of nature, why a man should not be paid for the lending of his money, as well as of any other property, whence arose the scruples that have been entertained upon this head, and upon the foundation of which, the receiving of interest or usury was once prohibited in almost all Christian countries?

A. From a passage in the law of MOSES, Deuteronomy, xxiii. 19, 20: "Thou shalt not lend upon usury to thy brother, &c."

Q. How is this prohibition now generally understood?

A. As intended for part of the civil or political law of the Jews alone, and calculated to preserve that distribution of property, to which many of their institutions were subservient; as the marriage of an heiress within her own tribe; &c.—regulations which were never thought to be binding upon any but the commonwealth of Israel.

Q. How is this interpretation confirmed?

A. By the distinction made between a Jew and a foreigner:—"unto a stranger thou mayest lend upon usury, but unto thy brother thou mayest not lend upon usury;" a distinction which could hardly have been admitted into a law, which the Divine Author intended to be of moral and universal obligation.

Q. How has the rate of interest in most countries been regulated?

A. By Law. The Roman allowed of £12. per cent., which Justinian reduced to 4. A statute of Elizabeth appointed it at 10. One of James I. reduced it to 8: of Charles II. to 6, and of Anne to 5, on pain of forfeiting treble the money lent; and thus the matter has ever since continued.

Q. What is the policy of these regulations?

A. To check the power of accumulating wealth

without industry; to give encouragement to trade, by enabling adventurers to borrow money at a moderate price; and of late years, to enable the state to borrow the subject's money itself.

Q. Why is compound interest, though forbidden by the law of England, agreeable to natural equity?

A. Because interest detained after it is due, becomes, to all intents and purposes, part of the sum lent.

Q. How ought money, borrowed in one country, to be paid in another, where its relative value is less?

A. More money ought to be returned until the actual value is the same; for it is to be presumed that the creditor would have made so much by his money if he had not lent it to me, and he neither intended, nor ought to be a sufferer by parting with the possession of it to me.

Q. If the relative value of the coin be altered by an act of the state, what is it enough to do?

A. It is enough to return an equal number of pieces of the same denomination, or their present value in any other.

Q. Whoever borrows money, knows that he is bound in conscience to repay it: but what does not every man see or reflect?

A. That he is, in consequence, bound to use the means necessary to enable himself to repay it. "If he pay the money when he has it, or has it to spare," he thinks he does all that an honest man can do, whilst he takes no previous measures to furnish himself with that money, which is as much his duty; such as selling a family estate, contracting his plan of expense, reducing his servants, or any of those sacrifices, which justice requires, the moment he perceives that he has no reasonable prospect of paying his debts without them.

Q. What law has been very much misunderstood?

A. That which authorizes the imprisonment of insolvent debtors.

Q. How has it been represented?

A. As a gratuitous cruelty, which contributed nothing to repair the creditor's loss, or benefit the community.

Q. How does this prejudice principally arise?

A. From considering the sending of a debtor to gaol, as an act of private satisfaction, instead of a public punishment. As an act of satisfaction or revenge, it is always wrong. Consider it as a public punishment, founded upon the same reason, and subject to the same rules, as other punishments; and the justice of it will be apparent: for there are frauds relating to insolvency, which require punishment, as much as any public crimes whatever: as where a man gets your money into his possession, and runs away with it; or, what is little better, squanders it in vicious expenses; or is conscious at the time he borrows it, that he can never repay it; or conceals his effects, or transfers them by collusion to another: or even obstinately prefers to rot in a gaol, rather than deliver up his estate.

Q. What is the only question?

A. Whether the punishment be properly placed in the hands of an exasperated creditor.

Q. For which what may be said?

A. That these frauds are so subtile, that nothing but a discretionary power can overtake them; and that no discretion is likely to be so vigilant, or active, as that of the creditor.

Q. Since however the confinement of a debtor is *punishment,* and every punishment supposes a crime, what ought we to abstain from doing?

A. From pursuing to extremity a sufferer, whom the fraud or failure of others, or disappointments and miscarriages have reduced to ruin, merely because we are provoked by our loss, and seek to relieve the pain we feel by that which we inflict; for this is repugnant to humanity, and justice, and a salutary provision of Law.

Q. How would any considerable mitigation of these laws encrease the hardships of the poor?

A. Whatever deprives the creditor of his power of coercion, deprives him of his security; and as this must add greatly to the difficulty of obtaining credit, the poor, especially the lower sort of tradesmen, are the first who would suffer by such a regulation.

CHAP. XI.

CONTRACTS OF LABOUR.

Q. What is the nature of service in this country?

A. It is, as it ought to be, voluntary, and by contract; and the master's authority extends no farther than the terms or equitable construction of the contract will justify.

Q. By what must the treatment of servants as to diet, discipline, and indulgence, be chiefly determined?

A. By custom; for where the contract involves so many particulars, the contracting parties express a few, and, by mutual understanding, refer the rest to the known custom of the country.

Q. In what is a servant not bound to obey his master?

A. In unlawful commands; to minister, for instance, to his unlawful pleasures; or to assist him by unlawful practices in his profession. For the servant is bound but by his own promise; and that obligation extends not to things unlawful.

For the same reason, the master's authority is no *justification* of the servant in doing wrong: for the servant's own promise, upon which that authority is founded, would be none.

Q. How ought clerks and apprentices to be employed?

A. Entirely in the profession or trade which they are to learn. Instruction is their hire; and to deprive them of it, by taking up their time with other occupations, is to defraud them.

Q. Why is the master responsible for what a servant does in the ordinary course of his employment?

A. Because it is done under a general authority committed to him, which is in justice equivalent to a specific direction. Thus, if I pay money to a banker's clerk, the banker is accountable; but not, if I had paid it to his butler or his footman, whose business it is not to receive money.

Q. Does the law of this country go far in inferring a kind of concurrence in the master, so as to charge him with the consequences of his servant's conduct?

A. It does: if an inn-keeper's servant rob his guests, the inn-keeper must make restitution; if your coachman or carter drive over a passenger in the road, the passenger may recover satisfaction from you. But these determinations stand rather upon the authority of law, than natural justice.

Q. What does Paley here designate as a great fraud committed upon society?

A. A carelessness and facility in "giving characters," as it is called, of servants, which are often given with so little veracity, "that we might as soon depend upon an acquittal at the Old Bailey." It is sometimes carelessness; and sometimes to get rid of a bad servant; than which nothing can be more ungenerous.

Q. There is a conduct the reverse of this, but more injurious, because the injury falls where there is no remedy; what is that?

A. The obstructing of a servant's advancement, because you are unwilling to spare his service; which is a poor return for his fidelity; and affords slender encouragement for good behaviour, in this numerous and important part of the community.

Q. Why is a master of a family culpable, if he permit any vices among his domestics, which he might restrain by proper discipline?

A. From the general obligation to prevent misery when in our power; and the assurance which we have, that vice and misery at the long run go together.

Q. What may be said of that which the Christian Scriptures have delivered concerning the relation and reciprocal duties of masters and servants?

A. It breathes a spirit of liberality, little known in ages when servitude was slavery; and which flows from a habit of contemplating mankind under the common relation in which they stand to their Creator, and with respect to their interest in another existence*. The idea of referring their service to God, of considering *him* as having appointed them their task, &c. was new; and affords a greater security to the master than any inferior principle. The exhortation also to masters, to keep in view their own subjection and accountableness, was no less seasonable.

* See St. Paul's Epist. to the Ephes. vi. 5—9.

CHAP. XII.

CONTRACTS OF LABOUR.

COMMISSIONS.

Q. What does he do who undertakes another man's business?

A. He makes it his own, that is, promises to employ upon it the same care and diligence as if it were his own; knowing that the business was committed to him with that expectation.

Q. But he promises no more than this; what, therefore, is an agent not obliged to do?

A. He is not obliged to wait, inquire, toil, or study, whilst there is a possibility of benefiting his employer; if he exert as much care as he thinks the value of the business deserves; that is, as he would have done if it had been his own, he has discharged his duty, although it should turn out, that by longer perseverance, he might have done better.

Q. Whose duty does this rule define?

A. That of factors, stewards, attorneys, and advocates.

Q. What is a principal difficulty in an agent's situation?

A. To know how far he may depart from his instructions, when, from some circumstances he sees reason to believe that his employer, if he were present, would alter his intention.

Q. How would the latitude allowed to agents in this respect, vary?

A. As the commission was confidential or ministerial; and as the general rule and nature of the service require a precise obedience to orders, or not. An attorney, sent to treat for an estate, if he found out a flaw in the title, would properly desist from his purchase; but if the commander of an army detach an officer upon a particular service, which turns out more difficult, or less expedient, than was supposed, so that he is convinced that his commander, if acquainted with it, would recall his orders, yet must this officer, if he cannot wait for fresh directions without prejudice to the service, pursue, at all hazards, those which he brought out.

Q. What is trusted to an agent, may be lost or damaged by misfortune. Is an agent who acts without pay, answerable for the loss?

A. No: for if he give his labour for nothing, it cannot be presumed that he gave also security for the success of it.

Q. If the agent be hired to the business, upon what will the question depend?

A. Upon the apprehension of the parties at the time of making the contract; which must be collected chiefly from custom. Whether a carrier ought to account for goods sent by him, or the owner of a ship for the cargo, where the loss is not through any fault or neglect of theirs, are questions of this sort. Any expression which implies a promise is binding on the agent, without custom;

as where the proprietors of a stage-coach advertise that they will *not* be accountable for money, plate, or jewels, this makes them accountable for every thing else; or where the price is so much for the labour, part may be considered as a premium for insurance. On the other hand, any caution of the owner against danger, proves that he considers the risk to be his; as cutting a bank-bill in two, to send by the post at different times.

Q. Universally, when must the loss fall upon the owner?

A. In all cases where a promise, either express or tacit, cannot be proved against the agent.

Q. If the agent be a sufferer in his own person or property by the business which he undertakes, can he, in such case, claim a compensation for the misfortune?

A. Not unless the same be provided for by express stipulation; for where the danger is not foreseen, there can be no reason to believe that the employer engaged to indemnify the agent against it: still less where it is foreseen; for whoever knowingly undertakes a dangerous employment, takes upon himself the danger and consequences; as where a fireman undertakes, for a reward, to rescue a box of writings from the flames.

CHAP. [illegible]

CONTRACTS OF LABOUR.

PARTNERSHIP.

Q. What, alone, requires explanation upon this subject?

A. How the profits are to be divided, where one partner contributes money, and the other labour.

Q. What is the Rule in this case?

A. Form the stock of the partnership out of the sum advanced, and divide the nett profits between the moneyed and the labouring partner, in the proportion of the interest of the money to the wages of the labourer, allowing such a rate of interest as money might be borrowed for upon the same security, and such wages as a journeyman would require for the same labour.

Q. The division of the profit is uniformly settled by express agreement; but what principle should these agreements [illegible]?

A. Those of the rule above laid down.

Q. Are all the questions [illegible] of them, [illegible]?

A. They are: [illegible] considered as an authorised agent [illegible]

CHAP. XIV.

CONTRACTS OF LABOUR.

OFFICES.

Q. In many offices, as schools, fellowships, or professorships in the universities, of what kind is the contract?

A. Two-fold; one with the founder, the other with the electors.

Q. What does the contract with the founder oblige the incumbent to do?

A. To discharge every duty appointed by the charter, statutes, or will of the founder; because the endowment was given, and accepted, upon these conditions.

Q. To what does the contract with the electors extend this obligation?

A. To all duties that have been customarily connected with the office, though not prescribed by the founder: for the electors expect from the person they choose, all the duties which his predecessors have discharged; and as he cannot be ignorant of their expectation, if he meant to have refused this condition, he ought to have apprised them of his objection.

Q. Why can the electors excuse the conscience of the person elected, from this last class of duties alone?

A. Because this class results from a contract to

which the electors and the persons elected are the only parties.

Q. What is a question of some magnitude and difficulty?

A. What offices may be conscientiously supplied by a deputy.

Q. How does Paley treat this subject?

A. He states the several objections to the substitution of a deputy; and then it is to be understood, that a deputy may be allowed in all cases to which these objections do not apply.

Q. In what cases, then, may an office not be discharged by deputy?

A. 1. Where a particular confidence is reposed in the judgment and conduct of the officer; as a [illegible], guardian, judge, &c.

2. Where custom [illegible]; as in the case of [illegible], &c.

3. Where the duty cannot, from its nature, be so well performed. The deputy-governor of a province may not possess the legal authority, or influence, of his principal.

4. When inconveniency would result to the service, from the permission of deputies in such cases: thus, military merit might be discouraged, if the duties of commissions in the army were allowed to be executed by substitutes.

Q. What case is worthy of a more distinct consideration?

A. The non-residence of the clergy, who supply the duty by curates.

Q. To draw this question to a point, what does Paley take for granted?

A. That the officiating curate discharges every duty of his principal, and with equal benefit to the parish.

Q. Under these circumstances, which alone of the foregoing objections is applicable to the absence of the principal?

A. The last.

Q. And how will the force of this be much diminished?

A. If the absent rector or vicar be engaged in any employment of equal, or of greater importance to the interest of religion. For the whole revenue of the church may be considered as a common fund to support the national religion; and if a clergyman be serving the cause of Christianity and Protestantism, it can make little difference out of what particular portion of this fund his service be requited; any more than it can prejudice the king's service that an officer who has signalised himself in America, should be rewarded with the government of a fort in Ireland, which he never saw; but for the custody of which, proper care is taken.

Q. Upon which principle, to whom is this indulgence especially due?

A. To those occupied in cultivating or communicating religious knowledge, &c.

Q. How does this idea of a common fund appear still more equitable?

A. As the value of particular preferments bears no proportion to the particular charge or labour.

Q. But what is the case where a man draws upon this fund whose employments bear no relation to its object?

A. It seems a misapplication little better than a robbery.

Q. Upon what supposition do all legal dispensations from residence proceed?

A. That the clergyman is detained from his living by some engagement of equal or of greater public importance.

Q. If therefore a person without such engagement pleads, that the Law which gives him the emoluments of a living, exempts him from residing upon it, and that he is excused in conscience, what may we answer?

A. That the law does not excuse him by its obligations; and that all other excuses are fraudulent.

CHAP. XV.

Q. What is a lie?

A. A breach of promise: for whoever seriously addresses his discourse to another, tacitly promises to speak the truth, because he knows that the truth is expected.

Q. How else may the obligation of veracity be made out?

A. From the direct ill consequences of lying to social happiness. Which consist either in some specific injury to individuals, or in the destruction of that confidence essential to social intercourse; for which reason, a lie may be pernicious in its general tendency, and therefore criminal, though it produce no particular or visible mischief.

Q. What are those falsehoods which are not lies, i. e. are not criminal?

A. 1. Where no one is deceived; as in parables, fables, ludicrous embellishments of a story, where the declared design is but to divert; a servant's denying his master, a prisoner's pleading not guilty, &c. here no confidence is destroyed, because none was reposed.

2. Where the person to whom you speak, has no right to know the truth, or, rather where little or no inconveniency results from want of confidence; as where you tell a falsehood to a madman for his own advantage; to a robber, to conceal your property, &c.

It is upon this principle, that it is allowable to deceive an enemy by false colours, spies, false intelligence, &c.; but not in treaties, signals of capitulation or surrender: and the difference is, that the former suppose hostilities to continue, the latter are calculated to terminate or suspend them. In one case there is no use, or rather no place, for confidence; but in whatever relates to the termination of war, the utmost fidelity is expected;

[illegible] but by the entire destruction of the vanquished.

Q. What does Paley observe respecting those persons who indulge in habitual lies and exaggeration in facts and narratives that appear indifferent?

A. (1) It is almost impossible to say beforehand, with certainty, of any lie, that it is inoffensive. *Volat irrevocabile*; and it collects sometimes accretions in its flight, which change its nature. It may owe its mischief to the officiousness of its circulators; but this is, in some degree, chargeable upon the original editor.

(2) This liberty in conversation defeats its own end. Much of the pleasure, and all the benefit, of conversation, depends upon our opinion of the speaker's veracity; for which this rule leaves no foundation.

Q. But beside both these reasons, what may be said of *white* lies?

A. They always introduce others of a darker complexion. Few who desert truth in trifles, can be trusted in matters of importance. The habit of lying, once formed, is easily extended, to serve the designs of malice or interest; and like all habits, it spreads of itself.

Q. What may be styled impositions of a more serious nature?

A. *Pious frauds*, pretended inspirations, counterfeit miracles, &c. Possibly they may sometimes have been set up with a design to do good: but this requires that the belief of them should be perpetual, which is hardly possible; and the detection of the fraud is sure to disparage the credit of such pretensions.

Q. As there may be falsehoods which are not lies, so can there be lies without literal or direct falsehood?

A. Yes. An opening is left for this species of prevarication, when the literal and grammatical signification of a sentence is different from the popular and customary meaning.

Q. What makes the lie?

A. The wilful deceit.

Q. And when do we wilfully deceive?

A. When our expressions are not true in the sense in which we believe the hearer to apprehend them.

Or a man may *act* a lie; as by pointing his finger in a wrong direction, when a traveller inquires of him his road; for speech is but a mode of action.

Or, lastly, there may be lies of *omission*. An historian, who, in his account of Charles the First, should suppress any evidence of his despotic measures, might be said to lie; for, by entitling his book a *History of England*, he engages to relate the whole truth, or all that he knows of it.

CHAP. XVI.

OATHS.

I. *Forms of Oaths.*

II. *Signification.*

III. *Lawfulness.*

IV. *Obligation.*

V. *What Oaths do not bind.*

VI. *In what cases Oaths are to be interpreted.*

Quest. 1. What does Paley say concerning the forms of oaths?

A. Like other religious ceremonies, they have in all ages been various; consisting generally of some bodily action, and of a prescribed form of words. Amongst the Jews, the juror held up his right hand towards heaven, which explains a passage in the 144th Psalm; "Whose mouth speaketh vanity, *and their right hand is a right hand of falsehood.*" The same form is retained in Scotland still. Amongst the same Jews, an oath of fidelity was taken, by the servant's putting his hand under the thigh of his lord, Gen. xxiv. 2.; whence is derived perhaps the form of doing homage at this day.

Amongst the Greeks and Romans, the form varied with the subject and occasion. In private contracts, they took each other's hand, whilst they swore to the performance; or they touched the altar of some god. Upon more solemn occasions, they slew a victim; whence the expressions τεμνειν ὁρκον, *ferire pactum*; and our phrase, translated from them, of "striking a bargain."

The forms in Christian countries are also very different; but in no country worse contrived, either to convey the meaning or impress the obligation of an oath, than in our own.

Our obscure elliptical form, together with the levity and frequency with which it is administered, has brought about a general inadvertency to the obligation of oaths; which, both in a religious and political view, is much to be lamented: and it merits public consideration, whether the requiring of oaths on so many frivolous occasions, has any other effect, than to make them cheap in the minds of the people. Let the law continue its own sanctions, if they be thought requisite; but let it spare the solemnity of an oath, and annex to prevarication penalties proportioned to the public mischief of the offence.

Q. II. What is observed concerning the signification of an oath?

A. Whatever be the form, the signification is the same. It is "the calling upon God to witness, *i. e.* to take notice of, what we say," and it is "invoking his vengeance, or renouncing his favour, if what we say be false, or what we promise be not performed."

Q. III. Quakers and Moravians found their

[illegible]

"But I say unto you, Swear not at all; neither by heaven; for it is God's throne; nor by the earth; for it is his footstool; neither by Jerusalem; for it is the city of the great King. Neither shalt thou swear by thy head, because thou canst not make one hair white or black. But let your communication be, Yea, yea; Nay, nay: for whatsoever is more than these, cometh of evil."

How can we reconcile with this passage of Scripture the practice of taking oaths, when required by law?

Answer: It does not appear, that swearing "by heaven," "by the earth," &c. was a form ever made use of by the Jews in judicial oaths: consequently, it is not probable that they were judicial oaths which Christ had in his mind.

As to the seeming universality of the prohibition, "Swear not at all," the emphatic clause "not at all" is to be read in connexion with what follows; "not at all" *i.e.* neither "by the heaven," nor by "the earth," &c. "*not at all*," does not mean upon no occasion, but by none of these forms. Our Saviour's argument supposes that they to whom he spake, made a distinction between swearing directly by the "name of God," and by inferior objects of veneration, "the heavens," "the earth," "Jerusalem," or "their own head." In opposition to which distinction, he tells them, that on account of the relation which these things

peal to the Supreme Being, (as certainly all of them, was in effect and substance swearing likewise.

3. Our Saviour himself being "adjured by the living God," answered the high-priest without objecting to the oath; for such it was. "God is my witness," says St. Paul to the Romans; and to the Corinthians still more strongly, "I call God for a record upon my soul, that to spare you I came not as yet to Corinth." Both these expressions contain the nature of oaths.

For these reasons, we explain our Saviour's words to relate to the practice of vulgar and unauthorised swearing. St. James's words, chap. v. 12, not so strong as our Saviour's, admit the same explanation with more ease.

Q. IV. In what case would oaths be nugatory, *i. e.* have no proper force or obligation?

A. If we did not believe that God will punish false swearing with more severity than a simple lie; for which belief, there are the following reasons:

1. Perjury is a sin of greater deliberation. The juror has the thought of God and of religion upon his mind at the time; he offends, therefore, with a high hand; in defiance of the sanctions of religion, and implies a disbelief or contempt of God's knowledge, power, and justice; which cannot be said of a lie, where nothing carries the mind to any reflection upon the Divine Attributes at all.

2. Perjury violates a superior confidence. Mankind must trust to one another; and they

have nothing better to trust to than one another's oath. Perjury, in its general consequence, strikes at the security of reputation, property, and even of life itself. A lie cannot do the same mischief, because the same credit is not given to it.

3. God directed the Israelites to *swear* by his name; and was pleased to confirm his covenant with that people by an oath: which probably he would not have done, had he not intended to represent oaths as having some meaning and effect beyond a bare promise; which effect must be owing to the severer punishment with which he will vindicate their authority.

Q. V. When are promissory oaths *not binding?*

A. When the promise itself would not be so: for the several cases of which see the Chapter on Promises.

Q. VI. What does Paley affirm respecting the interpretation of oaths?

A. As oaths are designed for the security of the imposer, it is manifest that they must be *interpreted* and performed in the sense in which he intends them; otherwise, they afford no security to *him*. And this is the meaning and reason of the rule, "*jurare in animum imponentis.*"

CHAP. XVII.

OATH IN EVIDENCE.

Q. What does the witness swear?

A. "To speak the truth, the whole truth, and nothing but the truth, touching the matter in question."

Q. Upon which, what may be observed?

A. That designed concealment is as much a violation of the oath as positive falsehood; whether the witness be interrogated as to any particular point or not. For when the witness is first sworn, to inquire whether he ought to give evidence in the cause at all, the form runs thus: "You shall true answer make to all such questions as shall be asked you:" but when he comes to be sworn *in chief*, he swears "to speak the whole truth," without restraining it, as before: which shows, that the law intends, in this latter case, to require of the witness, that he give a complete account of what he knows upon the subject, whether the questions proposed to him reach the extent of his knowledge or not."

Q. What single case may be cited, as an exception to this rule?

A. When a full discovery of the truth tends to accuse the witness himself of some legal crime. The law constrains no man to be his own accuser; consequently, imposes the oath of testimony with this tacit reservation. But the exception must be confined to *legal* crimes. A point of honour, delicacy, or reputation, will not justify his concealment of the truth.

Tenderness to the prisoner is no just excuse; for this transfers the administration of justice from judges and juries to prosecutors and witnesses.

Q. If questions irrelative to the cause be asked, of the propriety of which the witness doubts, what ought he to do?

A. To refer them to the court. The answer of the court is authority enough; for the law which imposes the oath, may remit what it will of the obligation: and the court declares what the mind of the law is. Yet the answer of the court is not universally conclusive upon the conscience of the witness; for his obligation depends upon what he apprehended, at the time of taking the oath, to be the design of the law in imposing it.

CHAP. XVIII.

OATH OF ALLEGIANCE.

Q. What is the form of this oath?

A. "I do sincerely promise and swear, that I will be faithful and bear true *allegiance* to his Majesty King George."

Q. How did it run before the Revolution?

A. "I do promise to be true and faithful to the king and his heirs, and truth and faith to bear, of life, and limb, and terrene honour; and not to know or hear of any ill or damage intended him, without defending him therefrom."

Q. As the present oath is a relaxation of the old one, and was intended to ascertain, not so much the extent of the subject's obedience, as the person to whom it was due, what does the legislature seem to have done?

A. To have wrapped up its meaning upon the former point, in a word purposely selected for its general and indeterminate signification.

Q. Into what considerations does Paley enter, with regard to this oath?

A. First, what the oath excludes as inconsistent with it; secondly, what it permits.

Q. What, then, does the oath exclude?

A. 1. The oath excludes all intention to support the claim of any other person to the crown, than the reigning sovereign. A Jacobite, persuaded of the Pretender's right, and designing to join with his adherents at a proper opportunity, cannot take this oath; or, if he could, the oath of abjuration follows, which contains a renunciation of all opinions in favour of the claim of the exiled family.

2. It excludes all design, at the time, of attempting to depose the reigning prince, for any reason whatever.

3. It forbids the taking up of arms against the reigning prince, with views of private advan-

ment, or from motives of personal resentment or dislike. If any engaged in the rebellion of forty-five with the expectation of titles or estates; or because they thought themselves neglected and ill-used at court; or because they entertained any animosity against the king or the minister; they added to the crime of unprovoked rebellion, that of wilful and corrupt perjury.

Q. What does the oath of allegiance permit, or not require?

A. 1. It permits resistance to the king, when his ill-behaviour or imbecility is such as to make resistance beneficial to the community. It may fairly be presumed that the very authority of that Parliament which introduced the oath was itself the effect of a successful opposition to an acknowledged sovereign. Some resistance, therefore, it is presumed, was meant to be allowed; and, if any, it must be that which has the public interest for its object.

2. It does not require obedience to commands of the king, unauthorised by law. No such is implied by the terms of the oath; the *fidelity* there promised, is fidelity in opposition to his enemies, not to law; and *allegiance*, at the utmost, can only signify obedience to lawful commands.

3. It does not require that allegiance be continued to the king, after he is actually deposed, driven into exile, or otherwise rendered incapable of exercising his office. The promise of allegiance implies, that the person to whom the promise is

made continues king; that is, exercises the power, and affords the protection, which belongs to the office: for, it is the possession of this power which makes such a particular person the object of the oath.

CHAP. XIX.

OATH AGAINST BRIBERY IN THE ELECTION OF MEMBERS OF PARLIAMENT.

Q. What is the form of this oath?

A. "I do swear, I have not received, or had, by myself, or any other person whatsoever in trust for me, or for my use and benefit, directly or indirectly, any sum or sums of money, office, place, or employment, gift, or reward, or any promise or security, for any money, office, employment, or gift, in order to give my vote at this election."

Q. Why do the several contrivances to evade this oath, as the accepting of money under plea of borrowing it, or the receiving it out of a drawer left open for that purpose, or the stipulating for a place, &c. incur the moral guilt, though they may escape the legal penalties of perjury?

A. They are manifestly within the design of the statute, and within the terms of the oath itself; for the word "indirectly" is inserted on purpose to comprehend such cases.

CHAP. XX.

OATH AGAINST SIMONY.

Q. Why has the obtaining ecclesiastical preferment by pecuniary considerations been termed simony?

A. From an imaginary resemblance between the purchase of a benefice and Simon Magus's attempt to purchase the gift of the Holy Ghost (Acts viii. 19).

Q. Since the law allows private patronage, and therefore the sale of advowsons, which is inseparable from it; what did it intend?

A. To restrain the patron, who possesses the right of presenting at the vacancy, from being influenced, in the choice of his presentee, by a bribe, or benefit to himself.

Q. In what does a similar distinction exist?

A. In the right of voting; that is, the freehold to which the right pertains, may be bought and sold as freely as any other property; but the exercise of that right, the vote itself, may not be purchased or influenced by money.

Q. What does the law adjudge to be simony?

A. 1. All payments, contracts, or promises, made by any person for a benefice *already vacant.*

2. A clergyman's purchasing of the *next turn* of a benefice *for himself*, "directly or indirectly." Also purchasing the perpetuity, and selling it again

with a reservation of the next turn, is inconsistent with the oath.

3. The procuring of a piece of preferment, by ceding to the patron any rights, or probable rights, belonging to it.

4. Promises to the patron of a portion of the profit, of a remission of tithes and dues, or other advantage out of the produce of the benefice.

5. General bonds of resignation, that is, bonds to resign upon demand.

Q. What does Paley remark upon this oath against simony?

A. He questions much the expediency of requiring it. It is very fit to debar public patrons from this kind of traffic: because from them may be expected some regard to the qualifications of the persons whom they promote. But the oath lays a snare for the integrity of the clergy; and the requiring of it in cases of private patronage produces no good effect, sufficient to compensate for this danger.

Where advowsons are holden *along* with manors, or other estates, it would be easy to forbid their separation; and thus keep preferment out of the hands of brokers.

CHAP. XXI.

OATHS TO OBSERVE LOCAL STATUTES.

Q. Members of colleges and of other ancient foundations, are required to swear to the observance of their statutes: which observance is become in certain cases unlawful, impracticable, useless, or inconvenient. How are unlawful directions countermanded?

A. By the authority which made them unlawful.

Q. How are impracticable directions dispensed with?

A. By the nature of the case.

Q. What is the only question?

A. How far the members of these societies may take upon themselves to judge of the *inconveniency* of any particular direction, and make that a reason for laying aside the observation of it.

Q. When does the *animus imponentis* seem to be satisfied?

A. When nothing is omitted, but what, from some change of circumstances, it may fairly be presumed that the founder himself would have dispensed with.

Q. To bring a case within this rule, what must the inconveniency be?

A. 1. It must be manifest; concerning which there is no doubt.

2. It must arise from some change in the cir-

cumstances of the institution: for, if it existed at the time of the foundation, it must be presumed that the founder did not deem the avoiding it of importance.

8. The direction of the statute must not only be inconvenient in the general, but prejudicial to the particular end of the institution: for, this alone proves that the founder would have dispensed with it.

Q. The statutes of some colleges forbid the use of any language but Latin within the walls, &c. &c.; what would be the case if they were to retain such rules?

A. Nobody would come near them. They are laid aside therefore, though parts of the statutes and included within the oath, not merely because they are inconvenient, but because there is reason to believe, that the founders would have dispensed with them, as subversive of their own designs.

CHAP. XXII.

SUBSCRIPTION TO ARTICLES OF RELIGION.

Q. Why may this, which is but a *declaration* of the subscriber's assent, be properly connected with the subject of oaths?

A. Because it is governed by the same rule of interpretation, the *animus imponentis*.

Q. What therefore will the inquiry be?

A. *Quis imposuit, et quo animo.* The bishop who receives the subscription is no more the imposer, than the crier of a court is the person that imposes the oath; nor, is the private opinion or interpretation of the bishop of any signification to the subscriber. Nor are the compilers of the Thirty-nine Articles to be considered as the imposers of subscription, any more than the drawer up of a law is the person that enacts it.

But the legislature of the 13th of Eliz. is the imposer, whose intention the subscriber is bound to satisfy.

Q. What must they suppose who contend that nothing can justify subscription but actual belief in all and every separate proposition of the 39 articles?

A. That the legislature expected the consent of ten thousand men in succession, not to one controverted proposition, but to many hundreds. It is difficult to conceive how this could be expected by any, who observed the incurable diversity of human opinion.

Q. If the authors of the law did not intend this, what did they intend?

A. To exclude from offices in the church,

1. All abettors of popery:

2. Anabaptists; at that time a powerful party on the Continent:

3. The Puritans; who were hostile to episco-

[illegible], and the members of such [illegible] foreign establishments as [illegible] our own.

Q. Who therefore ought not to subscribe?

A. Whoever finds himself comprehended within these descriptions. Nor any subscriber who [illegible] advantage which our rule may [illegible], who is not convinced that he is truly [illegible] the intention of the legislature.

CHAP. XXIII.

WILLS.

Q. What is the fundamental question upon this subject?

A. Whether Wills are of natural or of adventitious right? that is, whether the right of the disposition of property, after his death, belongs to a man by the law of nature, or be given him by the positive regulations of his country?

Q. The immediate produce of each man's personal labour are as much his own as the labour itself was; consequently, he may give or leave it to whom he pleases, there being nothing to limit the continuance, or restrain the alienation of his right. But how is the case with every other species of property, especially property in land?

A. It stands upon a different foundation in a

[illegible]

Q. How were the ancient apprehensions of mankind upon this subject?

A. Conformable to this account of it: for wills have been introduced into most countries by a positive act of the state; as by the Laws of Solon into Greece; by the Twelve Tables into Rome; [illegible]

Q. What are the beneficial purposes of extending the testator's power over property beyond his life and natural rights?

A. It incites to industry; it encourages marriage; it secures the dutifulness and dependency of children; but a limit must be assigned to the duration of this power.

Q. What is the limit of entails by the laws of England?

A. The life in existence at the death of the testator, and one-and-twenty years beyond that.

Q. From the consideration [illegible]

fore the municipal law, what question may be proposed?

A. Whether the intention of a testator in an informal will be binding upon the persons who, by operation of law, succeed to his estate; to suppose a man's will devising his freehold estate to his sister's son, being attested by two witnesses only, instead of three, witnesses; would the brother's son, who is heir at law, be bound in conscience to resign his claim, out of deference to his uncle's intention? or would not the devisee under the will be bound, upon discovery of this flaw in it, to surrender the estate to the heir at law?

Q. How does Paley decide this question?

A. Generally speaking, the heir at law is not bound by the intention of the testator, which can signify nothing, unless he have a right to govern the descent of the estate. Now, this the testator can only derive from the law of the land: but the law confers the right upon certain conditions, with which he has not complied; therefore, the testator can lay no claim to the power which he pretends to exercise. Consequently, the devisee under the will, who keeps possession of the estate, is like any other person who, through his neighbour's ignorance, detains from him his property. The will is so much waste paper, from the defect of right in the person who made it, the legislature deliberately enacting, that no will shall take effect upon real estates, unless authenticated in the [illegible]

[illegible] right, we [illegible] then have considered the law rather [illegible] its [illegible] to enforce the right of the devisee, [illegible] any [illegible] the right itself.

[illegible] where [illegible] of pity, duty, or gratitude [illegible] of justice.

Q. From what does the regard due to [illegible] ([illegible]) in a disposal of our fortune, arise?

[illegible] from the respect we owe to the presumed intention of the [illegible] from whom we received our fortunes, or from the expectations which [illegible] it only be presumed to be a father's intention, that his [illegible], after it had served one use, should remain a provision for the families of his other children, equally related and dear to him: whoever, therefore, without cause, leaves his patrimony from his brother's or sister's family is guilty of [illegible] to his parents. [illegible] accidentally [illegible] be involved.

[illegible] reasons; proximity of blood, and the like, [illegible] merely modes of speech, implying general obligation of themselves.

Q. What reason, however, always exists for providing for our poor relations, in preference to all others?

A. If we do not, no one else will; mankind, by an established consent, leaving the reduced members of good families to the bounty of their wealthy alliances.

Q. When is the not making a will a very palpable omission?

A. When it leaves daughters, or younger children, at the mercy of the eldest son; when it distributes a personal fortune equally amongst children, though there be no equality in their exigencies; where it leaves no opening for [illegible]; or principally, where it defrauds creditors through that defect in our laws, by which real estates are not subject to the payment of debts by simple contract, unless made so by will.

Q. What became of personal property anciently, when any one died without a will?

A. The bishop of the diocese took possession, to dispose of it for the benefit of the intestate's soul.

Q. As it thus became necessary that the bishop should be satisfied of the authenticity of the will, before he resigned his right, what took place?

A. Wills, and controversies relating to wills, came within the cognizance of ecclesiastical courts; under the jurisdiction of which, wills of personals (the only wills that were made formerly), still continue.

Q. How ought succession to intestates to be regulated?

A. By positive rules of law, there being no principal of natural justice whereby to ascertain the proportion of the different claimants.

Q. How should these regulations be guided?

A. By the duty and presumed inclination of the deceased, so far as these considerations can be consulted by general rules. The statutes of Charles II, which adopt the rule of the Roman law in the distribution of personals, are equitable. They assign one-third to the widow, and two to the children; in case of no children, one-half to the widow, and the other to the next of kin; where neither widow nor lineal descendants survive, the whole to the next of kin, and to be equally divided amongst kindred of equal degree.

Q. Why cannot we complain of the less reasonable descent of real estates, as that they shall in no wise go to the brother or sister of the half blood, though it came to the deceased from the common parent; that it shall go to the remotest relation the intestate has in the world, rather than to his own father or mother, &c.

A. Because any person may avoid this by so easy a provision as that of making his will.

Q. What may be a reason for making a difference in the course of inheritance with respect to land?

A. Its not being so divisible as money: but there ought to be no difference, except what is founded upon that reason. The Roman law made none.

BOOK III.

PART II.

OF RELATIVE DUTIES WHICH ARE INDETERMINATE.

CHAP. I.

CHARITY.

Q. How does Paley use the term Charity?

A. Neither in the common sense of bounty to the poor, nor in St. Paul's of benevolence to mankind; but to signify the *promoting the happiness of our inferiors.*

Q. What does he take charity to be in this sense?

A. The principal province of virtue and religion: for whilst worldly prudence will direct our behaviour towards our superiors, and politeness towards our equals, the consideration alone of duty, or habitual humanity, will produce a proper conduct towards our inferiors.

Q. What are the three principal methods of promoting the happiness of our inferiors?

A. 1. The treatment of our servants and other dependents. 2. Professional assistance. 3. Pecuniary bounty.

CHAP. II.

CHARITY.

THE TREATMENT OF OUR DOMESTICS AND DEPENDANTS.

Q. What is Paley's first observation on this subject?

A. He says, a party of friends journeying together, find it best, while they travel, that one should wait upon the rest; another procure food and lodging; a third carry the baggage; a fourth attend to the horses, and so on; not forgetting that as they started upon an equality, so they are to return to it at their journey's end—The same mild and forbearing conduct which their leader would think himself bound to use towards them, we ought to shew to those who happen to depend upon us in society.

Q. What other reflection of a like tendency does he make?

A. That our obligation to them is much greater than theirs to us—it is wrong to suppose, that the rich man maintains his servants, labourers, &c.—the truth is they maintain him: It is their industry which supplies him with his comforts and luxuries—their labour on his estate which pays his rent—He merely distributes what others produce.

Q. Does Paley subscribe to [illegible], that good usage is thrown away upon low and ordinary minds?

A. No: he observes that if by this expression we mean the minds of men in low stations, they seem to be affected by benefits and as ready to requite them as others; and it would be a very unaccountable law of nature if it were otherwise. Therefore whatever unnecessary uneasiness we occasion to our domestics, is wrong, were it only upon the principle of diminishing the sum of human happiness.

Q. By which rule what are we forbidden?

A. 1. To enjoin unnecessary labour or restraint from the mere love and wantonness of domination.

2. To insult our servants by harsh and opprobrious language.

3. To refuse them harmless pleasures.

By the same principle, also, is forbidden causeless or immoderate anger, habitual peevishness, and groundless suspicion.

CHAP. III.

SLAVERY.

Q. To what do the prohibitions of the last Chapter extend?

A. To the treatment of slaves; being founded on a principle independent of the contract between masters and servants.

Q. What is Paley's definition of slavery?

A. "An obligation to labour for the benefit of the master, without the contract or consent of the servant."

Q. How may this obligation arise, consistently with the Law of Nature?

A. From *crimes*, *captivity*, or *debt*. In the first case, the length of the punishment should be proportioned to the crime; in the second and third, it ought to cease when the demand of the injured nation, or private creditor, is satisfied.

Q. Is the African slave-trade excused upon these principles?

A. No: when slaves are sold in that country, the justice of the vendor's title is never asked, and probably is seldom founded in any of the above modes: in addition to this, the natives are excited to war for the sake of furnishing the market with slaves, who, torn from parents, friends, and country, *are transported like brutes to the American Settlements*, and subjected for life to the merciless authority of the plantation laws.

Q. May these enormities be justified by the pretended *necessity* of the case?

A. No: it has never been proved that the land there could not, with a small additional expense, be cultivated by hired servants.

Q. What are Paley's ideas upon the great revolution which has taken place in the Western world?

A. He considers that it may conduce to [illegible]

of slavery, and that [illegible] concluded [illegible] a legislature which had so long supported an institution replete with human misery, was fit to be trusted with the most extensive empire that ever existed in the world.

Q. As slavery was part of the civil constitution of most countries, when Christianity appeared, how may we account for its not being prohibited in the N. T.?

A. Christianity soliciting admission into all nations, abstained from intermeddling with the civil institutions of any; but it does not follow from the silence of Scripture that all those institutions were right, or that the bad should not be exchanged for better.

Q. What else may be said on this subject?

A. The discharging of slaves from all obligation to obey their masters, by pronouncing slavery unlawful, would have let loose one half of mankind upon the other, and have occasioned a *bellum servile*, to the reproach, if not the extinction of the Christian name.

Q. How does Paley conclude this chapter?

A. He asserts that the emancipation of slaves ought to be gradually carried on under the protection of civil government,—and that Christianity can act only as an alterative. By the diffusion of its light the minds of men may be led to perceive the enormities which folly, wickedness, or accident have introduced into public establishments: that

[illegible]

inasmuch as the contractors and overseers have an interest in opposition to the poor. A country gentleman of moderate fortune and income, by reading Dr. Burn's Justice, by acquainting himself with the prices of labour, etc., the wants of a family, and what is expected from their industry, may place out the one talent committed to him to great account.

CHAP. VI.

CHARITY.

PROFESSIONAL ASSISTANCE.

Q. Which of all professions puts it in a man's power to do the most good at the least [illegible]

A. That of medicine. [illegible]

Q. From whom is this kind of [illegible]

[illegible]

power which the law allows to Justices of the Peace over contractors and overseers?

A. He considers its judicious exercise and interposition as a most useful exertion of charity, inasmuch as the contractors and overseers have an interest in opposition to the poor. A country gentleman of moderate fortune and income, by reading Dr. Burn's Justice, by acquainting himself with the prices of labour, &c., the wants of a family, and what is to be expected from their industry, may place out the one talent committed to him to great account.

Q. Which of all private professions puts it in a man's power to do the most good at the least expense?

A. That of medicine. Health, which is precious to all, is to the poor invaluable; and their complaints, as agues, rheumatisms, &c., often yield to medicine. As to expense, drugs cost little, and advice nothing.

Q. What may be said upon the profession of the Law?

A. The rights of the poor are not so important or intricate, as their contentions are violent and ruinous. A lawyer of moderate knowledge may adjust them, without the expense of a suit; and may be said to give a man twenty pounds by preventing its being expended. A legal [illegible], whether of the profession or not, with a spirit of conciliation and the confidence of his neighbours, will be much resorted to for this purpose, especially since the great increase of legal costs.

[illegible] Peace, over contractors, and overseers?

A. [illegible] will often keep the rash and [illegible] from great difficulties.

Q. Lastly, what may be considered as a very exalted species of charity?

A. That which protects a child against the rapacity or persecution of a tyrant.

Q. What does Paley observe concerning the ministers of religion on this subject?

A. By argument, and by that authority which flows from respect and attends upon character, something may be done towards regulating the conduct and satisfying the thoughts of the lower orders. This office belongs to the ministers of religion; or rather, whoever undertakes it, becomes such. The inferior clergy, who are more on a level with their parishioners, and easily admitted to their confidence, have more in their power than their superiors. The discreet use of this power constitutes one of the most respectable functions of human nature.

CHAP. V.

CHARITY.

PECUNIARY BOUNTY.

I. *The obligation to bestow relief upon the poor.*

II. *The manner of bestowing it.*

III. *The pretences by which men excuse themselves from it.*

Q. What does Paley observe upon the first of these heads?

A. They who rank pity amongst the original impulses of our nature, rightly contend, that this principle indicates the Divine intention, and our duty. The same conclusion is deducible from the existence of the passion, whatever be its origin. Whether it be an instinct or a habit, it is in fact a property of our nature, which God appointed; and its final cause is to afford to the miserable, in the compassion of their fellow-creatures, a remedy for those distresses which God foresaw many would be exposed to, under every general rule for the distribution of property.

Beside this, the poor have a claim founded in the law of nature. All things were originally common. No one had any better title to a particular possession than his neighbour. There were reasons for agreeing upon a separation of this common fund; and God is therefore presumed to have ratified it. But this separation was made upon the expectation that each should have left a sufficiency for his subsistence, or the means of procuring it; and as no fixed laws for the regulation of property can provide for the relief of every case of distress, the cases of such, when their right and share in the common stock were given up, were supposed left to the voluntary bounty of those who might be acquainted with their exigencies, and able to afford assistance. Therefore, when the partition of property is rigidly maintained against the claims of indigence, it is in opposition to the intention of those who made it, and to his, who is the Supreme Proprietor, and who has filled the world with plenteousness, for the sustentation of all.

The Christian Scriptures are more copious and explicit upon this duty than upon almost any other. See Matt. xxv. 31:—"When the Son of man shall come in his glory," &c. It is not necessary to understand this as a literal account of what will actually pass on that day. Supposing it only a scenical description of the rules and principles by which God will regulate his decisions, it conveys the same lesson to us. The apostles also describe this virtue as eminently propitiating the Divine favour. And these recommendations have produced their effect; for it does not appear that, before the times of Christianity, a hospital, or public charity of any kind, existed in the world; whereas most Christian countries have long [illegible] with these instructions. A [illegible] of spirit of private liberality seems to furnish [illegible] the decay of many other virtues; not to mention the legal provision for the poor, which obtains in this country, and which was unthought of by all the nations of antiquity.

St. Paul adds upon the subject an excellent and practicable direction:—"Upon the first day of the week (or any other stated time) let every one of you lay by in store, as God hath prospered him." By which, he recommends what is the very thing wanting with most men, *the being charitable upon a plan*; that is, upon a deliberate comparison of our fortunes with the reasonable expenses and expectation of our families.

The effect of Christianity upon some of its first converts, was such as might be expected from a divine religion, coming with miraculous evidence upon the consciences of mankind. It overwhelmed all worldly considerations in the expectation of a more important existence.—See Acts, iv. 32.

Nevertheless, this community of goods is no precedent for our imitation. It was confined to the Church at Jerusalem; continued not long there; was never enjoined upon any (Acts, v. 4.); and, although it might suit with a small select society, is altogether impracticable in a large and mixed community.

The conduct of the apostles deserves notice. Their followers laid down their fortunes at their feet: but so far were they from taking advantage of this, to enrich themselves, that they soon afterwards transferred the custody and dispensing of the public fund to deacons, elected by the people at large. (Acts, vi.)

Q. What may be observed upon the second head, viz. *The manner of bestowing bounty; or the different kinds of charity*?

A. Every question between the different kinds of charity supposes the sum bestowed to be the same.

There are three kinds of charity which prefer a claim to attention.

The first, and in Paley's judgment one of the best, is to give stated and *considerable* sums, by way of pension or annuity, to individuals or families, with whose behaviour and distress we are acquainted. A poor fellow, who can find no better use for a *shilling* than to purchase half an hour's recreation for himself, would hardly break into a guinea for such purpose, or be so improvident as not to lay it by for an occasion of importance, *e. g.* for his rent, his clothing, &c. This kind of charity also is the only way by which we can prevent one part of a poor man's sufferings,—the *dread* of want.

2. But as this kind of charity supposes much which does not happen to all, a second method of doing good, in every one's power who has the money to spare, is by subscription to public charities. In this your money goes farther towards attaining the end for which it is given, than it can do by any private beneficence. A guinea contributed to an infirmary, becomes the means of providing one

patient at least with all suitable attendance, which would cost a sick person or family ten times as much.

3. The last, and lowest exertion of benevolence, is in the relief of beggars. Nevertheless, the indiscriminate rejection of all who implore our alms is not to be approved of. Some may perish by such a conduct, to whom all other relief would come too late. Beside which, resolutions of this kind compel us to offer such violence to our humanity, as may go near to suffocate the principle itself; which is a very serious consideration. A good man, will at least lend an ear to importunities accompanied with outward attestations of distress; and after a patient audience, will direct himself, not so much by any previous resolution, as by the circumstances and credibility of the account he receives.

There are other species of charity well contrived to make the money expended *go far*; such as lowering the price of fuel or provision, by purchasing articles at the best market, and retailing them at prime cost; or adding of a bounty to particular species of labour, when the price is accidentally depressed.

The proprietors of large estates have it in their power nobly to facilitate the maintenance, and encourage the establishment of families, by building cottages, splitting farms, cultivating wastes, draining marshes, &c. &c. If the profits of these undertakings do not repay the expense, let the authors of them place the difference to the account of charity.

It is a question of some importance, under what circumstances works of charity ought to be done in private, and when they may be made public without detracting from the merit of the action; J. C. having delivered a rule upon this subject which seems to enjoin universal secrecy:—(Matt. vi. 3, 4.) From the preamble to this prohibition it is however plain, that his sole design was to forbid *ostentation*, and all publishing of good works which proceeds from that motive. (see v. 2.) There are motives for doing our alms in public, beside those of *ostentation*, with which therefore our Saviour's rule has no concern: such as to recommend some particular species of charity, to take off the prejudice which the suppression of our name in the list of contributors might excite against it. And, so long as these motives are free from any mixture of vanity, they rather seem to comply with another direction which J. C. has left us: "Let your light so shine before men, that they may see your good works," &c. When our bounty is *beyond* our fortune, that is, more than could be expected from us, our charity should be private, if practicable: when it is not more than might be expected, it may be public: for we cannot hope to influence others to the imitation of *extraordinary* generosity.

Q. What remarks are made upon the third head; viz. *The pretences by which men excuse themselves from giving to the poor.*

A. 1. "They say that they have nothing to spare," *i.e.* nothing for which they have not provided some other use; nothing which their plan or expense, &c. will not exhaust: never reflecting whether it be their *duty*, to retrench their expenses, "that they may have to give to them that need:" or, rather, that this ought to have been part of their plan originally.

2. "That they have families of their own, and that charity begins at home." The extent of this plea will be considered hereafter.

3. "That charity does not consist in giving money, but in benevolence, philanthropy, goodness of heart," &c. upon this point see St. James, ii. 15, 16.

4. "That giving to the poor is not mentioned in St. Paul's description of charity, 1. Cor. xiii." This is not a description of charity, but of good-nature; and it is not necessary that every duty be mentioned in every place.

5. "That they pay the poor-rates." They might as well allege that they pay their debts: for the poor have the same right to that portion of a man's property which the laws assign to them, that he himself has to the remainder.

6. "That they employ many poor persons:"—for their own sake;—otherwise it is a good plea.

7. "That the poor do not suffer so much as we imagine; that habit has reconciled them to the evils of their condition." Habit can never reconcile human nature to the extremities of cold, hunger, thirst, &c.: besides, the question is not, how unhappy any one is, but how much more happy we can make him.

8. "That these people, give them what you will, will never thank you, or think of you for it." This is not true; and it was not for the sake of their thanks that you relieved them.

9. "That we are liable to be imposed upon." If due inquiry be made, our merit is the same: however the distress is generally real, though the cause be untruly stated.

10. "That they should apply to their parishes." This is not always practicable; besides there are many requisites to comfort, which parish relief does not supply; and some would suffer almost as much from receiving parish relief as by the want of it; there are many modes of charity to which this answer does not relate at all.

11. "That giving money encourages idleness." This is true only of indiscriminate generosity.

12. "That we have too many objects at home, to bestow any thing upon strangers; or, there are other charities more useful," &c. The value of this excuse depends upon the *fact*, whether we actually relieve those neighbouring objects, and contribute to those other charities.

Beside all these excuses, pride, or prudery, or love of ease, keep one half of the world out of the way of observing what the other half suffer.

CHAP. VI.

RESENTMENT.

Q. Into what may *resentment* be distinguished?

A. Into *anger* and *revenge*.

Q. What is meant by *anger*?

A. The pain we suffer upon the receipt of an injury or affront, with the usual effects of that pain upon ourselves.

Q. What by *revenge*?

A. The inflicting of pain upon the person who has injured or offended us, farther than the just ends of punishment or reparation require.

Q. Why may anger and revenge be considered separately?

A. Anger prompts to revenge; but it is possible to suspend the effect, when we cannot altogether quell the principle. We are bound also to endeavour to qualify and correct the principle itself. So that our duty requires two different applications of the mind.

CHAP. VII.

ANGER.

Q. "Be ye angry and sin not." Why is not all anger sinful?

A. Probably because some degree of it, and upon some occasions, is inevitable.

Q. When, however, does it become sinful, or contradict the rule of Scripture?

A. 1. When it is conceived upon slight provocations: for, "charity suffereth long, is not easily provoked." &c.

2. When it continues long: for, "let not the sun go down upon your wrath."

Q. What do these precepts, and all reasoning indeed upon the subject, suppose?

A. That the passion of anger is within our power: and this power consists not so much in any faculty we possess of appeasing our wrath at the time, as in so mollifying our minds by habits of just reflection, as to be less irritated by impressions of injury, and to be sooner pacified.

Q. What reflections are proper for this purpose, and which may be called the *sedatives* of anger?

A. The following: the possibility of mistaking the motives of offence; how often our own offences have been the effect of inadvertency, though construed into indications of malice; the inducements which prompted our adversary to act as he did; and how such have, at one time or other, operated upon ourselves: that he is suffering perhaps under a contrition, which he is ashamed, or wants opportunity, to confess; that the returns of kindness are sweet, and that there is neither honour nor virtue in resisting them. We may remember that others have their passions, their prejudices, their favourite aims, their sudden impulses, their varieties of apprehension, as well as we: we may recollect what has passed in our minds, when we have been in the wrong, and imagine the same to be passing in our adversary's mind; when we became sensible of our misbehaviour, what palliations we percived in it, and expected others to perceive; how we were affected by the kindness, and felt the superiority of a ready forgiveness; how persecution revived our spirits with our enmity, and seemed to justify the conduct in ourselves which we before blamed. Add to this, the indecency of extravagant anger; the inconveniences, or irretrievable misconduct, into which our irascibility has sometimes betrayed us; the friendships it has lost us; the distresses it has caused us; and the sore repentance which it always cost us.

Q. But what is the reflection best calculated to calm a haughty and impetuous temper?

A. That which the Gospel proposes; namely, that we ourselves shortly shall be suppliants for mercy and pardon at the judgment-seat of God. Imagine our secret sins brought to light; imagine us

themselves in an impotent [illegible] struggling under the hand of God and crying out furiously; imagine them [illegible] talk of satisfaction and revenge; refusing to be entreated, disdaining to forgive; imagine this, and you can hardly frame to yourself an instance of more impious and unnatural arrogance.

Q. What ought we principally to [illegible] these reflections?

A. To habituate ourselves to them, till they rise up of their own accord when wanted, that is, upon the receipt of an injury or affront, and with such force as to mitigate the anger at the time, and at length to produce an alteration in the temper itself.

CHAP. VIII.

Q. What is revenge?

A. All pain occasioned to another, in consequence of an offence or injury received from him, further than what is calculated to procure reparation or promote the just ends of punishment.

Q. Why can there be no difficulty in distinguishing [illegible] with [illegible] to the ends of punishment, from revenge?

A. In the one case we are pleased with [illegible]; in the other with pleasure.

Q. What is highly probable from the light of nature, concerning a passion which seeks its gratification immediately and expressly in giving pain?

A. That it is disagreeable to the benevolent will and counsels of the Creator. Other passions and pleasures may, and often do, produce pain to some one; but then pain is not, as it is here, the object of the passion and the direct cause of the pleasure.

Q. How is this probability turned into a certainty?

A. If we give credit to the Authority which dictated the several passages of the SS. that condemn revenge, or enjoin forgiveness.

Q. What are the principal of these passages?

A. "If ye forgive men their trespasses, your heavenly Father will also forgive you: but if ye forgive not men their trespasses, neither will your Father forgive your trespasses."—Math. vi. 14, 15, see also xviii. 34, 35, Col. iii. 12, 13, 1 Thess. v. 14, 15, Rom. xii. 19, 20, 21.

Q. What is evident from some of these, taken separately, and still more from all, collectively?

A. That revenge is forbidden in every degree, under all forms, and upon every occasion. We are likewise forbidden to refuse to an enemy even the most imperfect right; "if he hunger, feed him; if he thirst, give him drink;" if one who has offended us, solicit from us a vote to which his qualifications entitle him, we may not refuse it from motives of resentment. His right, and our obligation [illegible] are not altered by this enmity to us, or by his [illegible] to him.

Q. What, on the other hand, were these prohibitions not intended to interfere with?

A. The punishment or prosecution of public offenders. In xviii. chap. of St. Matthew, our Saviour tells his disciples, "If thy brother who has trespassed against thee neglect to hear the church, let him be unto thee as an heathen man, and a publican." Immediately after this, when St. Peter asked him, "How oft shall my brother sin against me, and I forgive him? till seven times?" Christ replied, "I say not unto thee until seven times, but until seventy times seven:" that is, as often as he repeats the offence. From these two adjoining passages compared together, we conclude that the forgiveness of an enemy is not inconsistent with the proceeding against him as a public offender; and that the discipline established in religious or civil societies, for the restraint or punishment of criminals, ought to be upholden.

If the magistrate be not tied down with these prohibitions, neither is the prosecutor, whose office is as necessary as that of the magistrate.

Nor, by parity of reason, are private persons withholden from the correction of vice, provided they be assured that it is the guilt which provokes them, and not the injury; and that their motives are quite free from that spirit which triumphs in the humiliation of an adversary.

Thus, it is no breach of Christian charity, to withdraw our company or civility when the same tends to discountenance any vicious practice. This is one branch of that extrajudicial discipline, which supplies the defects and the remissness of law; and is expressly authorised by St. Paul (1 Cor. v. 11).

We are likewise allowed to practise so much caution as not to put ourselves in the way of injury, or invite the repetition of it. If a servant or tradesman has cheated us, we are not bound to trust him again: for this is to encourage him in his dishonest practices, which is doing him much harm.

Where a benefit can be conferred only upon one or few, and the choice of the person is a proper object of favour, we are at liberty to prefer those who have not offended us to those who have; the contrary being no where required.

Q. What virtue does Christ, who estimated virtues by their solid utility, and not by their fashion or popularity, prefer to every other?

A. Forgiveness of injuries. He enjoins it oftener; with more earnestness; and with this peculiar circumstance, that the forgiveness of others is the condition upon which alone we are even to ask, from God, forgiveness for ourselves. And this preference is justified by the superior importance of the virtue. Feuds and animosities, which disturb the intercourse of human life, have their foundation in the want of a forgiving temper; and can never cease, but by the exercise of this virtue.

CHAP. IX.

DUELLING.

Q. Why is Duelling, as a punishment, absurd?

A. Because it is an equal chance, whether the punishment fall upon the offender, or the person offended.

Q. Is it much better, as a reparation?

A. No; it being difficult to explain in what the *satisfaction* consists, or how it tends to undo the injury, or to afford a compensation for it.

Q. Is it, indeed, considered as either?

A. No; a law of honour having annexed the imputation of cowardice to patience under an affront, challenges are given and accepted, merely to preserve the duellist's own reputation and reception in the world.

Q. The unreasonableness of this rule of manners is one consideration; the duty and conduct of individuals, while such a rule exists, is another: as to this, what is the proper and single question?

A. Whether a regard for our own reputation is, or is not, sufficient to justify the taking away the life of another?

Q. What does Paley observe upon this?

A. Murder is forbidden; and wherever human life is deliberately taken away, except by public authority, there is murder. No other idea or definition of murder can be admitted, which will not let in so much private violence, as to render society a scene of peril and bloodshed.

If unauthorised laws of honour be allowed to create exceptions to God's prohibitions, there is an end to all morality, as founded in his will; and the obligation of every duty is subjected to caprice and fashion.

Q. "But (it is said) a sense of shame is so much torture; and no relief presents itself otherwise than by an attempt upon the life of our adversary." What do we say to this?

A. The distress which a man suffers by want is often extreme, and there is no resource but that of removing a life between him and his inheritance. The motive in this case is as urgent, and the means much the same; yet it finds no advocate.

Take away the circumstance of the duellist's exposing his own life, and it becomes assassination; add this and what is the difference? None but this, that fewer perhaps will imitate the example. There is, however, fortitude enough in most men to undertake this hazard: and if not, the defence at best, would be only that of a highwayman, whose attempt had been so daring, that few were likely to repeat it.

Q. In expostulating with the duellist, what does Paley all along suppose?

A. His adversary to fall: because, if he have no right to kill his adversary, he has none to attempt it.

Q. In return, what does he forbear to apply to duelling?

A. The Christian principle of the forgiveness of injuries; because we may suppose the injury forgiven, and the duellist to act entirely for his own reputation: where this is not so the guilt is manifest, and greater.

Q. In this view what does it seem unnecessary to distinguish?

A. Between him who gives, and him who accepts a challenge: for they incur an equal hazard; and both act because they think it necessary to recover or preserve the good opinion of the world.

Q. What does Paley observe upon this?

A. Public opinion is not easily controlled by civil institutions; it is doubtful therefore whether any regulations can be contrived to suppress or change the rule of honour, which stigmatises scruples with the reproach of cowardice.

Q. What tempts many to redress themselves?

A. The insufficient redress which the law of the land affords for those injuries which affect a man in his sensibility and reputation. This ought to be remedied.

Q. What does he propose for the army?

A. He would establish a *Court of Honour*, with a power of awarding those submissions, which it is generally the purpose of a challenge to obtain; and it might grow into a fashion, with persons of rank of all professions, to refer their quarrels to this tribunal.

CHAP. X.

LITIGATION.

Q. What does the precept, "if it be *possible* live peaceably with all men," contain?

A. An indirect confession that this is not always *possible*.

Q. How are instances in the fifth chapter of St. Matthew to be understood?

A. As proverbial methods of describing the general duties of forgiveness and benevolence, and the temper we ought to aim at, rather than as directions to be specifically observed. "If thine enemy smite thee on thy right cheek, turn to him the other also;" yet, when one of the officers struck Jesus, we find him rebuking the man for the outrage. (John xviii. 43.) It may be observed, likewise, that the examples are drawn from instances of small and tolerable injuries.

Q. What would be the effect of a rule which forbade all opposition to, or defence against injury?

A. To put the good in subjection to the bad, and deliver one half of mankind to the depredation of the other half.

Q. What may be observed of St. Paul on this head?

A. Though no one more inculcated forgiveness and forbearance, he did not interpret either of them to require unresisting submission to contumely, or a neglect of the means of self-defence. He took refuge in the laws and privileges of a Roman citizen, from the conspiracy of the Jews (Acts xxv. 11.); and from the clandestine violence of the chief captain (Acts xxii. 25.); although he reproved the litigiousness of his Corinthian converts with so much severity.

Q. What therefore does Christianity, on the one hand, exclude?

A. All vindictive motives, and all frivolous causes of prosecution, where the injury is small, and no good purpose of public example is answered, &c.

Q. When, on the other hand, is a law-suit inconsistent with no rule of the Gospel?

A. 1. For the establishing of some important right.

2. For the procuring a compensation for some considerable damage.

3. For the preventing of future injury.

Q. But, since it is supposed to be undertaken simply with a view to the ends of justice and safety, to what is the prosecutor bound to confine himself?

A. To the cheapest process which will accomplish these ends, as well as to consent to any peaceable expedient for the same purpose; as to *a reference*, or to *a compounding of the dispute*, by accepting a compensation in the gross.

Q. As to the rest, how may the duty of the contending parties be expressed?

A. In the following directions:

Not by appeals to prolong a suit against your own conviction.

Not to undertake or defend a suit against a poor adversary, with the hope of intimidating or wearying him out by the expense, or delay.

Not to influence *evidence* by authority or expectation.

Nor to stifle any in your possession, although it make against you.

Q. Hitherto we have treated of civil actions; what ought to be observed in criminal prosecutions?

A. The private injury should be forgotten, and the prosecutor proceed with the same temper, and upon the same motives, as the magistrate, in a dispassionate care of the public welfare.

As the punishment of an offender is conducive, or his escape dangerous, to the interest of the community, so is the suffering party bound to prosecute, because such prosecutions must in their nature originate from the sufferer.

Therefore, great public crimes ought not to be spared on account of trouble or expense in carrying on the prosecution, or from misplaced compassion.

There are many offences, such as nuisances, neglect of public roads, smuggling, sabbath-breaking, profaneness, drunkenness, prostitution, &c. the prosecution of which, being of equal concern to the whole neighbourhood, cannot be a peculiar obligation upon any.

[illegible] proper [illegible].

An *informer* is in this country undeservedly odious. But where any public advantage is likely to be attained, a good man will despise a prejudice founded in no just reason, or will acquit himself of interested designs by giving away his share of the penalty.

On the other hand, prosecutions for the sake of the reward, or for private enmity, where the offence produces no public mischief, or arises from ignorance or inadvertency, are reprobated under the general description of *applying a rule of law to a purpose for which it was not intended*.

CHAP. XI.

GRATITUDE.

Q. In what does the mischief of ingratitude consist?

A. Examples of it check and discourage voluntary beneficence?

Q. Is this mischief small?

A. No; for after all is done that can be done towards providing for the public happiness, much must be left to those offices of kindness, which men may exert or withhold at pleasure; the quantity and even the existence of this sort of kindness in the world, depends in a great measure, upon the return which it receives.

Q. What is the second reason given for cultivating a grateful temper?

A. The same principle, which is touched with human kindness, is capable of being affected by the Divine goodness, and of becoming, under that influence, a source of the most exalted virtue. The love of God is the sublimest gratitude; and it is a mistake, to imagine, that this virtue is omitted in the SS. for every precept which commands us "to love God, because he first loved us," presupposes the principle of gratitude, and directs it to its proper object.

Q. Though it is impossible to particularise the various expressions of gratitude, what however may be observed?

A. That gratitude can never oblige a man to do what is wrong, and which he is previously obliged not to do. It is no ingratitude to refuse to do what we cannot reconcile to our duty; but it is both ingratitude and hypocrisy to pretend this reason, when it is not the real one.

Q. What has ever been considered a violation of delicacy and generosity?

A. To upbraid men with the favours they have received: but it argues a total destitution of moral probity, to take advantage of our ascendancy, to draw or drive them whom we have obliged, into mean or dishonest compliances.

CHAP. XII.

SLANDER.

Q. What does Paley observe with regard to *speaking*?

A. It is *acting*: for if the mischief and motive of our conduct be the same, the means which we use make no difference.

And this is in effect what our Saviour declares, Matt. xii. 37:—"By thy words thou shalt be justified, and by thy words thou shalt be condemned:" by thy words, as well, that is, as by thy actions; for they both possess the same property of voluntarily producing good or evil.

Q. How may slander be distinguished?

A. Into two kinds; *malicious* slander, and *inconsiderate* slander.

Q. What is malicious slander?

A. It is the relating of either truth or falsehood, for the purpose of creating misery.

Q. What indeed varies the degree of guilt?

A. The truth or falseness of what is related; for slander ordinarily signifies the circulation of mischievous *falsehoods*: but truth may be made instrumental to malicious designs; and if the end be bad, the means cannot be innocent.

Q. To what does Paley think the idea of slander ought to be confined?

A. To the production of *gratuitous* mischief. When we have an interest to advance, if we attempt it by falsehood, it is *fraud*; if by a publication of the truth, it is not criminal, without breach of promise, betraying of confidence, or the like.

To infuse suspicions, to kindle disputes, to avert the favour of benefactors from their dependents, to render some one whom we dislike contemptible, are all offences of slander; of which the guilt must be measured by the extent of the misery produced.

The disguises under which slander is conveyed, in a whisper, or with affected reluctance, &c., are all aggravations of the offence, as they indicate more design.

Q. What makes the difference between this and inconsiderate slander, though the same mischief follow, and might have been foreseen?

A. The not being conscious of that design which we have hitherto attributed to the slanderer.

Q. In what does the guilt here consist?

A. In the want of that regard to the consequences of our conduct, which a just concern for human happiness, and our own duty, would have produced in us.

Q. What is no answer to this crimination?

A. To say, that we entertained no evil *design*. A servant may be a very bad servant, and yet seldom or never design to act in opposition to his master's interest or will; and his master may justly punish such servant for a thoughtlessness and neglect nearly as prejudicial as deliberate disobedience.

Q. What is the opposite of slander ?

A. Indiscriminate praise: but, it is the opposite extreme ; and is commonly the effusion of a frivolous understanding, or of a settled contempt of all moral distinctions.

BOOK III.

PART III.

OF RELATIVE DUTIES WHICH RESULT FROM THE CONSTITUTION OF THE SEXES.

Q. What is the foundation of marriage?

A. The constitution of the sexes.

Q. What are collateral to the subject of marriage?

A. Fornication, seduction, adultery, incest, polygamy, divorce.

Q. What is consequential to it?

A. The relation and reciprocal duty of parent and child.

Q. In what order does Paley treat of these subjects?

A. 1. Of the public use of marriage-institutions; 2. of the subjects collateral to marriage; 3. of marriage itself; and, lastly, of the relation and reciprocal duties of parents and children.

CHAP I.

OF THE PUBLIC USE OF MARRIAGE-INSTITUTIONS.

Q. In what does the public use of marriage-institutions consist?

A. In their promoting the following beneficial effects:—

1. The private comfort of individuals, especially of the female sex. Though all are not interested in this, it is a reason to all for abstaining from any conduct which tends to obstruct marriage: for whatever promotes the happiness of the majority is binding upon the whole.

2. The production of the greatest number of healthy children, their better education, and provision.

3. The peace of human society, by assigning one or more women to one man, and protecting his exclusive right by sanctions of morality and law.

4. The better government of society, by means of separate families, and appointing over each the authority of a master, which has more influence than all civil authority.

5. The same end, in the additional security of the state from the good behaviour of its citizens, by the solicitude they feel for the welfare of their children, and by their being confined to permanent habitations.

6. The encouragement of industry.

Q. Do any ancient nations appear to have been more sensible of the importance of these institutions than we are?

A. The Spartans obliged their citizens to marry by penalties, and the Romans encouraged theirs by the *jus trium liberorum*, &c.

CHAP. II.

FORNICATION.

Q. In what consists the first and great mischief, as well as the guilt of promiscuous concubinage?

A. In its tendency to diminish marriages, and thereby to defeat the several beneficial purposes enumerated in the preceding chapter.

Q. How does this discourage marriage?

A. By abating the chief temptation to it. The male part of the species will not undertake the expense and restraint of married life, if they can gratify their passions cheaper; and they will undertake any thing, rather than not gratify them.

Q. How shall we learn to comprehend the magnitude of this mischief?

A. By attending to the important and various uses to which marriage is subservient; and by recollecting, that the malignity of each crime is not to be estimated by the particular effect of one offence, or of one person's offending, but by the general tendency of such crimes. The libertine may not be conscious that these irregularities hinder his own marriage, much less that *his* indulgences can hinder that of others; but what would be the consequence, if the same licentiousness were universal? or what should hinder its being so, if it be allowable in him?

2. Fornication supposes prostitution; and this brings and leaves the victims of it to almost certain want, disease, and insult. The whole of this is a *general consequence* of fornication, to the increase and continuance of which, every act contributes.

3. It produces habits of ungovernable lewdness, which introduce the more aggravated crimes of seduction, adultery, violation, &c. Likewise it corrupts and depraves the mind and moral character more than any other vice. It is in low life, usually the first stage to the most desperate villanies; and, in high life, to the utmost dissoluteness of principle, and contempt of religion and of moral probity. Its habit also incapacitates and indisposes the mind for all intellectual, moral, and religious pleasures.

4. It perpetuates one of the sorest maladies of human nature; the effects of which are said to visit the constitution of distant generations.

Q. The passion is natural: what does this prove?

A. That it was intended to be gratified; but under what restrictions, or whether without any, must be collected from different considerations.

Q. What do the Christian SS. say?

A. They condemn fornication absolutely and peremptorily. "Out of the heart proceed evil thoughts, murders, adulteries, *fornication*, &c.; these are the things which defile a man." These are Christ's own words; and one word from him upon the subject is final. It may be observed here too with what society fornication is classed.

Q. What do the apostles say upon this topic?

A. They are more full upon it. One well-known passage in the Epistle to the Hebrews, may stand in the place of all others; it is decisive: "Marriage and the bed undefiled is honourable amongst all men: but whoremongers and adulterers God will judge;" which was a great deal to say, at a time when it was not agreed, even amongst philosophers, that fornication was a crime.

Q. Do the Scriptures give any sanction to those austerities which have been imposed upon the world; as the celibacy of the clergy, the praise of perpetual virginity, &c.?

A. No; but with a just knowledge of, and regard to, our condition and interest, have provided in the marriage of one man with one woman, an adequate gratification for the propensities of their nature, and have *restricted* them to that gratification.

Q. What ought legislators who have patronized receptacles of prostitution, to have foreseen?

A. That whatever facilitates fornication diminishes marriages. And, as to the usual apology for this relaxed discipline, the danger of greater enormities, it will be time to look to that, when the laws and magistrates have done their utmost. After all, these pretended fears are without foundation in experience.

Q. What apology has been made for the more specious case of *kept-mistresses*, under the favourable circumstances of mutual fidelity?

A. It has been said, "That the marriage-rite being different in different countries, and amongst different sects, and with some scarce any thing; and not being prescribed or mentioned in Scripture, can be accounted only a ceremony of human invention; and that if a man and woman betroth and confine themselves to each other, their intercourse must be the same, as to all moral purposes, as if they were legally married."

Q. To this what may be replied?

A. 1. If the situation of the parties be the same thing as marriage, why do they not marry?

2. If the man choose to have it in his power to dismiss the woman at his pleasure, or to retain her in a state of dependence inconsistent with the rights of marriage, it is not the same thing.

It is not at any rate the same thing to the children.

Again, as to the marriage-rite being a mere variable form, the same may be said of bonds, wills, deeds of conveyance, &c. which yet make a great difference in the rights and obligations of the parties concerned in them.

And with respect to Scripture;—the SS. forbid fornication, that is, cohabitation without marriage, leaving it to the law of each country to pronounce what is, or what makes, a marriage; as they forbid thefts, or the taking another's property, leaving it to the municipal law to fix what makes the thing property, &c.

Q. Omitting the injunctions of Scripture, what seems a plain account of the question?

A. It is immoral, because it is pernicious, that men and women should cohabit, without undertaking certain irrevocable obligations, and mutually conferring certain civil rights; if, therefore, the law has annexed these rights and obligations to certain forms, and them only, which is the case here, it becomes in the same degree immoral, that men and women should cohabit without the interposition of these forms.

Q. If fornication be criminal, what are accessaries to the crime?

A. All those incentives which lead to it, as lascivious conversation, wanton songs, pictures, books; the writing and circulating of which is productive of so extensive a mischief from so mean a temptation, that few crimes have more to answer for, or less to plead in excuse.

Indecent conversation, and, by parity of reason, all the rest, are forbidden by St. Paul, Eph. iv. 29. Col. iii. 8.

The invitation, or voluntary admission, of impure thoughts into the imagination, falls within the same description, and is condemned by Christ, Matt. v. 28: who by thus enjoining a regulation of the thoughts, strikes at the root of the evil.

CHAP. III.

SEDUCTION.

Q. What may be remarked upon the system of *Honour*, as connected with this vice?

A. The seducer practises the same stratagem to draw a woman's person into his power, that a swindler does to get possession of your goods, or money; yet the *law of honour*, which abhors deceit, applauds the address of a successful intriguer.

Q. Seduction is seldom accomplished without fraud: to what extent is the fraud more criminal than other frauds?

A. As the injury effected by it is greater, continues longer, and less admits reparation.

Q. How may this injury be considered?

A. As threefold: to the woman, to her family, and to the public.

Q. I. How is this injury to the woman made up?

A. Of the *pain* she suffers from shame, or the *loss* she sustains in her reputation and prospects of marriage, and of the *depravation of her moral principle.*

1. This *pain* must be extreme, if we may judge of it from those barbarous endeavours to conceal their disgrace, to which women, under such circumstances, whose passionate fondness for

their children is remarkable, sometimes have recourse.

2. The *loss* which a woman sustains by the ruin of her reputation, and rejection from society, almost exceeds computation: for, every person's happiness depends in part upon the respect and reception which they meet with in the world. Moreover, a woman loses with her chastity the chance of marrying at all, or in any manner equal to the hopes she had been accustomed to entertain: and marriage is that from which every woman expects her chief happiness. Add to this, that where a woman's maintenance depends upon her character little is left to the forsaken sufferer, but to starve, or to have recourse to prostitution for food.

3. As a woman collects her virtue into this point, the loss of her chastity is generally the *destruction of her moral principle;* whether the criminal intercourse be discovered or not.

Q. II. How may the injury to the family be understood?

A. By the application of that infallible rule, "of doing to others what *we would* that others should do unto us."—Let a father or a brother say, for what consideration they would suffer this injury to a daughter or a sister. And let them distinguish, if they can, between a robbery, committed upon their property, and the ruin of their happiness by the treachery of a seducer.

Q. How does injury accrue to the public?

A. III. The public lose the benefit of the woman's service in her proper place, as a wife and parent. This may be little; but it is often more than all the good which the seducer does to the community can recompense. Moreover, prostitution is supplied by seduction; and in proportion to the danger there is of the woman's betaking herself to such a life, the seducer is answerable for the multiplied evils to which his crime gives birth.

Upon the whole, if we pursue the effects of seduction through the complicated misery which it occasions, we may perhaps assert that not one half of the crimes, for which men suffer death by the laws, are so flagitious as this.

CHAP. IV.

ADULTERY.

Q. What is the difference between this and the former crime?

A. A new sufferer is introduced, the injured husband, who receives a wound in his sensibility and affections, the most painful and incurable. In all other respects, adultery on the part of the man, includes the crime of seduction, and is attended with the same mischief.

Q. By what is the crime of the woman aggravated?

A. By cruelty to her children, who are generally involved in their parents' shame, and always made unhappy by their quarrel.

Q. If it be said that these are consequences, not of the crime, but of the discovery, what may we answer?

A. First, the crime could not be discovered, unless it were committed, and the commission is never secure from discovery; secondly, if we excuse such crimes, whenever we hope to escape detection, we leave the husband no security for his wife's chastity, but want of opportunity or temptation; which might either prevent marriage, or render it a state of such alarm to the husband, as must end in the slavery and confinement of the wife.

Q. What may be observed of the marriage-vow?

A. It "is witnessed before God," and accompanied with circumstances, which approach to the nature of an oath. The offender therefore incurs a crime little short of perjury, and the seduction of a married woman is little less than subornation of perjury;—this guilt is independent of the discovery.

Q. What may be observed of all behaviour that tends to captivate the affections of a married woman?

A. It is a barbarous intrusion upon the peace and virtue of a family, though it fall short of adultery.

Q. What is the usual and only apology for adultery?

A. The prior transgression of the other party.

Q. What may be said upon this point?

A. There are degrees, in this, as in other crimes; and so far as the bad effects are anticipated by the husband or wife who offends first, the guilt of the second offender is less. But this falls very far short of a justification; unless the obligation of the marriage-vow depended upon the condition of reciprocal fidelity; for which construction there is no foundation. Moreover, such a rule has a manifest tendency to multiply the offence, none to reclaim the offender.

Q. What may be said of considering the offence of one party as a *provocation*, and the other only *retaliation*?

A. It is a childish trifling with words. "Thou shalt not commit adultery," was an interdict delivered by God himself. By the Jewish law, adultery was capital to both parties in the crime:—(Levit. xx. 10.) Which proves, that the Divine Legislator placed a great difference between adultery and fornication. And with this agree the Christian Scriptures—(see Matt. xv. 19; 1 Cor. vi. 9; Gal. v. 19; Heb. xiii. 4.); which show that the crime of adultery was, in their apprehension, distinct from, and accumulated upon, that of fornication.

Q. The history of the woman taken in adultery, recorded in the eighth chapter of St. John's Gospel, has been thought by some to give countenance to that crime. How may a more attentive examination of the case convince us, that from it nothing can be concluded as to Christ's opinion concerning adultery, either one way or the other?

A. We may remark upon the words—"This they said tempting him, that they might have to accuse him;" that they meant to draw him into an exercise of judicial authority, that they might accuse him before the Roman governor, of intermeddling with the civil government. Christ's behaviour throughout the whole affair proceeded from a knowledge of this design, and a determination to defeat it. He gives them at first a cold reception, well suited to their insidious intention: "He stooped down, and with his finger wrote on the ground, as though he heard them not." "When they *continued* asking him," he dismissed them with a rebuke, which their impertinent malice, and the sacred character of many of them, deserved; "He that is without sin (that is, this sin) among you, let him first cast a stone at her." This had its effect. Stung with the reproof, and disappointed, they stole away one by one, and left Jesus and the woman alone. And then follows the conversation most material to our present subject. Now, when Christ asked the woman, "Hath no man *condemned* thee?" he certainly spoke, and was understood by her *to* speak, of a judicial condemnation; otherwise, her answer, "No man, Lord;" was not true. In every other sense of condemnation, as blame, censure, &c. many had condemned her. If then a judicial sentence was what Christ meant by *condemning* in the question, the common use of language requires us to suppose that he acquits the same in his reply, "Neither do I condemn thee;" *i.e.* I pretend to no judicial authority over thee; it is no office of mine to pronounce the sentence of the law.

When he adds, "Go, and sin no more," he in effect tells her, that she had sinned already: but as to the degree or quality of the sin, or Christ's opinion concerning it, nothing is declared, or can be inferred, either way.

CHAP. V.

INCEST.

Q. Upon what principle may the marriage or cohabitation of lineal kindred be said to be forbidden by the Law of Nature?

A. To preserve chastity in families, and between persons of different sexes brought up together in a state of unreserved intimacy, it is necessary by every method to inculcate an abhorrence of incestuous conjunctions; which abhorrence can only be upholden by the reprobation of *all* commerce of the sexes between near relations.

Q. Upon what are restrictions which extend to remoter degrees of kindred than what this reason makes it necessary to prohibit from intermarriage, families?

A. Upon the authority of the positive law which ordains them, and can only be justified by their tendency to diffuse wealth, connect families, or promote some political advantage.

Q. What does the Levitical law, which is retained in this country, and from which the rule of the Roman law differs very little, prohibit?

A. Marriage between relations, within *three* degrees of kindred; computing the generations, not from, but through the common ancestor, and accounting affinity the same as consanguinity. The issue, however, of such marriages are not bastardized, unless the parents be divorced during their life-time.

Q. What customs have prevailed in other countries?

A. The Egyptians allowed of the marriage of brothers and sisters. Amongst the Athenians, there was a very singular regulation; brothers and sisters of the half-blood, through the father, might marry; if through the mother, they were prohibited. The same custom also probably obtained in Chaldea so early as the age of Abraham; for he and Sarah his wife stood in this relation to each other.—Gen. xx. 12.

CHAP. VI.

POLYGAMY.

Q. What is it which intimates the intention of God that one woman should be assigned to one man?

A. The equality in the number of males and females born into the world; for, if to one man be allowed an exclusive right to five or more women, four or more men must be deprived of the exclusive possession of any.

Q. What else seems an indication of this?

A. Had God intended polygamy for the species, it is probable he would have begun with it; especially as the multiplication of the human race would have proceeded quicker.

Q. What bad effects does polygamy produce, besides violating the constitution of nature?

A. Contests and jealousies amongst the wives; distraction, or loss of affection in the husband; a voluptuousness in the rich, producing that indolence and imbecility both of mind and body, which have long marked the nations of the East; the abasement of one half of the human species; neglect of children; and the unnatural mischiefs which arise from a scarcity of women.

Q. What compensation does it offer for these evils?

A. None: in the article of population, the community gain nothing: for the question is not, whether one man will have more children by five wives than by one; but whether these five would not bear a greater number of children to separate husbands; whilst the care of the children when produced, &c. is less provided for, and less practicable, where twenty or thirty are to be supported by one father, than if they were divided into five or six families, to each of which were assigned the care of two parents.

Q. What may be said for this practice before the Mosaic Law and under it? as well as for the absence of any express law about it in the SS.?

A. The permission, if any, might be like that of divorce, "for the hardness of their heart," in condescension to their established indulgences, rather than from the propriety of the thing itself: manners in Judea had probably undergone a reformation in this respect before the time of Christ, for in the N. T. we find no trace of any such practice being tolerated.

For which reason, and because it was forbidden amongst the Greeks and Romans, we cannot expect to find any express law upon it in the Christian code. The words of Christ (Matt. xix. 9.) may easily be construed to prohibit polygamy: for, if "whoever putteth away his wife, and *marrieth* another, committeth adultery," he who marrieth another *without* putting away the first, is no less guilty of adultery. The several passages in St. Paul's writings, which speak of marriage, always suppose it to signify the union of one man with one woman. Upon this supposition he argues in Rom. vii. 1, 2, 3. When the same apostle permits marriage to his Corinthian converts, he restrains the permission to the marriage of one husband with one wife.

Q. How have the manners of different countries varied in this, as well as in other institutions, according as they have been less polished and more luxurious?

A. Polygamy is retained at this day in Turkey, and every part of Asia in which Christianity is not professed. In Christian countries, it is universally prohibited. In Sweden, it is punished with death. In England, besides the nullity of the second marriage, it subjects the offender to transportation, or imprisonment and branding, for the first offence, and to capital punishment for the second.

The ancient Medes compelled their citizens, in one canton, to take seven wives; in another, each woman to receive five husbands; as war had made an extraordinary havoc among the men, or the women had been carried away by an enemy.

Cæsar found amongst the inhabitants of this island a species of polygamy which was perfectly singular. *Uxores*, says he, *habent deni duodenique inter se communes; et maxime fratres cum fratribus, parentesque cum liberis: sed si qui sint ex his nati, eorum habentur liberi, quo primum virgo quæque deducta est.*

CHAP. VII.

OF DIVORCE.

Q. What does Paley mean by divorce?

A. The dissolution of the marriage-contract, by the act, and at the will, of the husband: which power was allowed to him among the Jews, Greeks, and the latter Romans; and is now exercised by the Turks and Persians.

Q. What may be observed of the congruity of such a right with the Law of Nature?

A. It is inconsistent with the duty which parents owe to their children: which can never be so well fulfilled as by their cohabitation and united care. It is also incompatible with the right which the mother possesses, as well as the father, to the gratitude of her children and the comfort of their society.

Q. What does Paley observe where this objection does not interfere?

A. He knows of no principles in the law of nature applicable to the question, beside that of general expediency.

For, if we say that arbitary divorces are excluded by the terms of the marriage-contract; it may be answered, that the contract might be so framed as to admit of this condition.

If we argue that the obligation of a contract naturally continues, so long as the purpose, which the parties had in view, requires; it will be difficult to show what purpose of the contract (the care of children excepted) should confine a man to a woman, from whom he seeks to be loose.

If we contend that a contract cannot, by the law of nature, be dissolved, unless the parties be replaced in the situation which each previously possessed; we shall be called upon to prove this to be an indispensable property of contracts.

He confesses himself unable to assign any circumstance in the marriage-contract, which proves that it contains, what many have ascribed to it, a natural incapacity of being dissolved by the consent of the parties. But if we trace the effects of such a rule upon the general happiness of married life, we shall perceive sufficient reasons to justify the policy of those laws which limit the power of divorce to a few extreme provocations: and we must pronounce that to be contrary to the law of nature, which can be proved detrimental to the common happiness.

Q. For what reason then, ought the marriage-contract to be indissoluble during the joint lives of the parties?

A. 1. Because this tends to preserve peace and concord between married persons, by perpetuating their common interest, and by inducing a necessity of mutual compliance.

An earlier termination of the union would produce a separate interest. This would beget peculation on one side, and mistrust on the other; evils which at present very little disturb the confidence of married life. Again, it necessarily happens that adverse tempers, habits, and tastes, often meet in marriage: when each party must take pains to give up what offends, and practise what may gratify the other. Love is neither general nor durable: where that is wanting, no lessons of duty, &c. will go half so far as this one intelligible reflection, that they must each make the best of their bargain; and that neither can find their own comfort, but in promoting the pleasure of the other. These compliances, though at first extorted by necessity, become in time easy, mutual, and consoling; though they may be less endearing than assiduities arising from affection.

II. Because new objects of desire would be continually sought after, if men could, at will, be released from their subsisting engagements; and there is no other security against the invitations of novelty, than the known impossibility of obtaining the object. Constituted as mankind are, and injured as the repudiated wife generally must be, it is necessary to add a stability to the condition of married women, more secure than the continuance of their husbands' affection; and to supply to both sides, by a sense of duty and of obligation, what satiety has impaired of passion and of personal attachment.

Q. Though we have considered divorces as depending solely upon the will of the husband, yet do the same objections apply, in a great degree, to divorces by mutual consent?

A. Yes: especially when we consider the indelicate situation and small prospect of happiness,

which injurious for the party who preferred his or her dissent to the liberty and desire of the other.

Q. When does the law of nature admit of an exception?

A. In favour of the injured party, in cases of adultery, of obstinate desertion, of attempts upon life, of outrageous cruelty, of incurable madness, and perhaps of personal imbecility.

Q. Why does it not grant the same privilege to dislike, opposition of temper and inclinations, neglect, severity, jealousy, &c.?

A. Because such objections may always be alleged, and cannot by testimony be ascertained; so that to allow implicit credit to them, and to dissolve marriages would lead in its effects to all the licentiousness of arbitrary divorces.

Q. To what does Paley assert, that the above consideration is a sufficient answer?

A. To the public vindication of himself by Milton, who, upon a quarrel with his wife, paid his addresses to another woman, and attempted to prove, that confirmed dislike was as just a foundation for dissolving the marriage-contract, as adultery.

Q. If a married pair, in irreconcileable discord, complain that their happiness would be better consulted, by permitting them to determine a connexion which is become odious to both; what may be told them?

A. That the same permission, as a general rule, would produce libertinism and misery, amongst thousands, who are now virtuous and happy in their condition: and it ought to satisfy them to reflect that when their happiness is sacrificed to an unrelenting rule, it is sacrificed to that of the community.

Q. How do the SS. draw this obligation tighter than the law of nature left it?

A. "Whosoever," saith Christ, "shall put away his wife, except it be for fornication, and shall marry another, committeth adultery," &c.—Matt. xix. 9. The law of Moses permitted the Jewish husband to put away his wife; but for what causes, appears to have been controverted amongst the interpreters of those times. Christ, the precepts of whose religion were calculated for more general use, revokes this permission as given to the Jews "for the hardness of their hearts," and promulges a law which was thenceforward to confine divorces to the single case of adultery in the wife. The rule was new. It surprised and offended his disciples; yet Christ added nothing to relax or explain it.

Q. What may inferior causes justify?

A. Separation, although not such a dissolution of the marriage-contract as would leave either party at liberty to marry again. If the ease of children does not require that they should live together, and it is become necessary for their mutual happiness that they should separate, let them separate by consent. Nevertheless, this necessity can hardly exist, without guilt and misconduct on one side, or on both. But cruelty, excessive violence, or other great and continued provocations, make it lawful for the party aggrieved to withdraw from the offender without his or her consent. The law which imposes the marriage-vow, whereby the parties promise to "keep to each other," must be understood to impose it with a silent reservation of these cases. St. Paul likewise distinguishes between a wife's merely separating herself from the family of her husband, and her marrying again.

Q. What is observed respecting the Law of this country on this head?

A. In conformity to our Saviour's injunction, it confines the dissolution of the marriage-contract to the case of adultery in the wife; and a divorce, even then, can only be had by an act of parliament founded on a sentence in the ecclesiastical court, and a verdict against the adulterer at common law; which proceedings compose a complete investigation of the complaint. It has lately been proposed to annex a clause restraining the offending party from marrying with the companion of her crime: for adulterous connexions are often formed with the prospect of bringing them to this conclusion; and the legislature, as the business is managed at present, assists the criminal design of the offenders, and confers a privilege where it ought to inflict a punishment. Something more penal, however, will probably be found necessary to check the progress of this depravity. Perhaps a law might be framed, directing *the fortune of the adulteress to descend as in case of her natural death*, reserving a certain proportion, by way of annuity, for her subsistence, and suspending the estate in the hands of the heir so as to preserve the inheritance to any children of a second marriage, in case there were none to succeed in the place of their mother by the first. An inordinate passion for splendor, for expensive amusements and distinction, is commonly found in that description of women who would become the objects of such a law; and a severity of this kind applies immediately to that passion. There is no room for any complaint of injustice, since the punishment is confined, so far as it is possible, to the person of the offender.

Q. What may be said of sentences of the ecclesiastical courts, which release the parties *a vinculo matrimonii* by reason of impuberty, frigidity, consanguinity, prior marriage, &c.?

A. They are not dissolutions of the marriage-contract, but judicial declarations that there never was any marriage. And the rite itself contains an exception of these impediments.

CHAP. VIII.

MARRIAGE.

Q. Whether it hath grown out of some tradition of Divine appointment in the persons of our first parents, or merely from a design to impress a solemn obligation upon the contract, the marriage rite, in almost all countries, has been made a religious ceremony: yet what is marriage, in its own nature, abstracted from the rules and declarations which the Jewish and Christian Scriptures deliver concerning it?

A. A civil contract, and nothing more.

Q. With respect to one main article in matrimonial alliances, what total alteration has taken place?

A. The wife now brings money to her husband, whereas anciently the husband paid money to the family of the wife: which alteration is of no small advantage to the female sex: for their importance in point of fortune procures to them that assiduity and respect, which are wanted to compensate for the inferiority of their strength.

Q. In treating of marriage as it is established in this country, why is it necessary to state the terms of the marriage-vow?

A. In order to shew:

1. What duties this vow creates.

2. What situation of mind at the time, is inconsistent with it.

3. By what subsequent behaviour it is violated.

Q. What is the marriage-vow?

A. The husband promises "to love, comfort, honour, and keep, his wife;" the wife "to obey, serve, love, honour, and keep, her husband;" in every variety of health and condition: and both stipulate "to forsake all others, and to keep only unto one another, so long as they both shall live."

This promise is witnessed before God and the congregation; accompanied with prayers to the Almighty for his blessing upon it; and attended with such circumstances as place the obligation of it nearly upon the same foundation as that of oaths.

Q. What may be observed upon this vow?

A. The parties by it engage their personal fidelity expressly; they engage likewise to consult and promote each other's happiness; the wife, moreover, promises *obedience* to her husband. Nature may have made the sexes nearly equal in their faculties, and perfectly so in their rights; but to guard against those competitions which a contested superiority, is almost sure to produce, the SS. enjoin upon the wife that obedience which she here promises, so absolutely, that it seems to extend to every thing not criminal, or not entirely inconsistent with the woman's happiness.

We cannot say, that no one can conscientiously marry, who does not prefer the person at the altar to all other men or women: but we can have no difficulty in pronouncing that whoever is conscious of such a dislike to the woman he is about to marry, or of such an attachment to another, that he cannot reasonably expect ever to entertain an affection for his future wife, is guilty, when he pronounces the marriage-vow, of a deliberate prevarication, aggravated by the presence of ideas of religion, and of the Supreme Being. The same likewise of the woman. This charge must be imputed to all who, from mercenary motives, marry the objects of their aversion; and to those who desert the object of their affection, and, without being able to subdue that affection, marry another.

Q. When is the marriage-vow violated?

A. I. By adultery.

II. By any behaviour which, knowingly, renders the life of the other miserable; as desertion, neglect, prodigality, drunkenness, jealousy, &c.

Q. What late regulation does Paley mention as having been made in the law of marriages in this country?

A. One which has made the consent of the father, if he be living, of the mother, if she survive the father and remain unmarried, or of guardians, if both parents be dead, necessary to the marriage of a person under twenty-one years of age. By the Roman law, the consent *et avi et patris* was required so long as they lived. In France, the consent of parents is necessary to the marriage of sons, until they attain to thirty years of age; of daughters, until twenty-five: in Holland, for sons till twenty-five; for daughters, till twenty. And this distinction between the sexes appears to be well founded; for a woman is usually as properly qualified for the domestic duties of a wife or mother at eighteen, as a man is for the business of the world, and the more arduous care of providing for a family at twenty-one.

The constitution also of the human species indicates the same distinction.

CHAP. IX.

OF THE DUTY OF PARENTS.

Q. Paley asserts, that although the virtue which confines its beneficence within the walls of a man's own house, is considered as little better than a more refined selfishness; yet it will be confessed, that the subject and matter of this class of duties are inferior to none in utility and importance; for virtue is most valuable where it does the most good; and no duty is more obligatory, than that on which the most depends. It will also be acknowledged that the good order and happiness of the world are better upholden whilst each man applies himself to the care of his own family, than if, from an excess of mistaken generosity, he should leave his own business, to undertake his neighbour's, which he must manage with less knowledge, conveniency, and success. To what, therefore, if the low estimation of these virtues be well-founded, must it be owing?

A. Not to their inferior importance, but to some defect or impurity in the motive: for, it cannot be denied, that *association* may so unite our children's interest with our own, as that we shall often pursue both from the same motive, and with little sense of duty in each pursuit. And when we find a solicitous care of a man's own family, in a total absence or penury of all other virtues, or directing itself solely to the temporal happiness of the children, in indulgence whilst they are young, or in advancement of fortune only when they grow up, this probably is the case. Thus, the common opinion of these duties may be accounted for. If we look to the subject of them, we perceive them to be indispensable: if to the motive, we find them often not very meritorious. Wherefore, although a man seldom rises high in our esteem who has nothing to recommend him but the care of his own family, yet we condemn the neglect of this duty with the utmost severity; both for the manifest and immediate mischief arising from this neglect, and because it argues a want not only of parental affection, but of those moral principles which ought to come in aid of it where it is wanting. And if our esteem of these duties be not proportioned to the good they produce, it is because virtue is most valuable, not where it produces the most good, but where it is the most wanted: which is not the case here; because its place is often supplied by instincts, or involuntary associations. Still, the offices of a parent may be discharged from a consciousness of their obligation; and a sense of this is sometimes necessary to stimulate parental affection; especially in stations where the wants of a family cannot be supplied without the continual hard labour and restraint of the father. Where the parental affection has fewer difficulties to surmount, a principle of duty may still be wanted to direct and regulate its exertions: for otherwise it is apt to degenerate into an excessive care to provide the externals of happiness, with little or no attention to the internal sources of virtue and satisfaction. Universally, wherever a parent's conduct is directed by a sense of duty, there is so much virtue.

Q. Having premised thus much concerning the place which parental duties hold in the scale of human virtues, what does Paley next proceed to state and explain?

A. The duties themselves.

Q. Why do moralists say more than is true, when they tell us, that parents are bound to do *all they can* for their children?

A. Because, at that rate, every expense which might have been spared, and every profit omitted which might have been made, would be criminal.

The duty of parents has its limits, like other duties; and admits, if not of perfect precision, at least of rules definite enough for application.

Q. Under what several heads may these rules be explained?

A. Under those of *maintenance*, *education*, and *a reasonable provision for the child's happiness in respect of outward condition*.

Q. What may be observed of the first head, or *maintenance*?

A. The wants of children make this necessary; and, as no one has a right to burthen others by his act, it follows, that the parents are bound to undertake this charge. Besides, the affection of parents, (if it be instinctive), and the provision which [illegible] of the [illegible] for the infant (concerning the design of which there can be no doubt), are manifest indications of the Divine will.

Hence the guilt of those who run away from their families, or (through idleness or drunkenness), throw them upon a parish; or who leave them destitute at their death, when they might have laid up a provision for their support; or who neglect and abandon their infant offspring; for the duty of maintenance, like the obligation which it is founded on, extends to them as well as to legitimate children.

The [illegible], although they contract themselves little with maxims of prudence or economy, [illegible] them of worldly mindedness, yet discover in explicit [illegible] their judgment of the obligation of this duty. (See 1 Tim. v. 8.)

Q. What [illegible] with respect to education?

A. Education (in the [illegible] by Paley in the most extensive sense), comprehending every preparation made in our youth for the sequel of our lives.

Some such preparation is necessary for all children, otherwise they must be miserable, and probably vicious when they grow up, either from want of subsistence, or of rational and inoffensive occupation. In civilized life, every thing is effected by art and skill. Whence a person who is provided with neither will be useless, and probably will be a burden to the community, [illegible] an uneducated child into the world, is injurious to the rest of mankind.

In the inferior classes, this principle condemns parents, who do not inure their children betimes to labour and regular employment, but who suffer them to waste their youth in idleness, or to betake themselves to some lazy and precarious calling: for having thus tasted the sweets of natural liberty, at an age when their passion for it is at highest, they become incapable of continued industry, or of persevering attention to any thing; spend their time miserably; and are prepared to embrace every experiment, which presents a hope of supply, without confining them to the plough, the shop, or the counting-house.

In the middle orders, those parents are most reprehensible, who neither qualify their children for a profession, nor enable them to live without one; and those in the highest, who omit to procure for their children those attainments which are necessary to make them useful in the stations to which they are destined, thus defrauding the community of a benefactor, and bequeathing them a nuisance.

Some, though not the same, preparation is necessary for youth of every description. Consequently, they who leave the education of their bastards to chance, contenting themselves with making provision for their subsistence, desert half their duty.

Q. What does Paley observe upon the last head, *a reasonable provision for the child's happiness, in respect of outward condition?*

A. That it requires three things: a situation suited to his habits and reasonable expectations; a competent provision for the exigencies of that situation; and a probable security for his virtue.

The first two articles vary with the condition of the parent. A situation somewhat approaching in condition to the parent's own, or, where that is not practicable, similar to what other parents of like condition provide for their children, bounds the reasonable, and (generally speaking) the actual, expectations of the child, and therefore contains the extent of the parent's obligation.

The providing a child with a situation, includes a competent supply for the expenses of it, until the profits enable the child to support himself. Noblemen and gentlemen of fortune may be bound to transmit a sufficient inheritance to their representatives, without the aid of a trade or profession, to which there is little hope that a youth, who has been flattered with other expectations, will apply himself with diligence or success. Public opinion has now assorted the members of the community into four or five general classes, each class comprising a great variety of employments, the choice of which must be left to the discretion of parents. All that can be expected as a *duty* is, that they endeavour to preserve their children in the *class* in which they are born, or in which others of similar expectations are accustomed to be placed;

and confine their hopes and habits of indulgence to objects which will continue to be attainable.

Rich parents ought not to bring up their sons to mean employments, to save the charge of a more expensive education: for these sons, when they become masters of their liberty and fortune, will hardly continue in occupations by which they think themselves degraded, and are seldom qualified for any thing better.

An attention to the exigencies of the children's respective conditions in the world; and a regard to their reasonable expectations (always postponing the expectations to the exigencies, when both cannot be satisfied) ought to guide parents in the disposal of their fortunes after their death. These exigencies and expectations must be measured by the standard of custom: for there is a certain appearance, and mode of living, which custom has annexed to the several orders of civil life, and which compose what is called *decency;* and a young person who is withheld from these for want of fortune, can scarcely be said to have a fair chance for happiness. As to what a child may reasonably expect from his parent, he will expect what he sees others in similar circumstances receive: and we can hardly call such an expectation unreasonable.

By this rule, a parent is justified in making a difference between his children, as they stand in greater or less need of assistance, in consequence of the difference of age, sex, or situation.

On account of the few lucrative employments

left to the female sex, and the little opportunity they have of adding to their income, daughters ought to be the particular objects of a parent's care; and as an option of suitable marriage is not presented to every woman who deserves it, a father should endeavour to enable his daughters to lead a single life with independence, though he subtract more from the portions of his sons, than is agreeable to modern usage, or than they expect.

But when exigencies are provided for, and not before, a parent ought to admit the satisfaction of his children's expectations; and upon that principle to prefer the eldest son to the rest, and sons to daughters; which constitutes the whole right of primogeniture, and the only reason for the preference of sex. The preference, indeed, of the first-born has one public good effect, that if the estate were divided equally, it would probably make all idle; whereas, by the present rule, it makes only one so; which is the less evil of the two. And it must further be observed, that if the rest of the community make it a rule to prefer *sons* to *daughters*, an individual ought to guide himself by it, upon the principles of mere equality. For, as the son suffers in the fortune he may expect by marriage, it is but reasonable he should receive the advantage in his own inheritance.

The point of actual expectations, together with the expediency of subjecting the illicit commerce of the sexes to every possible discouragement, makes the difference between the claims of legitimate children and of bastards. But neither reason will in any case justify the leaving of bastards to the world without provision, education or profession.

After a provision for the exigencies of his situation, a parent may diminish a child's portion, to punish any flagrant crime, or want of filial duty in instances not otherwise criminal: for a child who is conscious of bad behaviour, cannot reasonably expect the same instances of his munificence.

A child's vices may be such, and so incorrigible, as to afford the same reason for believing that he will waste his fortune, as if he were mad or idiotish, in which case a parent may treat him as a madman or an idiot; that is, provide for his support, by an unalienable annuity, equal to his wants and innocent enjoyments. This seems to be the only case in which a disinherison, nearly absolute, is justifiable.

A father must not hope to excuse a capricious disposition of his fortune, by alleging, that "every man may do what he will with his own." All the truth which this expression contains is, that this discretion is under no control of law: but this by no means absolves his conscience from the obligations of a parent, or imports that he may neglect, without injustice, the several wants and expectations of his family. Although in his domestic intercourse, a parent may not always resist his partiality to a favorite child (which, however, should be avoided, as productive of jealousies and discontents), yet, when he sits down to make his will, these tendernesses must give place to more manly deliberations.

A father is bound to adjust his economy with a view to these demands upon his fortune; and until a sufficiency for these ends is acquired, or in due time *probably* will be acquired, frugality and industry are duties. He is also justified in declining expensive liberality: for, to take from those who want, to give to those who want, adds nothing to the stock of public happiness. Thus far, only, the plea of "large families," "charity begins at home," &c. is an excuse for parsimony. Beyond this point, as the use of riches becomes less, the desire of *laying up* should abate. The truth is, our children gain not so much as we imagine, by setting out with large capitals. Of those who have died rich, a great part began with little. And, in respect of enjoyment, there is no comparison between a fortune acquired by well-applied industry, or a series of successes, and one received from another.

A principal part of a parent's duty is still behind, *viz.* the using of proper precautions and expedients, in order to form and preserve his children's virtue.

To us, who believe that virtue will conduct to happiness, and vice to misery; and who observe that men's virtues and vices are, to a certain degree, produced or affected by the management of their youth; the obligation to consult a child's virtue will appear to differ in nothing from that of his maintenance or fortune. The child's interest is concerned in the one means of happiness as well as in the other; and both are equally in the parent's power.

Hence we must impress upon children the idea of *accountableness*, that is, accustom them to look forward to the consequences of their actions in another world; for which reason parents must act with a view to these consequences themselves. Parents are seldom sparing of lessons of virtue and religion; in admonitions which cost little, and which profit less; whilst their *example* exhibits a continual contradiction of what they teach. A father will, with much apparent earnestness, warn his son against idleness, debauchery, and extravagance, who himself comes home every night drunk; is made infamous by some profligate connexion; and wastes the fortune which should support his family, in riot, or luxury. Or he will discourse gravely before his children of the obligation and importance of revealed religion, whilst they see the most frivolous, and oftentimes feigned, excuses detain him from its reasonable and solemn ordinances, &c. Now, even a child is not to be imposed upon by such mockery. He discovers that his parent is acting a part; and receives his admonitions as he would hear the same maxims from the mouth of a player. And this opinion has a fatal effect upon the parent's influence in all subjects; even where he may be sincere and convinced. Whereas, a silent, but observable, regard to his duties will take a sure and gradual hold of the child's disposition, beyond reproofs and chidings, which, being generally prompted by present provocation, discover more of anger than of principle, and are received with a temporary alienation and disgust.

A good parent's first care is, to be virtuous himself; his second, to make his virtues as easy and engaging to those about him as their nature will admit. Some virtues even may be urged to such excess, or brought forward so unseasonably, as to discourage, instead of exciting an imitation of them. Young minds are particularly liable to these unfortunate impressions: for instance, if a father's economy degenerate into a minute and teasing parsimony, it is odds but that the son, who has suffered under it, sets out a sworn enemy to all rules of order and frugality, &c.

Something likewise may be done towards the correcting or improving of those early inclinations which children discover, by placing them in situations the least dangerous to their particular characters. Thus, a retired life may be chosen for young persons addicted to licentious pleasures; liberal professions, and a town-life, for the mercenary and sottish: dissolute youths should not, according to the general practice of parents, be sent into the army; or penurious tempers to trade, &c. Also with a view to the particular frame and tendency of the pupil's character, we should make choice of a public or private education. The reserved, timid, and indolent, will have their faculties called forth and their nerves invigorated by a public education. Youths of strong spirits and passions will be safer in a [illegible] At [illegible] public [illegible] [illegible] is acquired, and more vice; quick parts are cultivated, slow ones are neglected. Under private tuition, a moderate proficiency in juvenile learning is seldom exceeded, but with more certainty attained.

CHAP. X.

THE RIGHTS OF PARENTS.

Q. From what do the rights of Parents result?

A. From their duties. If it be the duty of a parent to educate his children, to form them for a life of usefulness and virtue, to provide for them suitable situations; he has a right to such authority and exercise of discipline as may be necessary for these purposes. The law of nature acknowledges no other foundation of a parent's right over his children, besides his duty towards them. (Such rights are here meant as may be enforced by coercion.) This relation confers no property in their persons, or natural dominion over them.

Since it is necessary to determine the destination of children, before they are capable of judging of their own happiness, parents have a right to elect professions for them.

As the mother herself owes obedience to the father, in a competition of commands, the father is to be obeyed. In case of the death of either, the authority, as well as the duty, of both parents, devolves upon the survivor.

These rights, always following the duty, belong likewise to guardians; and so much of them as is delegated by the parents or guardians, belongs to tutors, school-masters, &c.

Q. From this principle, *that the rights of parents result from their duties*, what follows?

A. That parents have no natural right over the lives of their children, as was absurdly allowed to Roman fathers; nor any to exercise unprofitable severities; nor to command the commission of crimes; for these rights can never be wanted for the purpose of a parent's duty.

Nor, for the same reason, have parents any right to sell their children into slavery.

Q. Upon which latter point what may be observed?

A. That the children of slaves are not, by the law of nature, born slaves: for, as the master's right is derived to him through the parent, it can never be greater than the parent's own.

Q. What else also appears from hence?

A. That parents exceed their just authority, when they consult their own ambition, interest, or prejudice, at the expense of their children's happiness: as in the shutting up of daughters and younger sons in nunneries and monasteries, to preserve entire the estate and dignity of the family; in the urging of children to marriages from which they are averse, with the view of exalting or enriching the family, or for the sake of connecting estates, parties, or interests; or the opposing of a marriage, in which the child would probably find his happiness, from a motive of pride or avarice, or family hostility.

CHAP. XI.

THE DUTY OF CHILDREN.

Q. How may the duty of children be considered?

A. I. During childhood.

II. After they have attained to manhood, but continue in their father's family.

III. After they have attained to manhood, and have left their father's family.

Q. What does Paley observe, concerning the first of these divisions?

A. Children must have attained to some degree of discretion before they are capable of any duty. There is an interval between the dawning and the maturity of reason, in which it is necessary to subject their inclination to restraints, and direct their application to employments, of the tendency of which they cannot judge; for which cause, their submission during this period must be implicit, except any manifest crime be commanded them.

Q. What does he observe, concerning the second division?

A. If children, when grown up, voluntarily continue members of their father's family, they are bound, beside the general duty of gratitude, to observe such regulations of the family as the father shall appoint; contribute their labour to its support, if required; and confine themselves to such expenses as he shall allow. The obligation would be the same, if they were admitted into any other family.

Q. What does he observe, concerning the third division?

A. The duty to parents then becomes simply that of gratitude; but, *in degree*, just as much exceeding other obligations, by how much a parent has been a greater benefactor than any other friend. The services and attentions, by which filial gratitude may be testified, cannot be enumerated. It will show itself in compliances with the will of the parents, however contrary to the child's own taste or judgment, provided it be neither criminal, nor totally inconsistent with his happiness; in a constant endeavour to promote their enjoyments, and soften their anxieties, in small matters as well as in great; in assisting them in their business; in contributing to their support; in waiting upon their sickness or decrepitude; in bearing with their infirmities, peevishness, and complaints: for where must old age find indulgence, but in the piety and partiality of children?

Q. What are commonly the most serious contentions between parents and children?

A. Those which relate to marriage or the choice of a profession.

Q. What may be remarked on this subject?

A. A parent has, in no case, a right to destroy his child's happiness. If therefore there do exist such exclusive attachments between individuals of different sexes, that a particular marriage be really necessary for the child's happiness; or, if an aversion to a particular profession be involuntary and unconquerable; then parents ought not to urge their authority, and the child is not bound to obey it.

Q. What is the point, however, to discover?

A. How far, in any particular instance, this is the case. Whether the attachment of lovers ever continues so intense and long that its success constitutes, or its disappointment affects, a great portion of their happiness, it is difficult to determine: but it is certain that not one half of those attachments, which young people conceive so hastily, are of this sort. There are also few aversions to a profession, which resolution, perseverance, activity, and, above all, despair of changing, will not subdue: yet there are some such. Wherefore, a child who respects his parents' judgement, and is tender of their happiness, owes so much deference to their will, as to try fairly, in one case, whether time and absence will not cool an affection which they disapprove; and, in the other, whether a longer [illegible] in the [illegible] if they [illegible] choose for him may not [illegible] him [illegible]

Q. Upon what does the [illegible] depend?

A. Upon the [illegible] being [illegible] the child's [illegible] with sincerity, and not with a design of [illegible] his purpose [illegible] by [illegible] a simulated compliance. It is the nature of all violent affections to delude the mind with a persuasion that we shall always continue to feel them as we feel them at present. Experience of [illegible] greater changes in [illegible] giving credit to what others speak [illegible] this persuasion, otherwise it renders youth [illegible] tractable; for they see clearly that it is impossible to be happy under the circumstances proposed to them, in their present state of mind.

Q. How ought the parent to act after a [illegible] though ineffectual endeavour by the child to obey his parent?

A. When he has been [illegible] should acquiesce [illegible] the child is then at liberty to provide for his own happiness.

Q. What may be said concerning the right of parents to urge their children upon marriages to which they are averse?

A. They have no such right; nor ought they, in any shape, to [illegible] the children's [illegible] to such commands. This is different from [illegible] match of inclination, for misery is [illegible] probable consequence of being [illegible] to live with a person that we [illegible], than without [illegible] later. Add to this, that the reluctant party promises an affection, which is but expected to exist; and parental, like all human authority, ceases where obedience becomes criminal.

Q. In all contests between parents and children, what is the duty and best policy of the parent?

A. To represent to the child the consequences of his conduct with fidelity. By exaggeration parents lose all credit with their children; thus, in a great measure, defeating their own end.

Q. When are parents forbidden to interfere?

A. Where a trust is reposed personally in the son; and consequently, the son was expected, and by virtue of that expectation, is obliged, to pursue his own judgment: as is the case with magistrates in the execution of their office; members of the legislature in their votes, &c. The son may assist his own judgment by the advice of his father, or of any one else: but his own judgment ought finally to determine his conduct.

Q. What is said of the duty of children in the 2d.?

A. It was thought worthy to be made the subject of one of the Ten Commandments; and, as such, is recognised by Christ in various places of the Gospel.

His sentiments also concerning the relief of indigent parents, appear sufficiently from his manly indignation against the wretched casuistry of the Jewish expositors, who had contrived to evade this duty by converting, or pretending to convert, to the treasury of the temple, so much of their property, as their distressed parent might be entitled to by their law.

Q. Agreeably to this law of nature and Christianity, whom are children bound to support by the law of England?

A. As well their immediate parents, as their grandfather and grandmother, or remoter ancestors, who stand in need of support.

Q. How does St. Paul enjoin obedience to parents? and what was enacted by the Jewish law?

A. "Children, obey your parents in the Lord, for this is right;" and to the Colossians: "Children, obey your parents in all things, for this is well pleasing unto the Lord."

By the Jewish law, disobedience to parents was in some extreme cases capital. Deut. xxi. 18.

BOOK IV.

DUTIES TO OURSELVES.

CHAP. I.

THE RIGHTS OF SELF-DEFENCE.

Q. Does Paley agree to the assertion, that in a state of nature we might lawfully defend the most insignificant right, if determinate, by any means which the obstinacy of the aggressor rendered necessary?

A. He considers it doubtful whether the general rule be worth sustaining at such an expense; as apart from the general consequence, it cannot be for the increase of human happiness, that one man should lose his life, or limb, rather than another a pennyworth of his property. But as perfect rights can only be distinguished by their value, and we cannot ascertain the value at which the liberty of using extreme violence begins, the person attacked must endeavour to balance between the general consequence of yielding and the particular effect of resistance.

Q. How is this right, if it exist in a state of

nature, suspended by the establishment of civil society?

A. Because *thereby* other remedies are provided against attacks upon our property, and it is necessary to the safety of the community, that the prevention and redress of injuries be adjusted by public laws. Besides, as the individual is assisted by the public strength, it is expedient that he should submit to public arbitration the kind of satisfaction which he is to obtain.

Q. What case exists in which all extremities are justifiable?

A. When the death of the assailant is necessary for the preservation of our life. This is evident, in a state of nature, as we are bound neither by justice nor charity to love our enemy *better* than ourselves. Nor is the case altered by civil society; since, by the supposition, the laws of society cannot protect us.

Q. To what cases is this liberty restrained?

A. To those in which no other probable means of preserving life remain. The rule holds, whether the danger proceed from a voluntary attack, as by an assassin, &c. or from an involuntary one as by a madman, or person drowning and dragging us after him; or where two persons are in a situation in which one or both must perish, as in a shipwreck where two seize a plank which will save but one; these extreme cases however seldom happen, and are unworthy of long discussion. The defence of chastity justifies the same extremities.

T 8

Q. In all other cases how does it appear safest to consider the taking away of life?

A. As authorized by law, and the person who takes it as its minister or executioner. Under which view homicide, in England, is justifiable,

1. To prevent crimes which would be punishable with death. Thus it is lawful to shoot a highwayman, or a house-breaker by night, but not in the day; which distinction obtained both in the Jewish law and in that of Greece and Rome.

2. In necessary endeavours to put the law into execution, as in suppressing riots, &c.—The law does not authorize the destruction of a human being except in the above cases.

The rights of war are not here taken into account.

CHAP. II.

DRUNKENNESS.

Q. What may be observed of this vice?

A. That it is either actual or habitual; just as it is one thing to be drunk, and another to be a drunkard. What is here delivered upon the subject must principally be understood of a *habit* of intemperance; although *part* of the guilt and design described may be applicable to repeated excesses; and all of it, in a certain degree, for as much as every habit is only a repetition of single instances.

Q. To what do Paley's arguments principally apply?

A. To habitual intemperance; though part of the guilt attaches itself to equal excess, and all to a certain degree, inasmuch as every habit is but a repetition of single instances.

Q. From what bad effects must we compute the mischief and guilt of drunkenness?

A. 1. It betrays most constitutions either to extravagant anger or lewdness.

2. It disqualifies men for the duties of their station; first temporarily, and at length by a constant stupefaction.

3. It is attended with expenses, which can often be ill spared.

4. It is sure to occasion uneasiness to the family of the drunkard.

5. It shortens life.

Q. What else must be added to these consequences?

A. The peculiar danger of the example. Drunkenness is a social festive vice; and beyond any vice that can be mentioned, to draw in others by the example, till a whole neighbourhood be infected from the contagion of a single example. This is confirmed by what we often observe, that it is a *local* vice; found to prevail in certain countries, districts, or towns, without any pretence to be given for the fashion, but that it had been introduced by some popular example. To this, you may also connect a remark which belongs to the several evil effects above recited. The consequences of a vice, though they be all enumerated in the description, seldom all meet in the same subject. In this instance, the age and temperature of one drunkard may have little to fear from inflammations of lust or anger; the fortune of a second may not be injured; a third may have no family to be disquieted by his irregularities, &c. But if, as we ought, we comprehend the mischief and tendency of the example, the above circumstances will vary the guilt of the individual less, probably, than he supposes. The moralist may expostulate with him thus. Although the waste of time and of money be of small importance to you, it may be of the utmost to some one or other whom your society corrupts. Repeated or long-continued excesses, which hurt not *your* health, may be fatal to your companion. Other families, in which husbands and fathers have been invited to share in your ebriety, or encouraged to imitate it, may justly lay their misery or ruin at your door, whether by your persuasion or example. All these considerations must be assembled to judge truly of a vice which usually meets with more indulgence than it deserves.

Q. Why does Paley omit the violent outrages and sometimes maniacal effects of drunkenness?

[illegible]

[illegible]

Q. Is this vice forbidden by St. Paul? [illegible]

A. Repeatedly, [illegible] Ephes. v. 18. [illegible] 1 Cor. vi. 10. Also 1 Thess. v. 7. [illegible] it as peculiarly inconsistent with the Christian profession.

Q. It is a question of some importance, how far drunkenness is an excuse for the crimes which the drunken person commits; in the solution of this question, what does Paley first suppose?

A. The drunken person to be altogether deprived of moral agency, that is, of all reflection and foresight; in this case it is evident he is no more capable of guilt than a madman. His only guilt was incurred when he voluntarily brought himself into this situation. And as every man is responsible for the consequences which he foresaw, or might have foreseen, this guilt will be in proportion to the probability of such consequences ensuing. From which principle results this rule, viz. that the guilt of any action in a drunken man bears the same proportion to its guilt in a sober man, that the probability of its being the consequence of drunkenness bears to absolute certainty. Hence those vices which are the *known* effects of drunkenness, are to be deemed as criminal as if committed with full possession of the faculties and temper.

Q. If the privation of reason be only partial, how will the guilt be?

A. Of a mixed nature. For so much of his

self-government on the drunkard, [illegible] he is as responsible then as at any other time; [illegible] entitled to no abatement beyond the degree in which his moral faculties were impaired.

It is not meant that any rule can be applied to numbers, or the calculation be ever made with arithmetical precision; but this is the principle, and this the rule by which our general estimate of the guilt of such offences should be regulated.

Q. Since the appetite for intoxicating liquors appears, to Paley, almost always acquired, one proof of which is, that it is so apt to return at stated times and places;—what does he advise?

A. A change of habitation and society.

Q. What else does he remark upon the subject of drunkenness?

A. They commonly arise either from a fondness for, and connexion with, some company, or some companion, already addicted to this practice; or from want of regular employment, which is sure to let in many superfluous cravings; or, lastly, from grief or fatigue, which strongly solicit that relief which inebriating liquors administer. But the habit, when once set in, is continued by different motives. Persons addicted to excessive drinking suffer, in the intervals of sobriety, and near the return of their indulgence, a depression [illegible], which it exceeds ordinary patience to endure. This is speedily relieved for a short time by a repetition of the same excess; and to this relief, they who have once experienced it, are urged almost beyond the pursuit of [illegible]. This is not the principal [illegible] liquors [illegible] itself [illegible] [illegible] [illegible] all the [illegible]. Whoever reflects upon the violence of the craving in the advanced stages of the habit, and the fatal termination to which it leads, will, the moment he perceives in himself the first symptoms of a growing inclination to intemperance, collect his resolution to this point; or (what perhaps he will find his best security) arm himself with some peremptory rule, as to the times and quantity of his indulgences.

There is a difference between convivial intemperance, and that solitary sottishness which waits neither for company nor invitation. But the one commonly ends in the other; and this last is the basest degradation to which the faculties and dignity of human nature can be reduced.

CHAP. III.

SUICIDE.

Dr. Paley observes that there is no subject in morality in which the consideration of general consequences is more necessary than in this. Extreme cases of suicide may arise, of which it would be difficult to assign the particular mischief, or demonstrate the guilt; and these cases have being the chief occasion of confusion in the question: albeit this is no more than what is true of the most acknowledged vices. Which, however, is the true question in this argument?

A. May every man who chooses to destroy his life, innocently do so? Limit the subject as you can, it comes at last to this question.

For, shall we say, that we are at liberty to commit suicide when we find our continuance in life useless to mankind? Any one may make himself useless; and melancholy minds are prone to think themselves so, when they really are not. Besides no one is *useless* for the purpose of this plea, but he who has lost every capacity and opportunity of being useful, together with the possibility of recovering any degree of either; which is such complete destitution as cannot be predicated of any man.

Or rather, shall it be said that to depart voluntarily out of life, is lawful for those alone who leave none to lament their death? If this is to be taken into the account at all, the debate will be, not whether there are any to sorrow for us, but whether their sorrow will exceed that which we should suffer by continuing to live. Now this is a comparison of things so indeterminate, and capable of such different judgments, according to the state of the spirits, that in hypochondriacal constitutions, it would be an unqualified licence to commit suicide, whenever the distresses which men felt, or fancied, rose high enough to overcome the dread of death.

In like manner, whatever other rule be assigned, it will ultimately bring us to an indiscriminate toleration of suicide, in all cases in which there is danger of its being committed.

Q. What remains, therefore, to inquire?

A. What would be the effect of such a toleration: evidently, the loss of many lives to the community, of which some might be useful or important; the affliction of *many* families, and the consternation of *all*, when every disgust which is powerful enough to tempt men to suicide, shall be deemed sufficient to justify it; whilst the follies, vices, and calamities of life, so often make existence a burthen.

Q. What second consideration, distinct from the former, does Paley produce?

A. By continuing in the world, we retain the opportunity of meliorating our condition in a future state. This argument, it is true, does not prove suicide to be a crime; but it supplies a motive to dissuade us from committing it. Now there is no condition which is not capable of some virtue, active or passive. Even piety and resignation under suffering testify an edifying trust and acquiescence in the Divine counsels, and may hope for a recompense among the most arduous of human virtues. These qualities are always in the power of the miserable.

Q. The two considerations above stated, belong to all cases of suicide whatever. Beside which general reasons, how will each case be aggravated?

A. By its own proper and particular consequences; by the duties that are deserted; by the claims that are defrauded; by the loss, affliction, or disgrace, caused to our family; by the suspicion cast on the sincerity of our moral and religious professions; by the reproach we draw upon our order; in short, by a great variety of evil consequences with some or other of which every actual case of suicide is chargeable.

Q. Why does he refrain from the common topics of "deserting our post," "throwing up our trust," &c.?

A. Not because they are *common* (for that rather affords a presumption in their favour), but because he does not perceive in them much argument to which an answer may not easily be given.

Q. Hitherto the subject has been pursued by the light of nature alone; taking, however, into the account, the expectation of a future existence, what is to be met with in Scripture which may add to the probability of Paley's conclusions?

A. He acknowledges that there is to be found no sufficient evidence to prove that the case of suicide was in the contemplation of the law which prohibited murder. Any inference, therefore, deduced from the SS. can be sustained only by construction and implication; yet they have left enough to constitute a presumption how they would have decided the case, had it been proposed.

Q. What are the observations in which any thing to this purport occurs? And what does Paley remark upon them?

1. Human life is spoken of as a *term* assigned or prescribed to us: "Let us run with patience the race that is set before us."—"That I may finish my course with joy."—"Ye have need of patience, that, after ye have done the will of God, ye might receive the promise."—These expressions appear inconsistent with the opinion, that we may determine the duration of our lives for ourselves. If so, with what propriety could life be called a *race that is set before us*; or, "*our course*;" set out or appointed to us? The remaining quotation is equally strong:—"That, after ye have done the will of God, ye might receive the promise;" i. e. After ye have discharged the duties of life so long as God is pleased to continue you in it.

2. There is no quality which Christ and his apostles inculcate upon their followers so earnestly as that of patience under affliction. Now this virtue would have been in a great measure superseded, if their disciples had been at liberty to quit the world as soon as they grew weary of the ill usage they received in it. When evils pressed sore, they were to look forward to a "far more exceeding and eternal weight of glory;" they were to receive them, "as chastenings of the Lord."—"Consider him that endured such contradiction of sinners against himself, lest ye be wearied and faint in your minds." Now, would not a Christian convert, who had been impelled by his sufferings to destroy his own life, have been thought by the author of this text to have been

weary," and to have "fainted in his mind?" And yet, would not such an act have been attended with all the circumstances of mitigation which can extenuate suicide at this day?

3. The *conduct* of the apostles, and of the Christians of the first ages, affords no obscure indication of their sentiments upon this point. They experienced in this world every extremity of injury and distress. To die, was gain. Yet it never, that we can find, entered into the intention of any one of them to hasten this change by an act of suicide; from which no motive could have so universally withheld them, except an apprehension of unlawfulness in the expedient.

Q. What is the only argument in defence of suicide which Paley thinks worthy of notice?

A. If we deny to the individual a right over his own life, it seems impossible to reconcile with the law of nature that right which the state claims and exercises over the lives of its subjects. For this right can only be derived from the compact and virtual consent of the citizens which compose the state; and it seems self-evident, that no one, by his consent, can transfer to another a right which he does not possess himself. Whence is the power of the state to commit its subjects to the dangers of war, especially in offensive hostilities, and how, in such circumstances, can prodigality of life be a virtue, if the preservation of it be a duty of our nature?

Q. How does Paley answer this reasoning?

A. He observes, that it sets out from one error,

namely, that the state acquires its right over the life of the subject from the subject's own consent. The truth is, the state derives this right neither from the consent of the subject, nor through the medium of that consent; but immediately from the donation of the Deity. Finding that such a power in the sovereign is expedient for the community, it is justly presumed to be the will of God, that the sovereign should possess and exercise it. It is this *presumption* which constitutes the right, as it constitutes every other: and if there were the like reasons to authorise the presumption in the case of private persons, suicide would be as justifiable as war or capital executions.

BOOK V.

DUTIES TOWARDS GOD.

CHAP. I.

DIVISION OF THESE DUTIES.

Q. What are those duties which may be peculiarly called *duties towards God*?

A. Those of which God is the object as well as the author; silent piety in tracing out and referring our blessings to our Creator's bounty, &c. may possibly be more acceptable to him than visible expressions of devotion, though these alone may admit of disquisition by the moralist.

Q. How is our duty towards God, so far as it is external, divided?

A. Into worship and reverence; the first of which consists in action, the second in forbearance. When we go to church on the Lord's day, we perform an act of worship: when we rest in a journey upon that day, we discharge a duty of reverence.

CHAP. II.

OF THE DUTY AND OF THE EFFICACY OF PRAYER, SO FAR AS THE SAME APPEAR FROM THE LIGHT OF NATURE.

Q. What does a man do who desires to obtain any thing of another?

A. He betakes himself to entreaty; as may be observed in all ages and countries. Now what is universal, may be called natural; and it seems probable that God should expect that towards himself, which, by a natural impulse he has prompted us to pay to every other being on whom we depend.

The same may be said of thanksgiving.

Q. To what else is prayer necessary?

A. To keep up in our minds a sense of God's agency in the universe, and of our dependency upon him.

Q. Yet upon what, after all, does the efficacy of prayer, according to Paley's idea, depend?

A. Upon its efficacy: for he is unable to conceive, how any man can pray, or be obliged to pray, who expects nothing from his prayers; nor that they can produce the smallest impression upon the being to whom they are addressed.

Q. Now the efficacy of prayer imports that we obtain something by it, which we should not without it; against all expectation of which, what objection has been often alleged?

A. "If what we request be fit for us, we shall have it without praying; if it be not fit for us, we cannot obtain it by praying."

Q. What sole answer does this objection admit of?

A. That it may be agreeable to perfect wisdom to grant that to our prayers, which it would not have given us without.

Q. But what virtue is there in prayer, which should make a favour consistent with wisdom, which would not have been so without it? To this difficult question, what possibilities are offered in reply?

A. 1. A favour granted to prayer may be more apt, on that very account, to produce good effects upon the person obliged.

2. It may be consistent with the wisdom of the Deity to withhold his favors till they be asked for, as an expedient to encourage devotion in his rational creation.

3. Prayer has a natural tendency to amend the petitioner himself; and thus make him more worthy of God's favours.

Q. Why is it sufficient if these, or any other suppositions, remove the apparent repugnancy between the success of prayer and the character of the Deity?

A. The question with the petitioner is not from which, out of many motives, God may grant his petition, or in what particular manner he is moved; but whether it be consistent with his nature to be moved at all, to grant the petitioner what he wants, in consequence of his praying for it. It is sufficient for him, that he gains his end. It is not necessary to devotion that the circuit of causes, by which his prayers prevail, should be known to him. All that is necessary is, that there be no impossibility apprehended in the matter.

Q. How much must be conceded to the objection?

A. That prayer cannot reasonably be offered to God with all the same views, with which we often address our entreaties to men, *viz.* to inform them of our wants and desires; to tease them out by importunity; to work upon their indolence or compassion.

Q. Suppose there existed a prince, who was known to act, of his own accord, invariably for the best; the situation of a petitioner, who solicited a favour or pardon from such a prince, would resemble ours; and the question with him, as with us, would be, whether, the character of the prince considered, there remained any chance that he should obtain from him by prayer, what he would not have received without it. Would the character of such a prince necessarily exclude the effect of his subject's prayers?

A. No: for when he reflected that the supplication had generated in the suppliant a frame of mind, upon which the favour asked would produce a permanent sense of gratitude; that the granting of it to prayer would put others upon praying to him, and by that means preserve the love and submission of his subjects; also, that prayer had in other respects so disposed the mind of the petitioner, as to render capable of future services him who before was unqualified for any: might not that prince, although he proceeded only upon the strict rectitude and expediency of the measure, grant a favour or pardon to *this man*, which he did not to *another*, who was too proud, lazy, or indifferent whether he received it or not, or too insensible of his sovereign's power of giving or withholding it, ever to ask for it?

Q. As the objection to prayer supposes, that a perfectly wise being must necessarily be inexorable, what may be said in answer of this?

A. Where is the proof, that *inexorability* is any part of perfect wisdom; especially of that wisdom which is explained to consist in bringing about the most beneficial ends by the wisest means?

Q. What other principle does the objection likewise assume which is attended with considerable difficulty and obscurity?

A. That upon every occasion there is *one*, and only *one*, mode of acting *for the best*; and that the Divine Will is necessarily determined and confined to that mode.

Q. Now what do both these positions presume?

A. A knowledge of universal nature, much beyond what we are capable of attaining. When we use such expressions as these, "God *must* always do what is right," "God *cannot*, from the moral perfection and necessity of his nature, act otherwise than for the best," we ought to apply them with much indeterminateness and reserve; or rather confess, that there is something in the subject out of the reach of our apprehension; since in our apprehension a necessity of acting according to any rule, is inconsistent with free agency.

Q. But efficacy is ascribed to prayer without the proof, we are told, which can alone produce conviction,—the confirmation of experience. Concerning this appeal, what may be remarked?

A. That if prayer were suffered to disturb the order of second causes appointed in the universe too much, as to produce its effects with the same regularity that they do, it would introduce a change into human affairs, which in some important respects would be evidently for the worse; and it is easy to foresee that the conduct of mankind would, in proportion to their reliance, become careless and disorderly. It is possible that our prayers may, in many instances, be efficacious, and yet our experience of their efficacy be dubious and obscure. Also it appears probable, that this very ambiguity is necessary to the happiness and safety of human life.

Q. But some, whose objections do not exclude all prayer, are offended with the mode in use amongst us, and with many of the subjects introduced into public worship, and private devotion. To pray for particular favours by name, is to dictate to Divine wisdom: to intercede for others, especially for nations and empires, is to presume we possess vast interest with the Deity, and that upon the prosperity of communities, is to depend upon this interest, and our choice? What answer does Paley give to this?

A. How unequal soever our knowledge of the Divine economy may be to solve this difficulty, which requires perhaps a comprehension of the entire plan, and all the ends, of God's moral government, we can understand one thing, that it is, after all, nothing more than the making one man the instrument of happiness and misery to another; which is perfectly of a piece with the order that obtains, and which we must believe was intended to obtain, in human affairs. Why may we not be assisted by the prayers of other men, who are beholden for our support to their labour? Why may not our happiness be made in some cases to depend upon the intercession, as it does in many upon the good offices of our neighbours.

CHAP. III.

OF THE DUTY AND EFFICACY OF PRAYER AS REPRESENTED IN SCRIPTURE.

Q. Many of the preceding reflections, whatever truth they may contain, rise no higher than to negative arguments in favour of the propriety of prayer. To prove that its efficacy is not inconsistent with the attributes of the deity, does not prove that it is actually efficacious; and in the want of that unequivocal testimony, which experience alone could afford, the light of nature leaves us to controverted probabilities, drawn from the universal impulse of mankind to devotion, and from some beneficial purposes of it. What, however, supplies this defect of natural religion?

A. The revelations which we deem authentic. They require prayer to God as a duty, and contain positive assurances of its efficacy. We could have no reasonable motive for its exercise without believing that it may avail to our relief. This belief can only be founded in a sensible experience of the effect of prayer, or in promises of acceptance signified by Divine authority. Our knowledge would have come to us in the former way not only incapable of doubt, but subjected to the abuses and inconveniences briefly described above; in the latter way, we are encouraged to pray, but not to place such a dependence upon prayer as might relax other obligations, or confound the order of events and of human expectations.

Q. The Scriptures not only affirm the propriety of prayer in general, but furnish particular examples which justify some topics and modes of prayer that have been thought exceptionable. What texts does Paley adduce, as applicable to the five following heads: viz. to the duty and efficacy of prayer in general; of prayer for particular favours by name; for public national blessings;

of intercession for others; of the repetition of unsuccessful prayers.

A. 1. Texts enjoining prayer in general: "Ask, and it shall be given you; seek, and ye shall find," &c. &c.—Matt. vii. 7, 11; Luke xxi. 36; Rom. xii. 12; Philipp. iv. 6; 1 Thess. v. 17; 1 Tim. ii. 8. Add to these, that Christ's reproof of the ostentation and prolixity of pharisaical prayers, and his recommendation to his disciples, of retirement and simplicity in theirs, together with his dictating a particular form of prayer, all presuppose prayer to be an acceptable and availing service.

2. Examples of prayer for particular favours by name.—2 Cor. xii. 8; 1 Thess. iii. 10.

3. Directions to pray for national or public blessings: "*Pray for the peace of Jerusalem*," &c.—Psalm cxxii. 6; Zech. 10. 1; 1 Tim. ii. 1, 2, 3.

4. Examples of intercession and exhortations to intercede for others.—Exod. xxxii. 11; Acts xii. 5; Rom. i. 9. xv. 30; James v. 16.

5. Declarations and examples authorising the repetition of unsuccessful prayer.—Luke xviii. 1; Matt. xxvi. 44; 2 Cor. xii. 8.

CHAP. VI.

OF PRIVATE PRAYER, FAMILY PRAYER, AND PUBLIC WORSHIP.

Q. Concerning these three descriptions of devotion, what is first of all to be observed?

A. That each has its separate and peculiar use; and, therefore, that the exercise of one species of worship does not supersede the obligation of either of the other two.

Q. I. For what advantages is *private prayer* recommended?

A. Private wants cannot always be made the subject of public prayer; but whatever reason there is for praying at all, there is the same for making the grief of each man's own heart the business of his application to God.

Private prayer is generally more devout and earnest than the share we are capable of taking in joint acts of worship; affording leisure for the circumstantial recollection of those personal wants, by the ideas of which the earnestness of prayer is chiefly excited.

On this account, also, it has a greater tendency than other modes of devotion to revive and fasten upon the mind the general impressions of religion. Solitude powerfully assists this effect. Awful ideas concerning the universal agency, and invisible presence, of God; as well as concerning what is likely to become of ourselves, then gain admittance, and for a season overwhelm all others; leaving, when they depart, a solemnity upon the thoughts, that seldom fails, in some degree, to affect the conduct of life.

Private prayer, thus recommended by its own propriety and advantages, receives a superior sanction from the authority and example of Christ.—Matt. vi. 6; xiv. 23.

Q. II. What is the peculiar use of *family prayer?*

A. In its influence upon servants, and the young members of a family, who want sufficient seriousness and reflection to retire of their own accord to the exercise of private devotion, and whose attention you cannot easily command in public worship. The example also and authority of a father and master act in this way with the greatest force; for his private prayers act not at all upon them as examples; and his attendance upon public worship they will readily impute to a care to preserve appearances, to a concern for decency and character, &c. Add to this, that forms of public worship are always less interesting than family prayers, in which the ardour of devotion is better supported, and the sympathy more easily propagated than in the presence of a mixed congregation.

Q. III. What may be said concerning *public worship?*

A. If the worship of God be a duty of religion, public worship is a necessary institution; forasmuch say, without it the greater part of mankind would exercise no religious worship at all.

These assemblies afford also, at the same time, opportunities for moral and religious instruction to those who otherwise would receive none.

The two reasons above stated, bind all the members of a community to uphold public worship by their presence and example, although the helps and opportunities which it affords may not be necessary to the devotion or edification of all; and to some may be useless: for it is easily foreseen, how soon religious assemblies would fall into contempt and disuse, if that class of mankind who are above seeking instruction in them, and want not that their own piety should be assisted by either forms or society in devotion, were to withdraw their attendance; especially when it is considered, that all who please, are at liberty to rank themselves of this class. The same consideration should over-rule many small scruples concerning the rigorous propriety of some things, contained in the forms, or administration of the public worship: for it seems impossible that even "two or three should be gathered together" if each require from the rest submission to his objections, and if no man will attend upon a religious service which in any point falls short of his ideas of perfection.

There are also other valuable advantages growing out of the use of religious assemblies, without being designed in the institution, or thought of by the individuals who compose them.

1. Joining in prayer and praises to their common Creator, has a sensible tendency to unite mankind, and to cherish the generous affections.

So many pathetic reflections are awakened, that most men carry away from public worship a better temper towards the rest of mankind, than they brought with them. Sprung from the same extraction, preparing together for the period of all worldly distinctions, reminded of their mutual infirmities and common dependency, having all one interest to secure, one Lord to serve, one judgment to look towards; it is hardly possible then to behold mankind as strangers or enemies; or not to regard them as children of the same family, assembled before their common parent. A single effect of this kind will probably not be considerable or lasting; but the frequent return of such sentiments may generate in time a permanent and productive benevolence.

2. Assemblies for the purpose of divine worship, placing men under impressions by which they are taught to consider their relation to the Deity, and to contemplate those around them with a view to that relation, force upon their thoughts the natural equality of the human species, and thereby promote humility and condescension in the highest orders, and inspire the lowest with a sense of their rights. If ever the poor man holds up his head, it is at church: if ever the rich man views him with respect, it is there: and both will be the better, and the public profited, the oftener they meet where

the [illegible] of dignity in the one is tempered and mitigated, and the spirit of the other quickened and confirmed.

The public worship of Christians is a duty of Divine appointment. "Where two or three," says Christ, "are gathered together in my name, there am I in the midst of them." Again, in the epistle to the Hebrews; "not forsaking the assembling of ourselves together, as the manner of some is;" which reproof seems as applicable to the desertion of public worship at this day, as in the age of the Apostle. Independently of these passages, a disciple of Christianity will hardly think himself at liberty to dispute a practice set on foot by the inspired preachers of his religion, coeval with its institution, and retained by every sect into which it has been since divided.

CHAP. V.

OF FORMS OF PRAYER IN PUBLIC WORSHIP.

Q. Liturgies, or preconcerted forms of public devotion, being neither enjoined in Scripture, nor forbidden, what is the only good reason for receiving or rejecting them?

A. That of expediency; which is to be gathered from a comparison of the advantages and disadvantages of this mode of worship, with those which usually accompany extemporary prayer.

Q. What are the advantages of a liturgy?

A. I. That it prevents absurd, extravagant, or impious addresses to God, which the folly and enthusiasm of many must be in danger of producing, where the conduct of the public worship is intrusted, without restraint to the discretion of the officiating minister.

II. That it prevents the *confusion* of extemporary prayer, in which the congregation are confounded between their attention to the minister, and to their own devotion: where before a hearer can assent to a petition, that is, before he can address the same request to God for himself, and from himself, his attention is called off to what succeeds. Add to this, that the mind is held in continual expectation, and detained from its proper business, by the very novelty with which it is gratified. A congregation may be pleased and affected with the prayers and devotion of their minister, without joining in them. *Joint* prayer, which amongst all denominations of Christians is the declared design of "coming together," is a prayer in which all *join*; and not that which one alone conceives and delivers, and of which the rest are merely hearers. This objection seems fundamental, and holds even where the minister's office is discharged with every possible advantage and accomplishment.

Q. With what two principal inconveniences are these advantages of a liturgy connected?

A. First, that forms of prayer composed in one age become unfit for another, by the unavoidable change of language, circumstances, and opinions: secondly, that the perpetual repetition of the same form of words produces weariness and inattentiveness in the congregation. However, both these are in their nature vincible. Occasional revisions may obviate the first, and devotion will supply a remedy for the second: or they may both subsist in a considerable degree, and yet be outweighed by the objections which are inseparable from extemporary prayer.

Q. How does our Saviour appear, if not to have prescribed, at least to have authorized the use of fixed forms?

A. When he complied with the request of the disciple, Luke xi. 1. and gave the Lord's prayer as a precedent and pattern.

Q. What are the properties required in a public liturgy?

A. I. That it be compendious.

It were no difficult task to contract the liturgies of most churches into half their present compass, and yet retain the substance of every petition and sentiment, which can be found in them. But brevity may be studied too much. The composer of a liturgy must not hope, that the devotion of the congregation will be uniformly sustained throughout, or that every part will be attended to by every hearer. If this could be depended upon, a very short service would be sufficient; but seeing that the attention of most men is apt to wander and return at intervals, he will admit a certain degree of amplification and repetition, to the end that the attention, which has been absent during one part of the service, may be recalled by another; and the assembly kept together until it may be presumed, that the most inadvertent have performed some act of devotion. On the other hand, the too great length of church-services is very unfavourable to piety. It begets, in many, an early and unconquerable dislike to public worship: so that they come to church seldom; and when they do, it is under apprehension of a tedious attendance, which they soon relieve, by composing themselves to a drowsy forgetfulness of the place and duty.

The length and repetitions complained of in our liturgy, are not so much the fault of the compilers, as the effect of uniting into *one* service what was originally distributed into *three*. Notwithstanding the prevalent dread of innovations in religion, few would be displeased with such omissions, abridgements, or change in the arrangement, as the combination of separate services must necessarily require. The church of England would then be in possession of a liturgy, in which those who assent to her doctrines would have little to blame, and the most dissatisfied must acknowledge many beauties. As it is, a Christian petitioner can have few things to ask of God, or to deprecate, which he will not find there expressed in it, and for the most part with inimitable tenderness and simplicity.

II. That it express just conceptions of the Divine Attributes.

In this no care can be too great. The popular notions of God are formed, in a great measure, from the accounts the people receive in their religious assemblies. An error here, becomes the error of multitudes: and as it leads the way to some practical consequence, the purity or depravation of public manners will be affected by the truth or corruption of the public forms of worship.

III. That it recite such wants as the congregation are likely to feel, and no other.

Of forms which offend not egregiously against truth and decency, that has the most merit which is best calculated to keep alive devotion. It were to be wished, therefore, that every part of a liturgy were personally applicable to the congregation; and that nothing were introduced to damp the flame, which it is not easy to rekindle. Upon this principle, the *state prayers* in our liturgy should be fewer and shorter. Besides, they ill accord with that annihilation of human greatness, of which every act that carries the mind to God presents the idea.

IV. That it contain as few controverted propositions as possible.

We allow to each church the truth of its own tenets, and all the importance zeal can ascribe to them. We dispute not the right or expediency of framing creeds, or of imposing subscriptions. But why should every position which a church maintains, be woven with so much industry into her forms of public worship? Some are offended and some are excluded; this is an evil, at least to them; and what advantage or satisfaction can be derived to the rest, from the separation of their brethren, it is difficult to imagine, unless it were a duty to agree in religious exercises with those from whom we differ in some religious opinions. If sectaries are blameable for taking unnecessary offence, established churches are no less so for unnecessarily giving it; they are bound at least to produce a command, or a reason of equivalent utility, for shutting out any from their communion, by mixing with divine worship doctrines which, whether true or false, are unconnected in their nature with devotion.

CHAP. VI.

OF THE USE OF SABBATICAL INSTITUTIONS.

Q. What produces a necessity of appropriating set seasons to the social offices of religion?

A. An assembly cannot be collected, unless the time be fixed and known before hand: and if the design of the assembly require that it be holden frequently, it is easiest that it should return at stated intervals.

Q. Why is it also highly convenient that the same seasons be observed throughout the country?

A. That all may be employed, or all at leisure, together; otherwise one man's business will perpetually interfere with another man's devotion. A general intermission of labour and business therefore, during times previously set apart for public worship, is founded in the reasons which make public worship itself a duty.

Q. What remains of Sunday, beside the part employed at church, is a mere rest from ordinary occupations: he therefore who would defend the institution, as required by law to be observed, unless he can produce a command for a Christian *sabbath*, must point out the uses of it in that view: what are these?

A. *First*, that interval of relaxation afforded to the laborious part of mankind, contributes greatly to their comfort, both as it refreshes them for the time, and as it relieves their six days' labour by the prospect of a day of rest; which could not be said of *casual* indulgences of leisure. Moreover holydays which come seldom and unexpected, are unprovided, when they do come, with any duty or employment; and are commonly consumed in stupid sloth, or brutish intemperance.

Nor is any thing lost to the community by the intermission of public industry one day in the week. For, in countries tolerably advanced in population and the arts of civil life, there is always enough of human labour, and to spare. The difficulty is not so much to procure, as to employ it.

2. Sunday, by suspending many public diversions, and ordinary employments, leaves to men

of all ranks and professions, leisure both for the external offices of Christianity, and the equally necessary duties of religious meditation and inquiry. It is true, many do not convert their leisure to this purpose; but it is of moment, that to every one be allowed the opportunity.

3. They, whose humanity embraces the whole sensitive creation, will esteem it no inconsiderable recommendation, that it affords a respite to the toil of brutes. This was among the uses for which the Divine Founder of the *Jewish* sabbath expressly appointed the institution.

None of these reasons, indeed, show why Sunday should be preferred to any other day, or one day in seven to one day in six, or eight: but these points being established to our hands, our obligation applies to the subsisting establishment, so long as we confess that some such institution is necessary, and cannot substitute any other in its place.

CHAP. VII.

OF THE SCRIPTURE ACCOUNT OF SABBATICAL INSTITUTIONS.

Q. The subject, so far as it makes any part of Christian morality, is contained in two questions: what are these?

A. I. Whether the command, by which the Jewish sabbath was instituted, extends to Christians?

II. Whether any new command was delivered by Christ; or any other day substituted in the place of the Jewish Sabbath by the authority or example of his apostles?

Q. In treating of the first question, what is necessary?

A. To collect the accounts which are preserved of the institution in the Jewish history: for the seeing these accounts in one point of view, will be the best preparation for judging of any arguments on one side or the other.

In the second chapter of Genesis, we read, that "God *blessed* the seventh day and *sanctified* it, because that in it he had rested from all his work which God created and made." After this, we hear no more distinct mention of the sabbath, or of the seventh day, until the sojourning of the Jews in the wilderness, in a remarkable account of God's provision for their relief by the miraculous supply of manna. In which account we find the following expressions: "This is that which the Lord hath said, *To-morrow is the rest of the holy sabbath unto the Lord*." "Eat that to-day: *for to-day is a sabbath unto the Lord*;" "See, *for that the Lord hath given you the sabbath*, therefore he giveth you on the sixth day the bread of two days." Exodus xvi.

Not long after this, the sabbath was established with great solemnity, in the fourth commandment.

Q. Now, in Paley's opinion, what was the first actual institution of the Sabbath?

A. The transaction in the wilderness above recited. For if the sabbath had been instituted at the time of the creation, as the words in Genesis may seem at first sight to import, and had been observed from that time to the departure of the Jews out of Egypt; it appears unaccountable that no mention of, or allusion to it, should occur, either in the general history of the world before the call of Abraham, or, in that of the lives of the first three Jewish patriarchs. Nor is there, in the passage above-mentioned from Exodus, any intimation that the sabbath, when appointed to be observed, was only the revival of an ancient institution, which had been neglected; nor is any such neglect imputed either to the inhabitants of the old world, or to any part of Noah's family; nor is any permission recorded to dispense with the institution during the captivity of the Jews in Egypt, or on any other emergency.

Q. Is the passage in 2nd. chapter of Genesis, inconsistent with this opinion?

A. No; for as the seventh day was erected into a sabbath, on account of God's resting from the work of creation, it was natural in the historian, when he had related the history of the creation, and of God's ceasing from it on the seventh day, to add; "And God blessed the seventh day, and sanctified it, because that on it he had rested from all his work;" although the blessing, and sanctification, i. e. the religious appropriation of that day, was not actually made till many ages afterwards. The words do not assert that God *then* "blessed" and "sanctified" the seventh day, but that he blessed and sanctified it *for that reason*; and if any ask, why the sanctification of the seventh day, was *then* mentioned, if it was not *then* appointed, the answer is at hand: the order of connexion, and not of time, introduced the mention of the sabbath, in the history of the subject which it was ordained to commemorate.

Q. How is this interpretation strongly supported?

A. By a passage in the prophet Ezekiel, where the sabbath is plainly spoken of as *given*, (and what else can that mean, but as *first instituted*?) in the wilderness. Ezek. xx. 10, 11, 12.

Q. What else supplies an argument on the same side?

A. Nehemiah recounts the promulgation of the sabbatic law amongst the transactions in the wilderness: Nehem. ix. 12.

Q. If it be inquired what duties were appointed for the Jewish sabbath, and under what penalties and how it was observed amongst the ancient Jews: what do we find?

A. That, by the fourth commandment, a strict cessation from work was enjoined, not only upon Jews, but upon all who resided within the limits of the Jewish state; that the same was to be permitted to their slaves and cattle; that this rest was not to be violated, under pain of death: Exod. xxxi. 15. Beside which, the seventh day was to be solemnnised by double sacrifices in the temple: Numb. xxviii. 9, 10. Also by *holy convocations*, which mean, we presume, assemblies for the purpose of public worship or religious instruction. Levit. xxiii. 3.

Q. What accordingly do we read as regards the Jews on this point?

A. That the sabbath was in fact observed amongst them by a scrupulous abstinence from every thing which, by any construction, could be deemed labour. In the Maccabean wars, they suffered a thousand of their number to be slain, rather than do any thing in their own defence on the sabbath-day. In the final siege of Jerusalem, they refused any operation on the sabbath-day, by which they might have interrupted the enemy in filling up the trench. After the establishment of synagogues it was the custom to assemble in them on the sabbath-day, for the purpose of hearing the law rehearsed and explained, and for the exercise, it is probable, of public devotion. The seventh day is *Saturday*; and, agreeably to the Jewish computation, the sabbath held from six o'clock on the Friday, to six o'clock on Saturday evening.

Q. These observations being premised, what may be said on the main question, Whether the command by which the Jewish sabbath was instituted, extends to us?

A. If the Divine command was delivered at the creation, it was addressed to the whole human species alike, and continues, unless repealed by some subsequent revelation, binding upon all who know it. If it was published for the first time in the wilderness, then it was directed to the Jews alone; and something farther will be necessary to show, that it was designed for any other. It is on this account, that the question concerning the date of the institution was first to be considered. The former opinion precludes all debate about the extent of the obligation; the latter admits, and, *primâ facie*, induces, a belief that the sabbath ought to be considered as part of the Jewish policy.

Q. From what arguments does this belief receive great confirmation?

A. The sabbath is described as a sign between God and the people of Israel; "*It is a sign between me and the children of Israel for ever.*" Exodus xxxi. 17. Also the same is declared Ezek. xx. 12.—Now it does not seem easy to understand how the sabbath could be a *sign* between God and the people of Israel, unless the observance of it was peculiar to that people, and designed to be so.

The distinction of the sabbath is, in its nature, as much a positive ceremonial institution, as that of many other seasons appointed by the Levitical law to be kept holy, which in the twenty-third chapter of Exodus are recited together with the sabbath.

If the command be binding upon Christians, it must be so as to the day, the duties, and the penalty; in none of which it is received.

The observance of the sabbath was not one of

the articles enjoined by the Apostles, in the fifteenth chapter of Acts.

St. Paul appears to have considered the sabbath as part of the Jewish ritual, and not obligatory upon Christians as such.—Col. ii. 16, 17.

Q. What two objections may be opposed to the force of these arguments?

A. One is, that the reason assigned for hallowing the seventh day, "because God rested on the seventh day from the work of the creation," pertains to all mankind; the other, that the command is inserted in the Decalogue, of which all the other precepts and prohibitions are of moral and universal obligation.

Q. What may be remarked upon the first objection?

A. That although in Exodus the commandment is founded upon God's rest from the creation, in Deuteronomy the commandment is repeated with a reference to a different event:—"And remember that thou wast a servant in the land of Egypt, and that the Lord thy God brought thee out thence, through a mighty hand, and by a stretched out arm; *therefore*, the Lord thy God commanded thee to keep the sabbath-day." It is further observable, that God's rest is proposed as the reason of the institution, even where the institution itself is spoken of as peculiar to the Jews:—"Wherefore the children of Israel shall keep the sabbath," &c.—"*for* in six days the Lord made heaven and earth, and on the seventh day he rested and was refreshed." These different reasons were assigned, to account for different circumstances in the command. If a Jew inquired, why the *seventh day* was sanctified rather than the sixth or eighth, his law told him, because God rested on the *seventh day*. If he asked, why was the same rest indulged to *slaves*? his law bade him remember, that he also was a *slave* in the land of Egypt, and "that the Lord his God brought him out thence." In this view, the two reasons are perfectly compatible with each other, and with a third end of the institution, its being a *sign* between God and the people of Israel; but in this view they determine nothing concerning the extent of the obligation.

Q. What may be said respecting the second objection?

A. That this argument will have less weight when it is considered, that the distinction between positive and natural duties, like other distinctions of modern ethics, was unknown to the simplicity of ancient language; and that there are various passages in Scripture, in which duties of a political or ceremonial nature, and of partial obligation, are enumerated without any discrimination, along with others which are natural and universal. Of this, there is an incontestable example in Ezekiel xviii. 5—9. The same may be observed of the apostolic decree recorded in the fifteenth chapter of the Acts:—"That ye abstain from meats offered to idols, and from blood, and from things strangled, and *from fornication*: from which if ye keep yourselves, ye shall do well."

Q. 19. If the law by which the sabbath was instituted, was a law only to the Jews, what becomes an important question with the Christian inquirer?

A. Whether the founder of his religion delivered any new command upon the subject; or, if that should not appear to be the case, whether any day was thus appropriated by the authority or example of his Apostles.

Q. What may be remarked on this head?

A. The practice of holding religious assemblies upon the first day of the week, was so early and universal in the Christian Church, that it carries with it considerable proof of having originated from some precept of Christ, or of his Apostles, though none such be now extant. It was upon the *first* day of the week that the disciples were assembled, when Christ appeared to them for the first time after his resurrection. (John xx. 19.) This might appear, as to the day, to have been accidental; but in the 26th verse we read that "after eight days," that is, on the *first day* of the week *following*, "*again* the disciples were within;" which looks like an appointment and design to meet on that particular day. In the 20th ch. of the Acts, we find the same custom in a Christian Church at a great distance from Jerusalem:—"And we came unto them to Troas in five days, where we abode seven days; and *upon the first day of the week, when the disciples came together to break bread*, Paul preached unto them." Acts xx. 6, 7. This makes it appear very probable that the practice was now familiar and established. St. Paul to the Corinthians writes thus: "upon the *first day of the week* let every one of you lay by him in store as God hath prospered him." Which affords a probable proof, that the *first* day of the week was already, amongst Christians, distinguished from the rest by some religious application or other. When St. John wrote his Revelation, the first day of the week had obtained the name of the *Lord's day.*"—"I was in the spirit," says he, "*on the Lord's day.*" Rev. i. 10. Therefore the name and its appropriation was known to the Churches of Asia. No doubt by the *Lord's day* was meant the *first* day of the week; for we find no distinction of days, which could entitle any other to that appellation. The subsequent history of Christianity corresponds with the accounts delivered on this subject in Scripture.

Q. What, must it be remembered, is contended for by these proofs?

A. No other duty upon the first day of the week, than that of holding and frequenting religious assemblies. A general cessation upon that day from labour, is not intimated in any passage of the N. T. nor did Christ or his Apostles deliver, that we know of, any command for a discontinuance of common offices; a reserve which we shall not wonder at, if we consider that, in the primitive condition of Christianity, the observance of a new sabbath would have been useless, or inconvenient, or impracticable. During Christ's personal ministry, his religion was preached to the Jews alone. *They* already had a sabbath, [illegible] fore enjoin another day of rest in conjunction with this. When the new religion came to the Gentiles, converts to it were, for the most part, made from those classes who have not their time and labour at their own disposal; and it was scarcely to be expected, that unbelieving masters would permit their slaves and labourers to rest from their work every seventh day: or that civil government would have submitted to the loss of a seventh part of the public industry, in addition to their other numerous festivals; this might have greatly retarded the reception of Christianity.

For the opinion, that Christ and his Apostles meant to retain the duties of the Jewish Sabbath, shifting only the day from the seventh to the first, there seems not sufficient proof, nor does any evidence remain (of what, however, is not improbable), that the first day was thus distinguished in commemoration of our Lord's resurrection.

Q. What is the conclusion from the whole enquiry?

A. The assembling upon the first day of the week for the purpose of public worship and instruction, is a law of Christianity, of Divine appointment; the resting from our employments longer than we are detained in attendance upon those assemblies, is an ordinance of human institution, binding upon the conscience of every individual for the sake of the beneficial purposes which the public and regular observance of it promotes, and recommended perhaps to the Divine approbation, by its resemblance to what God made a part of the law de-

[illegible]

of our time as [illegible]

ligious reflection; as journies, visits, letter-writing, studies, or reading of books which bear no relation to the business of religion.

4thly, By unnecessary encroachments on the rest which Sunday ought to bring to the inferior orders; as by keeping [illegible] on that day busied in preparations for our table, or dress, &c.

[illegible]

[illegible] shooting, frequenting taverns, playing at cards or [illegible]

Q. Since the obligation upon Christians [illegible]

[illegible] a game of cards, or in conversation [illegible] the like questions [illegible]

Q. [illegible] retained at all, must be upholden by some [illegible] where [illegible] you will, many actions situated on its [illegible]

[illegible] merely in custom — [illegible]

Q. [illegible] disrespectful to the institution, but as [illegible]

[illegible]

[illegible] towards [illegible] light [illegible]; [illegible] journies, visiting, letter-writing, [illegible] reading of books which bear no relation to the business of religion.

[illegible] By unnecessary encroachments on the rest which Sunday ought to bring to the [illegible] as by keeping servants on that day busied in preparations for our table, or dress, &c.

[illegible] shooting, frequenting taverns, playing at cards or [illegible]

[illegible] a game of cards, or in conversation [illegible] to the like questions what answer may we return? [illegible] the observance of Sunday, if it is to be retained at all, must be upholden by some [illegible] draw the line of distinction where you will, many actions situated on its confines, [illegible] yet lie on the opposite side. [illegible] to the service of religion [illegible] Christian faith;—

[illegible]

CHAP. IX.

OF REVERENCING THE DEITY.

[illegible]

[illegible]
[illegible] be destroyed?

A. By indecent appeals to them, and by speaking with that familiar levity with which some speak of the Deity, of his attributes, providence, revelation, or worship.

Q. God hath been pleased to forbid the vain mention of his name. Now the mention is vain, when it is useless: when then is it useless?

A. When it is neither likely nor intended to serve any good purpose; as when it flows from idle lips, or is applied, on occasions inconsistent with any consideration of religion and devotion, to express our anger, earnestness, courage, or mirth.

Q. Is the prohibition of the third commandment recognized by Christ?

A. Yes, in his sermon upon the mount; which adverts to none but the moral parts of the Jewish law: "Swear not at all: but let your communication be Yea, yea; Nay, nay: for whatsoever is more than these, cometh of evil."

Q. How did the Jews probably interpret the prohibition?

A. As restrained to the name JEHOVAH, which the Deity had appointed and appropriated to himself; Exod. vi. 3. The words of Christ extend the prohibition beyond the name of God, to every thing associated with the idea: Matt. v. 35.

Q. By what is the offence of profane swearing aggravated?

A. By the consideration, that in it duty and decency are sacrificed to slender temptations.—Suppose the habit already formed, it must always lie in the power of common resolution to correct it; and it cannot cost a great deal to relinquish the pleasure and honour which it confers.

Q. What disposition does a contempt of positive duties, or rather of those duties for which the reason is not so plain as the command, indicate?

A. One upon which the authority of Revelation has obtained little influence.—This remark is very applicable to those who are most addicted to profane swearing.

Q. What else falls within the meaning of the law which forbids the profanation of God's name, especially as extended by Christ's interpretation?

A. Mockery and ridicule, when exercised upon the SS. or even upon the places, persons, and forms, set apart for the ministration of religion.

Q. With what, moreover, are they inconsistent?

A. With a religious frame of mind: for as no one ever feels himself disposed to pleasantry upon matters in which he is deeply interested, so a mind intent upon the acquisition of heaven, rejects with indignation every attempt to entertain it with jests calculated to degrade or deride subjects which it never recollects but with seriousness and anxiety.

Q. Finally; what may the knowledge of what is due to the solemnity of those interests, concerning which Revelation professes to inform and di-

[illegible] over those who are least inclined to respect the prejudices of mankind.

III. To observe a decorum in the style and conduct of religious disquisitions, with the neglect of which many adversaries of Christianity are justly chargeable. Serious arguments are fair on all sides. Christianity refuses not audience or toleration to objections. But whilst we would have freedom of inquiry restrained only by decency, we are entitled to demand, for a religion which holds forth assurances of immortality, that its credit be assailed by no other weapons than sober discussion and legitimate reasoning:—that its truth or falsehood be not made a topic of raillery, an exercise of wit, or a contention for literary fame and victory:—that all applications to fancy, passions, or prejudices, all attempts to pre-occupy, ensnare or perplex the judgment, without proper grounds and evidence, be rejected from a question which involves the hopes, the virtue, and the repose, of millions:—that nothing be produced, in the writings of either side, contrary to, or beyond, the writer's own knowledge and persuasion: that objections be proposed, from no other motive than an honest and serious desire to promote the discovery and progress of truth:—that in conformity with this, every thing be stated with integrity, precision, and simplicity; and above all, that whatever is published in opposition to received and confessedly beneficial persuasions, be set forth under a form which is likely to invite inquiry and to meet examination.

[illegible] equitable [illegible] compared the manner in which hostilities [illegible]
waged against Christianity, what will every [illegible]
who looks forward with anxiety to the destination
of his being, see?

[illegible] Much to blame and to complain of. By one,
[illegible] all the follies which have adhered in
a long course of dark and superstitious ages to
the popular creed, are assumed as so many [illegible],
for the purpose of subverting the system by the absurdities which it is *thus* represented to contain.
By *another*, the ignorance and vices, dissensions
and persecutions, of the sacerdotal order, have
been displayed, not so much to guard the Christian
laity against a repetition of the same injuries, as
to prepare the way for an insinuation, that the religion itself is but a profitable fable, imposed upon
the multitude by the frauds and influence of an interested priesthood. And yet, how remotely is
the character of the clergy connected with the
truth of Christianity! What, after all, do the
most disgraceful pages of ecclesiastical history
prove, but that the passions are not altered by
distinctions of name, and that the characters of
men are formed more by the temptations than the
duties of their profession? A *third* delights in
repeating accounts of wars, massacres, and tumults, excited by religious zeal; as though the
vices of Christians were parts of Christianity; or
as if its spirit could be judged of from the counsels
of princes, the intrigues of statesmen, or the unauthorised cruelties of some gloomy and virulent

superstition. By so framing the succession and variety of popular religions; the vicissitudes with which sects and tenets have flourished and decayed; the little share which reason appears to have had in framing the creed, or regulating the religious conduct of the multitude; the indifference with which the religion of the state is generally received; the caprice and vehemence with which it is sometimes opposed; the equal confidence with which we hear the doctrines of Christ or of Confucius, the law of Moses or of Mahomet, maintained or anathematized, taught or abjured, according as we keep within or step over the boundaries of a state; or even in the same country, as often as the event of a battle, or a negociation, delivers them to a new master;—points of this sort are exhibited to the public attention, as so many arguments against the *truth* of Christianity;—and with success. For being brought together, and set off with aggravation of circumstances, and with a vivacity of style familiar enough to free-thinkers, they insensibly lead the imagination into a habit of classing Christianity with other delusions, and of regarding it as what they represent *the superstition of the day*.

Q. Now is this to deal honestly by the subject or with the world?

A. No: the same things may be said, and the same prejudices excited by these representations, whether Christianity be true or false, or by what proofs its truth be attested. Truth, as well

[illegible]

[illegible]

A. In the system under which they are disguised. Infidelity is served up in every shape likely to allure, surprise, or beguile the imagination; in a fable, a tale, a poem; in broken hints, detached surmises; in philosophy and natural history; in any form rather than the right one, that of a professed and regular disquisition. And because the coarse buffoonery of the old and rude adversaries of Christianity, would offend the taste, perhaps, rather than the virtue, of this cultivated age, a graver irony, a more skilful and delicate banter, is substituted in their place. Who can refute a *sneer*? Who computes the number, or scrutinizes the justice, of a multitude of disparaging insinuations? What reader calls off his attention from the principal narrative, to examine references, or to weigh the reason and propriety of every transient sarcasm, or sly allusion, by which the Christian testimony is depreciated; and by which, nevertheless, he may find his persuasion afterwards unsettled and perplexed?

Nay more, obscenity itself has been the vehicle of infidelity. The awful doctrines of our religion, together with all the appendages of its worship,

[illegible] been [illegible] employed, [illegible]
[illegible] with [illegible].
The feeling for ridicule is universal, and [illegible]
to many minds is irresistible, [illegible]
obscenity, and employed upon religion. [illegible]
these noxious principles take hold of the imagination, they infatuate the judgment, and [illegible]
disposed to receive either [illegible]
of impressions from authority. And this effect
being exerted upon the sensitive part of our [illegible]
is independent of argument, proof, or [illegible]
formidable to a true religion, as to a false and fabulous one. Neither is the crime of [illegible] less,
because impure ideas are exhibited under a veil,
in covert and chastised language.

Q. With what remarks does Paley conclude this topic?

A. Seriousness is not constraint of thought, nor levity, freedom. Every mind which wishes to advance truth and knowledge, in the most important of human researches, must abhor this licentiousness, as violating the laws of reasoning, with the rights of decency. There is but one description of men to whom it can be tolerable; viz. that class of reasoners who see *little* in Christianity, even supposing it to be true. To such this reflection is addressed.—Had Christ delivered no other declaration than the following—"The hour is coming, in the which all that are in the grave shall hear his voice, and shall come forth; they that have done good, unto the resurrection of life; and they that have done evil, unto the resurrec-

feel of immortality,—he has pronounced a message of inestimable importance, worthy of that splendid apparatus of prophecy and miracles with which his mission was attended; a message in which the wisest would rejoice to find an answer to their doubts, and rest to their inquiries. It is idle to say, that a *future state* had been discovered already:—it had been discovered as the Copernican system was;—it was one guess among many. He alone discovers, who *proves*; and no man can prove this point, but the teacher who testifies by miracles that his doctrine comes from God.

OF THE ORIGIN OF CIVIL GOVERNMENT.

Q. What was Government at first?

A. Either patriarchal or military: that of a parent over his family, or of a commander over his fellow-warriors.

Q. What is observed upon the first of these kinds?

A. 1. Paternal authority, and the order of domestic life, supplied the foundation of civil government. The condition of infancy prepares man for society, by combining individuals into small communities, and by placing them from the beginning under direction and controul. A family contains the rudiments of an empire. The authority of one, and the disposition to govern and to be governed, are incidental to man's nature, and coeval with his existence.

The constitution of families was formed in the first steps of the process by which empires are

BOOK VI.

CHAP. I.

OF THE ORIGIN OF CIVIL GOVERNMENT.

Q. What was Government at first?

A. Either patriarchal or military: that of a parent over his family, or of a commander over his fellow-warriors.

Q. What is observed upon the first of these kinds?

A. 1. Paternal authority, and the order of domestic life, supplied the foundation of civil government. The condition of infancy prepares men for society, by combining individuals into small communities, and by placing them from the beginning under direction and controul. A family contains the rudiments of an empire. The authority of *one*, and the disposition to govern and to be governed, are incidental to man's nature, and coeval with his existence.

The constitution of families also furnishes the first steps of the process by which empires have been reared. A parent would retain considerable authority, after his children had formed families of their own. Their obedience would be considered as natural; and would scarcely be withdrawn during the parent's life. Here then is the second stage in the progress of dominion.

Although the original progenitor was the centre of union to his posterity, yet it is not probable that the association would be immediately dissolved by his death. Connected by intercourse, affection, and by some common rights and interests, they would consider themselves as allied to each other in a nearer degree than to the rest of the species. Almost all would feel an inclination to continue in the society in which they had been brought up; and soon experiencing many inconveniences from the absence of that authority which their common ancestor exercised, they might be induced to supply his place by a formal choice of a successor; or rather might almost imperceptibly transfer their obedience to some one respectable elder of the family: or, the apprehended inconveniences might prompt the first ancestor to appoint a successor; and his posterity, from the same motive, united with an habitual deference to his authority, might receive the appointment with submission. Here, then, we have a tribe incorporated under one chief. Such communities might increase, and fulfil the purposes of civil union, without any more regular convention or form of government. Every branch slipped off from the primitive stock, would in like manner, take root, and grow into a separate clan. Two or three of these clans were frequently, we may suppose, united into one. Marriage, conquest, mutual defence, common distress, &c. might produce this effect.

Q. What does Paley remark upon the second kind of government?

A. A source of personal authority, which might extend, or sometimes perhaps supersede, the patriarchal, is that which results from military arrangement. In wars, either of aggression or defence, necessity would prompt those on the same side to array themselves under one leader. And although their *leader* was thus advanced for the purpose only, and during the operations, of a single expedition, yet his authority would not always terminate with the reasons for which it was conferred. A warrior who had led forth his tribe in war with repeated success, would acquire, even in the deliberations of peace, a powerful influence. If this were added to patriarchal authority, or any previous distinction of ancestry, it would not be difficult for such a person to obtain the almost absolute direction of affairs; especially if he was careful to procure proper auxiliaries, and to practise the art of gratifying or removing opponents.

Q. What are the causes why sovereign power, which may easily be acquired by merit and management, descends in hereditary succession?

A. The influence of association, which communicates to the son a portion of the respect which was paid to the virtues of the father; the mutual jealousy of other competitors; the envy with which all behold the exaltation of an equal; a reigning prince leaving behind him many adherents, who can preserve their own importance only by supporting the succession of his children; and the destructive calamities which, upon trial, have proceeded from elections to the supreme power.

Q. Does the ancient state of society and the modern condition of some uncivilized nations, exhibit that appearance which this account of the origin of civil government would lead us to expect?

A. Yes; the earliest histories of Palestine, Greece, Italy, Gaul, Britain, inform us, that these countries were occupied by many small independent nations, not much perhaps unlike those which are now found amongst the savages of North America, and upon the coast of Africa. These nations may be considered as amplifications of so many single families; or derived from the junction of two or three families, through society in war, or the approach of some common danger. Suppose a country to have been first peopled from shipwreck, or by emigrants: the new settlers, occupied only with the care of personal subsistence, would think little of digesting a system of laws, policy or government; but each settler would remain at the head of his own family, and each family would include all who were descended from him. So many of these families as were holden together after the death of the original ancestor, by the reasons above recited, would in time wax into tribes, clans, or nations, as the ancient inhabitants of many countries are known to have been divided, and are still found wherever the state of society is immature and uncultivated.

Nor need we be surprised at the early existence of some vast empires, or at the rapidity with which they advanced to their greatness. Whilst people were broken into numerous communities, unconnected, and often contending; before experience had taught them to see their own danger in their neighbour's ruin, or had instructed them in the necessity of resisting an aspiring power, by alliences, and timely preparations; in this state, a particular tribe, which had gotten the start in strength or discipline, and was under an ambitious chief, by directing their first attempts where success was most secure, and by assuming those whom they conquered into a share of their future enterprises, might soon gather a force which would infallibly overbear any opposition.

Q. Lastly, what presumption does this theory afford?

A. That the earliest governments were monarchies, because the government of families, and of armies, from which civil government derived its institution, and probably its form, is universally monarchical.

CHAP. II.

HOW SUBJECTION TO CIVIL GOVERNMENT IS MAINTAINED.

Q. Could we view our own species from a distance, or as we remark the *manners* of any other animal, what would particularly surprise us?

A. The almost universal subjugation of strength to weakness;—the sight of millions of robust and courageous men, in the complete exercise of their personal faculties, waiting upon the will of a child, a woman, or a driveller. And although we thus suppose an extreme case; yet in all, even in the most popular forms of civil government, *the physical strength resides in the governed.*

Q. By what motives the many are induced to submit to the few, becomes an inquiry which lies at the root of almost every political speculation. What removes, but does not resolve, the difficulty?

A. To say that civil governments are now almost universally upholden by standing armies; for, the question still returns; how are these armies themselves kept in subjection, or made to obey and carry on the designs of a prince or state?

Q. What does Paley observe upon this point?

A. Although we should look in vain for any *single* reason which will account for this general submission; yet it may not be difficult to assign for every class and character in the community considerations to dissuade each from any attempts to resist established authority. In this, as in other instances, the conduct is similar, but the principles which produce it, various.

There are three distinctions of character, into which the subjects of a state may be divided: who obey from prejudice; from reason; and from self-interest.

Q. I. How are they who obey from *prejudice* determined?

A. By an opinion of right in their governors, founded upon *prescription*. In monarchies and hereditary aristocracies, the prescription operates in favour of particular families; in republics and elective offices, in favour of particular forms of government. Nor can we wonder, that mankind should reverence authority founded in prescription, when they observe that the whole course, and all the habits of civil life, favour this prejudice. Upon what other foundation stands any man's right to his estate? the right of primogeniture, the descent of property, the inheritance of honours, the right of way, the privileges of nobility, the immunities of the clergy? upon what else are they all founded, in the apprehension at least of the multitude? It is natural therefore to transfer the same principle to government, and to regard those exertions of power which have been long exercised, as so many *rights* in the sovereign; and to consider obedience to his commands, as enjoined by that rule, which requires us to render to every man his due.

In hereditary monarchies, the *prescriptive title* is corroborated by an accession of religious sentiments, and by that sacredness which men are wont to ascribe to the persons of princes: of which disposition princes themselves have not failed to take advantage. For this purpose were introduced the titles of Sacred Majesty, of God's Anointed, his Vicegerent, together with the ceremonies of investitures and coronations, not so much to recognise their authority, as to consecrate their persons. Where a fabulous religion permitted it, the public veneration has been challenged by bolder pretensions. The Roman emperors usurped the titles and arrogated the worship of gods. Some princes, like the heroes of Homer, and the founder of the Roman name, derived their birth from the gods; others, with Numa, pretended a secret communication with some divine being; and others, again, like the incas of Peru, and the ancient Saxon kings, extracted their descent from the deities of the country. In all these instances the purpose was the same,—to engage the reverence of mankind, by an application to their religious principles.

In this article, every opinion, whether true or false, is denominated a *prejudice*, which is not founded upon argument, in the mind of the person who entertains it.

Q. II. What is said of those who obey from *reason?*

A. They who so obey, from conscience, as instructed by reasonings and conclusions of their own, are determined by the consideration of the necessity of some government or other; the certain mischief of civil commotions; and the danger of re-settling the government of their country better, or at all, if once subverted.

Q. III. What of those who obey from *self-interest?*

A. They are kept in order by want of leisure; by a succession of private cares, pleasures, and engagements; by a sense of the ease, plenty, and safety, which they enjoy; or lastly, by fear, foreseeing that they might bring themselves by resistance into a worse situation than their present, inasmuch as the strength of government, each discontented subject reflects, is greater than his own, and he knows not that others would join him.

This last consideration has often been called *opinion of power*.

Q. What cautions may this account of the principles by which mankind are retained in their obedience to civil government suggest?

A. 1. Civil governors may learn hence to respect their subjects; considering that *the physical strength resides in the governed;* that this strength need only be roused, to lay prostrate the most confirmed dominion; that civil authority is founded in opinion, which, therefore, ought always to be treated with deference, and managed with delicacy.

2. *Opinion of right*, always following *the*

cation, and lending one principal support to government, every innovation in the constitution diminishes the stability of government. Hence some absurdities are to be retained, and many small inconveniences endured, rather than that the usage should be violated, or the course of public affairs diverted from their old and smooth channel. Even *names* are not indifferent; for when the multitude are to be dealt with, there is a *charm* in sounds.

3. *Government may be too secure.* The greatest tyrants have been those whose titles were the most unquestioned. Whenever, therefore, the opinion of right becomes too predominant and superstitious, it is abated by *breaking the custom.* Thus, the Revolution broke the *custom of succession*, and thereby moderated, both in the prince and in the people, those lofty notions of hereditary right, which in the one were become a continual incentive to tyranny, and disposed the other to invite servitude, by undue compliances and dangerous concessions.

4. As ignorance of union, and want of communication, appear amongst the principal preservatives of civil authority, it behoves every state to keep its subjects in this want and ignorance, by vigilance in guarding against actual confederacies, and by a timely care to prevent great collections of men of any separate religious party or profession, or in any way connected by a participation of interests, from being assembled in the same vicinity. Hence, one danger of an overgrown me-

tropolis, and of those great cities and crowded districts, into which the inhabitants of trading countries are commonly collected. The worst effect of popular tumults is, that they discover to the insurgents the secret of their own strength, both producing and diffusing sentiments of confidence and assurances of mutual support. Such leagues may overset the power of any state; and the danger is greater, as, from the propinquity of habitation and intercourse, the passions and counsels of a party can be circulated with ease and rapidity.

CHAP. III.

THE DUTY OF SUBMISSION TO CIVIL GOVERNMENT EXPLAINED.

Q. In order to prove civil obedience to be a moral duty, and an obligation upon the conscience, what has it been usual with many political writers (at the head of whom we find the venerable name of Locke) to state?

A. A compact between the citizen and the state, as the ground and cause of the relation between them: which compact, binding the parties like private contracts, resolves the duty of submission to civil government, into the universal obligation of fidelity in the performance of promises.

Q. What further then is said of this compact?

A. That it is twofold. First, An *express* compact by the primitive founders of the state, who are supposed to have convened for the purpose of settling the terms of their political union, and future constitution. The whole body is supposed to have unanimously consented to be bound by the resolutions of the majority; that majority to have fixed certain fundamental regulations; and then to have constituted, either in one person, or in an assembly, a *standing legislature*, to whom, under these pre-established restrictions, the government was thenceforward committed, and whose laws the several members of the convention were thus personally engaged to obey.—This transaction is sometimes called the *social compact*, and these supposed original regulations compose what are meant by the *constitution*, the *fundamental laws of the constitution*; and form, on one side, the *inherent indefeasible prerogative of the crown*; and, on the other, the unalienable, imprescriptible *birthright* of the subject.

Secondly, A *tacit* or *implied* compact, by all succeeding members of the state, who, by accepting its protection, consent to be bound by its laws; in like manner, as whoever *voluntarily* enters into a private society, is understood to promise a conformity with its rules and obedience to its government, as the known conditions upon which he is admitted to a participation of its privileges.

Q. Under what objections does this account of the subject, although specious, and patronized by names the most respectable, appear to labour?

A. That it is founded upon a supposition false in fact, and leading to dangerous conclusions.

No such social compact, or original convention, was, or ever could be, entered into in reality, antecedent to the existence of civil government. It is to call savages out of caves and deserts, to deliberate upon topics, which the experience, studies, and refinements, of civil life, alone suggest. Therefore no government *began* from this original: though some imitation of a social compact may have taken place at a *revolution*. The present age has been witness to a transaction, which bears the nearest resemblance to this political idea, of any in history: the establishment of the United States of North America. Yet even here much was presupposed; and many important parts of the constitution were presumed to be already settled. The qualifications of constituents, admitted to vote in the election of congress, as well as the mode of election, were taken from the old forms of government: that was wanting, from which every social union should set off, and which alone makes the resolutions of the society an act of the individual—the unconstrained consent of all to be bound by the decision of the majority; and yet, without this previous consent, the revolt, and the repudiation which followed it, were compulsory upon dissentients.

Q. But the original compact, we are told, is not proposed as a *fact*, but as a fiction, which furnishes a commodious explication of the mutual rights and duties of sovereigns and subjects. What may be said in answer to this representation of the matter?

A. That the original compact, if it be not a fact, is nothing; can confer no actual authority upon laws or magistrates; nor afford any foundation to rights which are supposed to be real and existing. But the truth is, that in the books, and in the apprehension, of those who deduce our civil rights and obligations *a pactis*, the original convention is appealed to and treated of as a reality. They would teach us, that certain ordinances were established by the people, when they settled the government, and the powers and the form of the future legislature; that this, consequently, deriving its commission and existence from the act of the primitive assembly (of which it is the standing deputation) continues subject to the rules, reservations, and limitations, which the same assembly then made and prescribed to it.

Q. "As the first members of the state were bound by stipulation to obey the government which they had erected, so the succeeding inhabitants are understood to promise allegiance to the constitution they find established, by accepting its protection, claiming its privileges, and acquiescing in its laws; more especially, by the purchase or inheritance of lands, to the possession of which, allegiance to the state is annexed, as the very price and condition of the tenure." Similarly, as this train of argument proceeds, will it explain much examination?

A. No: the native subjects of modern states are not conscious of any stipulation with the sovereign; of any alternative being proposed to their choice; of a promise either required or given; nor do they apprehend that the validity of the law depends upon their recognition or consent. In all stipulations whatever, whether they be expressed or implied, the parties stipulating must possess the liberty of assent and refusal, and also be conscious of this liberty; which cannot with truth be affirmed of the subjects of civil government as it is now, or ever was, administered. All presumptions of consent, without this consciousness, or in opposition to it, are vain and erroneous. Still less can we reconcile with any idea of stipulation, the practice of founding allegiance upon the circumstance of nativity; or, of claiming it from those who, though born within the confines of one country, have removed to another in their youth or infancy. Here, certainly, a consent is not presumed. Also, if the subject be bound only by his own consent, and if the voluntary abiding in the country be the proof and intimation of it, how can we defend the right, which sovereigns assume, of prohibiting the departure of subjects out of the realm?

Again, when it is contended that the taking and

[illegible] of the sovereign, and a virtual [illegible] for the argument, [illegible] prove, that the inhabitants who first [illegible] collectively possessed a right to the [illegible] they pleased, and [illegible] their own conditions. [illegible] this right? An agreement [illegible] would not [illegible] already belonged to them; [illegible] of men could [illegible] the [illegible] of a region of the world. Yet the [illegible] right [illegible] by which the duty of allegiance is inferred from the [illegible]

Q. [illegible] appear to lead to conclusions unfavourable to the improvement, and to the peace, of human society. What are these?

A. Supposing the government [illegible] by a convention; it might be pretended, that many points were settled by [illegible] in the [illegible] which the legislature, [illegible] no right to alter, or interfere with. These points are called the fundamentals of the constitution: and as [illegible] they are, the suggesting of any such, [illegible] to the [illegible] of the legislature, and a dangerous pretence for disputing the authority of the laws.

2dly, If it be by virtue of a compact, that the subject owes obedience to civil government, it will follow that he ought to abide by the form of government which he finds established, be it ever so absurd or inconvenient. He is bound by his bargain. The law of contracts is universal: and to call the relation between the sovereign and the subjects a contract, yet not to apply to it the rules of a contract, is an arbitrary and unsteady use of names. Resistance to *encroachments* may be justified upon this principle; recourse to arms, for bringing about an amendment of the constitution, never can. No form of government contains a provision for its own dissolution; and few governors will consent to the extinction, or even to any abridgment, of their own power. It does not therefore appear, how despotic governments can ever, in consistency with the obligation of the subject, be changed or mitigated.

3dly. Every violation of the compact by the governor, releases the subject from allegiance, and dissolves the government. We cannot avoid this consequence, if we found the duty of allegiance upon compact, and confess any analogy between the social compact and other contracts. Now, the terms and articles of the social compact being no where extant or expressed; the imaginary and controverted line of prerogative being so liable to be overstepped; the position, that every such transgression amounts to a forfeiture of the government, and authorise the people to withdraw their obedience, and provide for themselves by a new settlement, would endanger the stability of every political fabric in the world.

Q. The intervention therefore of a compact being rejected, as unfounded in its principle, and dangerous in the application, what may be assigned for the only ground of the subject's obligation?

A. *The will of God as collected from expediency.*

Q. What are the steps by which the argument proceeds?

A. They are few and direct.—"It is the will of God that the happiness of human life be promoted:"—"Civil society conduces to that end:" "Civil societies cannot be upholden, unless, in each, the interest of the whole society be binding upon every part and member of it:"—this conducts us to the conclusion, namely, "that so long as the interest of the whole society requires it, that is, so long as the established government cannot be resisted or changed without public inconveniency, it is the will of God (which *will* universally determines our duty) that the established government be obeyed,"—and no longer.

Q. This principle being admitted, to what is the justice of every particular case of resistance reduced?

A. The computation of the quantity of danger and grievance on the one side, and of the probability and expense of redressing it on the other.

Q. But it may be said, who shall judge this?

A. "Every man for himself." In contentions between the sovereign and the subject, the parties acknowledge no common arbitrator; and it would be absurd to refer the decision to *those* whose conduct has provoked the question, and whose own interest and fate, are immediately concerned in it. The danger of error and abuse is no objection to the rule of expediency, because every other rule is liable to the same or greater.

Q. Paley proceeds to point out some easy but important inferences, which result from the substitution of *public expediency* into the place of all implied compacts or conventions. What are these?

A. I. It may be a duty, at one time, to resist government, as it is, at another, to obey it; to wit, whenever more advantage will, in our opinion, accrue to the community from resistance, than mischief.

II. The lawfulness of resistance, or the lawfulness of a revolt, does not depend alone upon the grievance which is sustained or feared, but also upon the probable expense and event of the contest.

III. Irregularity in the first foundation of a state, or subsequent violence, fraud, or injustice, in getting possession of the supreme power, are not sufficient reasons for resistance, after the government is once peaceably settled. Thus no subject of the British empire conceives himself engaged to vindicate the justice of the Norman claim or conquest.

IV. Not every invasion of the subject's rights, or liberty, or of the constitution; not every stretch of prerogative, abuse of power, or neglect of duty, &c. justifies resistance, unless these crimes draw after them public consequences of sufficient magnitude to outweigh the evils of civil disturbance; although every violation of the constitution ought to be watched with jealousy, and resented, and because security is weakened by every encroachment which is made without opposition, or opposed without effect.

V. No usage, law, or authority is so binding, that it ought to be continued, when it may be changed with advantage to the community. The family of the prince, the order of succession, the prerogative of the crown, the form and parts of the legislature, &c. are all only so many *laws*, mutable like other laws, when expediency requires, either by the ordinary act of the legislature, or, if the occasion deserve it, by the interposition of the people. These points are wont to be approached with a kind of awe, as principles of the constitution settled by our ancestors, and, being settled, to be no more committed to innovation or debate; as the terms and conditions of the social compact. Such reasons have no place in our system; if there be any good reason for treating these with more deference than other laws, it is either the advantage of the present constitution of government, or because in all countries it is of importance that the form and usage of governing be acknowledged and understood by all.

VI. As all civil obligation is resolved into expediency, what, it may be asked, is the difference between the obligation of an Englishman and a Frenchman? or why, is a Frenchman bound in conscience to bear any thing from his king, which an Englishman would not be bound to bear? How can this comparison be explained, unless we refer to a difference in their compacts?—This is a fair question, and the answer will afford a further illustration of our principles. We admit then that there are many things which a Frenchman is bound in conscience to endure at the hands of his prince, to which an Englishman would not be obliged to submit: but it is for these two reasons alone: *first*, because the same act of the prince is not the same grievance, where it is agreeable to the constitution, and where it infringes it; *secondly*, because redress in the two cases is not equally attainable. Resistance cannot be attempted with equal hopes of success, or with the same prospect of receiving support from others, where the people are reconciled to their sufferings, as where they are alarmed by innovation.

VII. "The interest of the whole society is binding upon every part of it." No rule, short of this, will provide for the stability of civil government, or for the peace and safety of social life. Wherefore, as individual members of the state are not permitted to pursue their private emolument to the prejudice of the community, so is it equally a consequence of this rule, that no particular colony, province, town, or district, can justly concert measures for their separate interest, which shall appear at the same time to diminish the sum of public prosperity. The contested claims of sovereign states and their remote dependencies may be submitted to the adjudication of this rule with mutual safety. A public advantage is measured by the advantage which each individual receives, and by the number of those who receive it. A public evil is compounded of the same proportions. Whilst, therefore, a colony is small, if a competition of interests arise between the original country and their acquired dominions, the former ought to be preferred; because it is fit that, if one must be sacrificed, the less give place to the greater; but when, by an increase, the interest of the provinces begins to bear a great proportion to the entire interest of the community, it is possible that they may suffer so much by their subjection, that the whole happiness of the empire may be obstructed by their union. The rule and principle of the calculation being still the same, the *result* is different: and this difference begets a new situation, which entitles the subordinate parts of the states to more equal terms of confederation, and, if these be refused, to independency.

CHAP. IV.

OF THE DUTY OF CIVIL OBEDIENCE, AS STATED IN THE CHRISTIAN SCRIPTURES.

Q. Paley affirms that, as to the extent of our civil rights and obligations, *Christianity* hath left us where she found us; that she hath neither altered nor ascertained it;

What are the only passages of the N. T. which have been seriously alleged in the controversy, or which it is necessary to state and examine?

A. One extracted from St. Paul's Epistle to the Romans, another from the First General Epistle of St. Peter.

ROMANS. xiii. 1—7.

"Let every soul be subject unto the higher powers: for there is no power but of God; the powers that be, are ordained of God," &c.

1 PETER ii. 13—18.

"Submit yourselves to every ordinance of man, for the Lord's sake; whether it be to the King, as supreme; or unto Governors, as unto them that are sent by him," &c.

Q. To comprehend the proper import of these instructions, what must the reader reflect?

A. That upon the subject of civil obedience there are two questions: the first, whether to obey government be a moral duty upon the conscience of all; the second, how far that obedience ought to extend? that these two questions are so distinguishable, that it is possible to treat of the one, without any thought of the other; and lastly, that if expressions relating to one be transferred to the other, it is with great danger of giving them a signification very different from the author's meaning.

Q. How does Paley illustrate this?

A. He says, that if he met with a person who entertained doubts, whether civil obedience were a voluntary moral duty, or whether it were not a mere submission to force, he should represent to him the use of civil government, and the end of civil subjection; or, if he preferred a different theory, he should explain to him the social compact, urge him with the obligation and the equity of his implied promise, &c.; or, he should argue, perhaps, that Nature herself dictated the law of subordination, &c. From whatever principle he set out, he should labour to infer from it this conclusion, "That obedience is to be numbered amongst the relative duties of life, for the transgression of which we shall be accountable at the tribunal of Divine justice." He should then stop, having delivered the conclusion itself, and all along expressed the obedience, which he inculcated, in the most general and unqualified terms; all reservations and restrictions being superfluous, and foreign to the doubts he was employed to remove.

Q. If, in a short time afterwards, he should be accosted by the same person, with complaints of public grievances, of acts of cruelty and oppression, of tyrannical encroachments, &c. and should be consulted whether it were lawful to join in an attempt to shake off the yoke, what part would he take?

A. He should certainly consider the case and question very different from the former. He should now define and discriminate. He should reply, that if public expediency be the foundation, it is also the measure, of civil obedience: that the obligation of subjects and sovereigns is reciprocal; that the duty of allegiance, is neither unlimited nor unconditional; that patience becomes culpable pusillanimity, when it serves only to encourage our rulers to increase the weight of our burthen; that the submission which entails slavery upon future generations, is enjoined by no law of rational morality; finally, he should instruct the inquirer to compare the peril and expense of his enterprise with the effects it was expected to produce, and to choose the alternative by which not his own present relief and profit, but the whole and permanent interest of the state, was likely to be best promoted.

Q. If any one should upbraid him with inconsistency of opinion, or retort upon him the passive doctrine which he before taught, what would he reply?

A. That the only difference between the language of the two conversations was, that he added necessary exceptions and limitations, which were omitted or unthought of; such exceptions being not necessary to the subject of the present conference, as they would have been [illegible] in the former.

Q. What further does he observe respecting the difference in these two conversations?

A. That it is precisely the distinction to be taken in interpreting the above-mentioned passages of Scripture. They inculcate the duty, they do not describe the extent of it. They enforce the obligation by the proper sanctions of Christianity, without intending either to enlarge or contract, without considering, indeed, the limits by which it is bounded; just as when the duty of servants to their masters, of children to their parents, is enjoined, the same concise form of expression occurs; the same silence as to any exceptions or distinctions: yet the commands of masters, parents, &c. are often so unjust, and inconsistent with other obligations, that they both may and ought to be resisted. In all these cases we find the apostles more solicitous to impress the duty, than curious to enumerate exceptions.

Q. This distinction is alone sufficient to vindicate these passages from any indication in favour of unlimited passive obedience: but what other supposition may fairly be assumed?

A. One asserted by many commentators, that the first Christians privately cherished an opinion, that their conversion entitled them to new immunities; to an exemption, as of right, from the authority of the Roman sovereign; in this view a most apt and satisfactory interpretation.

Q. How do the two passages apply with great propriety to the refutation of this error?

A. They teach the Christian convert to obey the magistrate "for the Lord's sake;" "not only for wrath, but for conscience sake;" "that there is no power but of God;" "that the powers that be," even the present rulers of the Roman empire, though heathens and usurpers, seeing they are in possession of the actual and necessary authority of civil government, "are ordained of God;" and, consequently, entitled to receive obedience from those who profess themselves the peculiar servants of God. They greatly simplify the office of "civil governors, the punishment of evil-doers, and the praise of them that do well;" from which description of the use of government, they justly infer the duty of subjection; which, being as extensive as the reason of it, belongs to Christians, no less than to the other members of the community.

Q. What is the only defect in this solution?

A. That neither the history nor any history of the early ages of the church, directly attest the existence of such disaffected sentiments amongst the primitive converts, though they supply some circumstances which render probable the opinion, that extravagant notions of the political rights of the Christian state were at that time entertained by many proselytes to the religion.

Q. Paley observes, that after this account of the general design of these much agitated passages, little need be added in explanation of particular clauses. What may be observe respecting the passage of St. Paul, "whosoever resisteth the power, resisteth the ordinance of God;" which, by many, is so interpreted as to authorise the most superstitious ideas of the [illegible]

[illegible]

tue only of [illegible]

[illegible] of man.

Q. What does the definition of civil liberty above laid down import?

A. That the laws of a free people impose no restraints upon individuals which do not conduce in a greater degree to the public happiness, by which it is [illegible], than the restraint itself

CHAP. V.

OF CIVIL LIBERTY.

Q. What is civil liberty?

A. *Civil Liberty is the not being restrained by any law, but what conduces in a greater degree to the public welfare.*

To do what we will, is natural liberty; to do what we will consistently with the interest of the community, is civil liberty; the only liberty to be desired in a state of civil society.

I should wish, no doubt, to act in every instance as I pleased; but all mankind would then do the same; in which state of universal independence, I should meet with so many checks to my own will, from the interference of others, that not only my happiness, but my liberty, would be less, than whilst all are subject to equal laws.

Natural liberty exists only in a state of solitude. In civil life, the liberty of the individual may be augmented by the very laws which restrain it; for he may gain more from the limitation of other men's freedom, than he suffers by the diminution of his own.

Q. What does the definition of civil liberty above laid down import?

A. That the laws of a free people impose no restraints upon an individual, which do not conduce in a *greater degree* to the public happiness; by which it is intimated, 1st, that restraint itself is an evil; [illegible] that this evil ought to be over-balanced by some public advantage; [illegible] that the proof of this advantage lies upon the legislature; 4thly, that a law being found to produce no sensible good effects, is a sufficient reason for repealing it, as adverse and injurious to the rights of a citizen, without demanding specific evidence of its bad effects.

Q. The degree of civil liberty [illegible] according to [illegible] the restraint ; what follows?

[illegible]

be conveyed to a [illegible] by an order of [illegible] that. The manifest expediency of the measure justifies and reconciles the most absolute confinement with the perfect possession, and [illegible] enjoyment of civil liberty. And if this be true of the coercion of a prison, it cannot be disputed of those more moderate constraints imposed upon the will of individuals. It is the inexpediency of laws and acts of authority, alone, which makes them tyrannical.

Q. What other idea of civil liberty, though neither so simple nor so accurate, agrees better with the usage of common discourse, and the example of many respectable writers?

A. This places liberty in security; not merely in an actual exemption from the constraint of useless and noxious laws, &c.; but in being free from the danger of having such imposed or exercised. Thus, we are accustomed to say of Sweden, that she lost her *liberty* by a revolution; and yet the people are governed by the same laws as before, or by others milder and more equitable. What then have they lost? The power and functions of their diet; that constitution whose deliberations and concurrence were required in every public law; and thereby they have parted with their security against any attempts of the crown to harass its subjects, by oppressive and useless exertions of prerogative. They have changed, not their laws, but their legislature; not their enjoyment, but their safety; and this is a change from the condition of freemen to that of slaves. Were it probable that the welfare of the people would be as studiously consulted in the edicts of a despotic prince, as by the resolutions of a popular assembly, there would an absolute government be no less free than a pure democracy. The degree of care and knowledge of the public interest which may reasonably be expected from the different form of the legislature, constitutes the distinction, in respect of liberty, as well between the two extremes, as between all the intermediate modifications of civil government.

Q. The different definitions which have been formed of civil liberty, are most of them adapted to this idea. Thus one writer makes the subject's liberty to consist in his being governed by no laws but those to which he hath actually consented; another is satisfied with an indirect and virtual consent; a third places civil liberty in the separation of the legislative and executive offices; a fourth, in the being governed by *law*, that is, by known preconstituted rules, &c. &c. Concerning which, and some other similar accounts what may be observed?

A. That they all labour under one inaccuracy, viz. that they describe not so much liberty itself, as its safeguards and preservatives: for a man's being governed by no laws but those to which he has given his consent, were it practicable, is no otherwise necessary to civil liberty, than as it affords a probable security against laws which impose superfluous restrictions upon his private will. This remark is applicable to the rest.

Q. What consideration will prevent our being surprised at the diversity of these definitions?

A. That there is no contrariety or opposition amongst them whatever: for by how many different precautions civil liberty is protected, so many different accounts of it, all sufficiently consistent with truth and each other, may, thereby, be framed and adopted.

Q. Truth cannot be offended by a definition, but propriety may. In which view, what definitions of liberty ought to be rejected?

A. Those which, by making that essential to civil freedom which is unattainable in experience, inflame expectations that can never be gratified, and raise complaints, which no wisdom or benevolence of government can remove.

Q. Of the two ideas that have been stated of civil liberty, a subject so difficult to define, whichever we assume, and whatever reasoning we found upon them, concerning its extent, nature, value and preservation—what is the conclusion?

A. That *that* people, government, and constitution is the *freest*, which makes the best provision for the enacting of expedient and salutary laws.

CHAP. VI.

OF DIFFERENT FORMS OF GOVERNMENT.

Q. As a series of appeals must be finite, there necessarily exists in every government a power from which the constitution has provided no appeal; which power, for that reason, may be termed absolute, uncontrollable, despotic, and is alike in all countries: what is the person, or assembly, in whom this power resides, called?

A. The sovereignty, or supreme power of the state.

Q. Since to the same power universally appertains the office of establishing public laws, what is it called also from hence?

A. The legislature of the state.

Q. A government receives its denomination from the form of the legislature; what do we commonly mean by that form?

A. The constitution of a country.

Q. Writers enumerate three principal forms of government, which, however, are to be regarded rather as the simple forms, by some combination of which all governments are composed, than as any where existing in a pure elementary state. What are these forms?

A. I. Despotism, or absolute MONARCHY, where the legislature is in a single person.

II. An ARISTOCRACY, where the legislature is in a select assembly, the members of which succeed to places in it by election, inheritance, or property, or some personal qualification.

III. A REPUBLIC, or democracy, where the people at large, either collectively or by representation, constitute the legislature.

Q. What are the separate advantages of MONARCHY?

A. Unity of counsel, activity, decision, secrecy, dispatch; the military strength and energy which result from these qualities; the exclusion of popular and aristocratical contentions; the preventing by a known rule of succession, of all competition for the supreme power; and thereby repressing the intrigues, and dangerous ambition, of aspiring citizens.

Q. What are the mischiefs, or rather the dangers of MONARCHY?

A. Tyranny, expense, exaction, military domination; unnecessary wars; risks of the character of the reigning prince; ignorance in the governors of the interests of the people, and deficiency of salutary regulations; want of constancy and uniformity in the rules of government, and, thence, insecurity of person and property.

Q. In what consists the separate advantage of an ARISTOCRACY?

A. In the wisdom which may be expected from experience and education:—a permanent council naturally possesses experience; and the members who succeed to their places in it by inheritance will, probably, be trained and educated with a view to their stations.

Q. What are its evils?

A. Dissensions in the ruling orders, which, from want of a common superior, are liable to proceed to extremities; oppression of the lower orders by the privileges of the higher; and by laws partial to their separate interests.

Q. What are the advantages of a REPUBLIC?

A. Exemption from needless restrictions; equal laws; regulations adapted to the wants of the people; public spirit, frugality, averseness to war; the opportunities which democratic assemblies afford to all men, of producing their abilities and counsels to public observation, and the exciting thereby, and calling forth the faculties of the best citizens.

Q. What are its evils?

A. Dissensions, tumults, faction; the attempts of powerful citizens to possess themselves of the empire; the confusion, rage, and clamour, which are the consequences of assembling multitudes, and of popular discussion; the delay and disclosure of public counsels; measures retarded by the necessity of obtaining the consent of numbers; lastly, the oppression of the provinces not admitted to a participation in the legislative power.

Q. What is a mixed government?

A. It is composed by the combination of two or more of the simple forms above described; and in whatever proportion each form enters into the constitution of a government, in the same proportion may both the advantages and evils which we have attributed to that form, be expected; that is, those are the uses to be maintained and cultivated, and these are the dangers to be provided against in each part.

Hence is afforded a rule to direct the construction, improvements, and administration of mixed governments,—subjected however to this remark, that a quality sometimes results from the conjunction of two simple forms, which belongs not to either separately: thus corruption, which has no place in an absolute monarchy, and little in a pure republic, is sure to exist in a constitution which divides the supreme power between an executive magistrate and a popular council.

Q. Why is an *hereditary* MONARCHY to be universally preferred to an *elective* one?

A. The confession of every writer, the experience of ages, the example of Poland, and of the papal dominions, seem to place this amongst the few indubitable maxims in the science of politics. A crown is too splended a prize to be conferred upon merit: the passions or interests of the electors exclude all consideration of the qualities of the competitors. The same may be said of any office attended with a great share of power and emolument. Nothing is gained by a popular choice, worth the dissensions, tumults, and interruption of regular industry, with which it is attended. Add to this, that a king, so called, will be apt to regard one part of his subjects as the associates of his fortune, and the other as conquered foes. Moreover as plans of national improvement are seldom brought to maturity by the exertions of a single reign, a nation cannot attain to the degree of happiness and prosperity of which it is capable unless an uniformity of counsels, a consistency of public measures, be continued through a succession of ages. This benefit may be expected rather where the power descends in the same race, and each prince succeeds, in some sort, to the aim and pursuits of his ancestor, than if the crown, at every change, devolve upon a stranger, who will commonly wish to pull down what his predecessor had built up.

Q. Of how many kinds are ARISTOCRACIES?

A. Two.—First, where the power of the nobility is in their collective capacity alone; that is, where, although the government reside in an assembly of the order, yet its members separately and individually possess no authority or privilege beyond the rest of the community,—as in the ancient constitution of Venice. Secondly, where the nobles are severally invested with great personal power and immunities, and where the power of the senate is little more than the aggregated power of the individuals who compose it:—this is the constitution of Poland.

Q. Of these two forms of Government, which is most tolerable?

A. The first; for although the members of a senate should many, or even all, be profligate enough to abuse their authority in the prosecution of private designs, yet, not being all under a temptation to the same injustice, it would be difficult to obtain the consent of a majority to any specific act of oppression which an individual might propose, as if the will were the same, the power is more confined. Of all species of domination the most odious is that of a numerous nobility over their vassals: the freedom and satisfaction of private life are more constrained by it than by the most vexatious laws, or even by the lawless will of an arbitrary monarch, from whose knowledge, and injustice, most of his subjects are removed by distance, or concealed by obscurity.

About the middle of the last century, the commons of Denmark, weary of the oppressions which they had long suffered from the nobles, and exasperated by some recent insults, presented themselves at the foot of the throne, with a formal offer of their consent to establish unlimited dominion in the king. The revolution in Sweden, owed its success to the same cause. In England, the people beheld the depression of the barons, under the house of Tudor, with satisfaction, though they saw the crown acquiring thereby an almost unlimited power.

Q. What is the lesson to be drawn from such examples as these?

A. That a mixed government, which admits a patrician order into its constitution, ought to circumscribe the personal privileges of the nobility, especially claims of hereditary jurisdiction and local authority, with a jealousy equal to the solicitude with which it wishes its own preservation.

Q. Do you suggest the inference, that [illegible]

advantages of a DEMOCRATIC constitution, in which the people partake of the power of legislation, what ought not to be neglected?

A. I. The direction which it gives to the education, studies, and pursuits, of the higher orders. The share which this has in forming the manners and national character, is very important. In countries where the gentry are excluded from all concern in the government, scarcely any thing leads to advancement, but the profession of arms. They who do not addict themselves to this profession are commonly lost by the mere want of object and destination; they either fall into the most sottish habits of animal gratification, or devote themselves to the attainment of those futile arts which compose the business and recommendations of a court: but where any effective portion of civil power is possessed by a popular assembly, more serious pursuits, purer morals, and a more intellectual character, will engage the public esteem; those deliberative faculties which are the fruit of sober habits, and long-continued application, will be roused by the animating reward of political dignity and importance.

II. Popular elections procure to the common people courtesy from their superiors; while contemptuous and overbearing insolence is greatly mitigated where the people have something to give. The assiduity with which their favour is sought, generates settled habits of condescension and respect; and whatever contributes to procure civility of manners towards those who are most liable to suffer from a contrary behaviour, corrects greatly the evil of inequality, and is among the most generous institutions of social life.

III. The satisfactions which the people in free governments derive from the knowledge and agitation of political subjects; and, in general, from the discussion of public measures and questions. Such subjects excite just enough of interest and emotion, without rising to any painful degree of anxiety. And what is this, but the end and aim of all those amusements which compose so much of the business of life and of the value of riches? Even all the money paid in taxes to government, is well compensated by the pleasure we receive from expecting, hearing, and relating public news; reading parliamentary debates; conversing on political arguments, projects, and intelligence. These topics, exciting universal curiosity, and being such as almost all are ready to deliver their opinion about, greatly promote, and improve conversation; render it more rational and more innocent; and supply a substitute for drinking, gaming, scandal, and obscenity. Now the secrecy, the jealousy, the solitude, and precipitation, of despotic governments, exclude all this.

Q. We have been accustomed to an opinion, that a REPUBLICAN form of government suits only with the affairs of a small state: on what is this opinion founded?

A. In the consideration, that unless the people, in every district of the empire, be admitted to a share in the representation, the government is not, as to them, a republic; that elections, where the constituents are numerous, and widely dispersed, are conducted with difficulty, or rather, managed by the intrigues of a few, situated near the place of election; that whilst we contract the representative so as to admit of orderly debate, the interest of the constituent becomes too small, that of the representative too great. It is difficult also to maintain any connexion between them. He who represents two hundred thousand, must be a stranger to the greatest part of those who elect him; and when his interest amongst them ceases to depend upon an acquaintance with them, or a care and knowledge of their affairs; when he finds the treasures and honours of a great empire at the disposal of a few, and himself one of the few; there is little reason to hope that he will not prefer to his public duty those temptations which his situation offers. All appeal to the people is precluded by the impossibility of collecting them in sufficient force and numbers. The factions and the unanimity of the senate are equally dangerous. Add to this, that in a democratic constitution the mechanism is too complicated, and the motions too slow, for the operations of a great empire; whose defence and government require execution and dispatch.

Q. Though there is weight, no doubt, in these reasons; yet how does much of the objection seem to be done away?

A. By the contrivance of a *federal* republic, which, distributing the country into contermined districts, and leaving to each its internal legislation, reserves to a convention of the states the adjustment of their relative claims; the requisition of subsidies; the making of peace and war; the entering into treaties; the regulation of foreign commerce, &c. &c. To what limits such a republic might, without inconveniency, enlarge its dominions, by assuming neighbouring provinces into the confederation; or how far it is capable of uniting the liberty of a small commonwealth with the safety of a powerful empire; or whether, amongst co-ordinate powers, dissensions and jealousies would not be likely to arise, which, for want of a common superior, might proceed to fatal extremities; we cannot decide. The experiment will be tried in America upon a large scale.

CHAP. VII.

OF THE BRITISH CONSTITUTION.

Q. What is meant by the constitution of a country?—and what is that of England?

A. So much of its law as relates to the designation and form of the legislature; the construction, rights, and functions of the legislative body and courts of justice. The constitution is one principal division, or section, of the code of public laws; distinguished from the rest only by the superior importance of its subject. Therefore, the terms *constitutional* and *unconstitutional*, mean legal and illegal. The distinction and the ideas which they denote, are founded in the same authority with the law of the land upon any other subject. In England, the system of public jurisprudence is made up of acts of parliament, of decisions of courts of law, and of immemorial usages; consequently, these are the principles of which the English constitution itself consists, the authorities to which all appeal ought to be made, and by which every constitutional doubt and question can alone be decided. This plain definition is the more necessary, as some writers absurdly confound what is constitutional with what is expedient; pronouncing a measure to be unconstitutional, which they adjudge in any respect detrimental or dangerous: whilst others ascribe a kind of mysterious sanctity to the constitution, as if it were founded in some higher original than the ordinary laws and statutes of the realm, or were inviolable on any other account than its intrinsic utility. An act of parliament in England can never, strictly speaking, be unconstitutional; in a lower sense it may, *viz.* when it militates with the spirit, or defeats the provision, of other laws, made to regulate the form of government.

Q. How do most of those who treat of the British constitution consider it?

A. As a scheme of government formally contrived by our ancestors, in some certain æra and as set up in pursuance of such regular plan and design. Something of this sort is secretly referred to, in the expressions of those who speak of "the principles of the constitution," of bringing back the constitution to its "first principles," &c.

Q. How does this appear to Paley?

A. As an erroneous conception of the subject. No such plan was ever formed, consequently no such first principles, original, model, or standard, exist: that is, there never was a date or point of time in our history, when the government of England was to be set up anew, or when a constitution, prepared and digested, was by common consent received and established. Between the death of Charles the First and the restoration of his son, many such projects were published, but none carried into execution. The Great Charter, and the Bill of Rights, were wise and considerable measures; but these were much too partial modifications of the constitution, to give it a new original.

Q. How has the constitution of England been formed?

A. Like that of most countries of Europe, it has grown out of occasion and emergency; from the fluctuating policy of different ages; from the contentions, successes, interests, and opportunities, of different orders and parties of men in the community.

Q. What may be observed in the British, and possibly in all other constitutions?

A. That there exists a wide difference between the actual state of the government and the theory; though the one results from the other. When we contemplate the theory of the British government, we see the king invested with personal impunity; with a power of rejecting laws, of conferring upon any set of men he pleases, the privilege of sending representatives into one house of parliament, as by his mandate he can place whom he will in the other. What is this, a foreigner might ask, but a more circuitous despotism? Yet, when we turn from the legal extent, to the actual exercise of royal authority in England, we see these formidable prerogatives dwindled into mere ceremonies; and, in their stead, a commanding influence, of which the constitution is totally ignorant, growing out of that enormous patronage which the increase and opulence of the empire have placed in the disposal of the executive magistrate.

Q. Upon questions of reform, what habit of reflection is to be encouraged?

A. A sober comparison of our constitution, not with models of speculative perfection, but with the actual chance of obtaining a better. This will generate a political disposition, equally removed from that puerile admiration of establishments, which sees no fault, and can endure no change; and that sensibility, which is alive only to perceptions of inconveniency, and is too impatient to compute either the peril or expense of the remedy. Political innovations commonly produce many effects beside those that are intended. The direct consequence is often much less important than the incidental, remote, and unthought-of evil or advantages. It is from the silent operation, and the obscure progress of causes set at work for different purposes, that the greatest revolutions take their rise. When Elizabeth, and her successor, applied themselves to the encouragement of trade by many wise laws, they knew not, that with wealth and industry, they were diffusing a consciousness of strength and independency which would not long endure the dominion of arbitrary princes. When it was debated whether the mutiny act should be temporary or perpetual, little else probably occurred to the advocates of an annual bill, than the expediency of retaining a control over the most dangerous prerogative of the crown,—the direction and command of a standing army; whereas, in its effect, this single reservation has altered the whole frame and quality of the British constitution. For since, in consequence of the military system in other nations, as well as on account of the internal exigencies of government, a standing army has become essential to its safety and administration, it enables parliament, by discontinuing this necessary provision, so to enforce its resolutions upon any other subject, as to render the king's dissent to a law which has received the approbation of both houses, a dangerous experiment.

Q. One end of civil government peculiar to a good constitution is the happiness of its subjects? what other is essential to it, but common to it with many bad ones?

A. Its own preservation. Observing that the best form would be defective, which did not provide for its own permanency, we consider all such pro-

vindicate as expedient; and accept as a sufficient ground for a measure, or law, that it is conducive to the preservation of the constitution.

Q. Yet when only are such provisions expedient and such excuse final?

A. Only whilst the constitution is worth preserving; that is, until it can be exchanged for a better. This distinction is premised, because many things in the English, as in every constitution, are to be vindicated and accounted for solely from their tendency to maintain the government in its present state; and because it must be remarked that such a consideration is always subordinate to another,—the value and usefulness of the constitution itself.

Q. How is *the Government of England*, which has been sometimes called a mixed government, sometimes a limited monarchy, formed?

A. By a combination of the three regular species of government: the monarchy, residing in the King; the aristocracy, in the House of Lords; and the republic, represented by the House of Commons.

Q. What is the perfection intended by such a scheme of government?

A. To unite the advantages of the several simple forms, and to exclude the inconveniencies.

Q. How can we judge to what degree this purpose is attained or attainable in the British constitution; wherein it is lost sight of or neglected; and by what means it may in any part be promoted with better success?

A. By a separate recollection of the advantages and inconveniences, enumerated in the preceding chapter, and a distinct application of each to the political condition of this country.

Q. How does Paley present his remarks upon the subject?

A. In a brief account of the expedients by which the British constitution provides,

1. For the interest of its subjects.
2. For its own preservation.

Q. 1. What are the contrivances for the first of these purposes?

A. In order to promote the establishment of salutary laws, every citizen is capable of becoming a member of the senate; and every senator possesses the right of propounding for deliberation whatever law he pleases.

Every district enjoys the privilege of choosing representatives, informed of the interests and circumstances of their constituents, and entitled to communicate that information to the national council.

By annexing the right of voting for members of the House of Commons to different qualifications in different places, each order and profession of men in the community become virtually represented; that is, men of all orders and professions obtain seats in parliament.

The elections are so connected with the influence of landed property, as to afford a certainty that a considerable number of men of great estates will be returned to parliament; and are also so modi-

pected from an assembly so constituted, that it will receive the approbation of a majority.

To prevent those evil contentions for the supreme power, which take place where the members of the state do not live under an acknowledged head, and a known rule of succession; to preserve the people in tranquillity at home, by a speedy and vigorous execution of the laws; to protect their interest abroad, by strength and energy in military operations;—for these purposes, the executive government is committed to the administration and limited authority of an hereditary king.

In the defence of the empire; in the maintenance of its power and privileges with foreign nations; in the advancement of its trade by treaties; and in the providing for the general administration of municipal justice; the inclinations of the king and of the people usually coincide; in this part, therefore, of the regal office, the constitution entrusts the prerogative with ample powers.

The dangers principally to be apprehended from regal government, relate to taxation and punishment. In every form of government from which the people are excluded, it is the interest of the governors to get as much, and of the governed to give as little, as they can; the power also of punishment, with an arbitrary prince, often becomes an engine of extortion and revenge. The British constitution has guarded the safety of the people in these two points, by the most studious precautions.

[illegible] in the prosecution, the law in that case, sensible of the unequal contest in which the subject is engaged, has assisted his defence with extraordinary indulgence. Every person indicted for high treason, shall have a copy of the indictment, a list of witnesses, and of the jury, delivered to him ten days before the trial; he is also permitted to make his defence by counsel; and, what is of still more importance, the testimony of two witnesses, at least, is required to convict a person of treason; whereas, one positive witness is sufficient in almost every other accusation.

Q. How has the constitution provided for its preservation; that is, in what manner is each part of the legislature secured in the exercise of the powers assigned to it, from the encroachment of the other parts? Which security is sometimes called the *balance of the constitution*?

The political equilibrium, which this phrase denotes, consists in two contrivances—a balance of power, and a balance of interest. By a balance of power is meant, that there is no power possessed by one part of the legislature, the abuse of which is not checked by some power, residing in another part. Thus the power of the two houses to frame laws, is checked by the king's negative; that, by [illegible] his prerogative, if need be, he may [illegible] his necessary rights and authority. On the other hand, the arbitrary application of this negative is checked by the privilege of parliament to refuse supplies to the exigencies of the king's ad-

[illegible] authority, by [illegible], the House of Lords [illegible] ordinary power [illegible] of the republic; each would [illegible] pageantry of a despotic court [illegible], if the House of Commons should [illegible] upon the established prerogative of the crown, the House of Lords would [illegible], and oppose every [illegible] power, from an attachment to the [illegible], from which they derive their own distinction; and the [illegible] of a [illegible] in which they have been brought up; and [illegible] attempt to revive the [illegible] exercised under the [illegible] king and the people would [illegible], by [illegible]

[illegible] in the community [illegible] prejudices and interests. Hence [illegible] of an hereditary nobility, invested with [illegible] legislative [illegible] toned to condemn the clamour of the [illegible] [illegible] not only an [illegible] [illegible] jority of the [illegible]

[illegible] the public opinion, [illegible] this [illegible] there is little [illegible] number; for it is only [illegible] which is [illegible] public [illegible] for; [illegible]

[illegible] or of propriety. Or, to describe the [illegible] sentation as it exists, it may be affirmed, [illegible], [illegible] half of the House of Commons [illegible] tain their seats by the election of the people, the other half by purchase, or by the [illegible] of proprietors of great estates.

Q. [illegible] Paley [illegible] in a Constitution? [illegible]

[illegible]

[illegible] distinguish, that we may be assured, [illegible] [illegible] of the evil justifies the danger of the [illegible]

[illegible] Paley profess to [illegible]?

A. [illegible] the form of government [illegible] with [illegible] be considered [illegible] right [illegible] in public [illegible] of good laws, and the [illegible] them. [illegible]

[illegible]

[illegible] contribute to the [illegible] purely popular are in this unequal [illegible] with "property" but when [illegible] [illegible] to introduce into parliament a [illegible] pending [illegible] with the representatives of small boroughs [illegible] which [illegible] not only [illegible] given by the [illegible] part of the House of Commons [illegible] be tolerated with more danger? For what [illegible]

[illegible] consequence.

But whilst we dispute concerning different schemes of reformation, all directed to the same end, a previous doubt occurs, whether the end itself be good or safe; whether the influence so complained of can be destroyed without danger to the state. Whilst nothing but its entire abolition can appease the jealousy of some, other wise and virtuous politicians deem a portion of it to be as necessary a part of the constitution as any other ingredient; to be that, indeed, which gives cohesion and solidity to the whole. Were the measures of government, say they, opposed only from principle, they ought to have nothing but rectitude to support them; but since opposition springs from other motives, government must possess an influence to counteract these motives; to produce, not a bias of the passions, but a neutrality. It is the nature of power, always to press upon the boundaries which confine it. Licentiousness, faction, envy, impatience of control, &c.; above all, that love of power, and of showing it, which resides in every human breast, and which, in popular assemblies, is inflamed by communication and encouragement: these motives, added to private designs and resentments, [illegible] House of Commons [illegible]:

[illegible] ceas or satisfaction [illegible] have its weight with the [illegible] the general [illegible] Q. [illegible] A. The third [illegible] Q. [illegible] Agitaty which the subject [illegible] which it will appear, and to the greatest part of those to whom it is proposed, for want of information, reflection, experience, or capacity, &c. These are subjects of apparent indifference. What province do these cases compose?

A. That of influence; that is, the decision, in these cases will inevitably be determined by influence of some sort or other.

Q. What is the only doubt or question?

A. What influence shall be admitted. If you remove that of the crown, it is only to make way for influence from a different quarter. If motives of expectation and gratitude be withdrawn, others will succeed equally foreign and external to the merits of the question. There exist passions in the human heart, which will always make a strong party against the executive power. According as parliament is friendly or adverse to the recommendation of the crown in matters *really* or *apparently indifferent*, the business of the empire will be transacted with ease, or embarrassed with endless contention and difficulty. Nor are we warranted by justice or experience, to say that because men are induced by views of interest to consent to measures on which their judgment decides nothing, they may be brought by the same influence to act in opposition to knowledge and duty. Whoever reviews the operations of government in this country since the Revolution, will find few even of the most questionable measures, about which the best-instructed might not be understood at the time; but of which we may af-

[illegible] that a similar application would procure the [illegible] of parliament [illegible] to [illegible] the prerogative, deprived [illegible] belong [illegible] For what [illegible] power of the House of Commons to enforce compliance with its resolutions, or to put to death the constitution by a refusal of the [illegible] grants of money [illegible] the necessary [illegible] [illegible] we reflect [illegible] there are, [illegible] in the vicissitudes of things, [illegible] one day [illegible] push this power against [illegible], we shall perhaps [illegible] apothegm, [illegible] independent parliament is incompatible with the existence of the monarchy.

CHAP. VIII.

OF THE ADMINISTRATION OF JUSTICE.

Q. What is the first maxim of a free state?

A. That the laws be made by one set of men, and administered by another; in other words, that the legislative and judicial characters be kept sepa-

[illegible] particular, many general laws are made by one body of men, without foreseeing whom they may affect; and, when made, must be applied by the other.

Q. How may this be illustrated?

A. Suppose either that, the judicature being laid aside, the courts of Westminster Hall made their own laws, or that the two houses of parliament, with the King at their head, tried and decided causes at their bar; it is evident, in the first place, that the decisions of such a judicature would be so many laws; and in the second place, that, when the parties and the interests to be affected by the law were known, the inclinations of the law-makers would inevitably attach on one side or the other; and that where there were any fixed rules to regulate their determinations, nor any superior power to control their proceedings, these inclinations would interfere with the integrity of public justice.

Q. How are these dangers guarded against in this country?

A. By the division of the legislative and judicial functions. Parliament knowing not the individuals upon whom its acts will operate; and having no private designs to serve, its resolutions will be suggested by the consideration of universal effects and tendencies, from which spring impartial, and advantageous regulations. When laws are made, courts of justice must abide by them; for the legislative being the supreme power, the judicial and

[illegible]

Q. When is this fundamental rule of civil jurisprudence violated?

A. In acts of attainder or confiscation, in bills of pains and penalties, and in all ex post facto laws in which parliament exercises the double office of legislature and judge. And whoever understands the value of the rule, will acknowledge, that it had been wiser and safer never to have departed from it; or at least, that nothing but the most manifest and immediate peril will justify a repetition of these dangerous examples. If the laws do not punish an offender, let him go unpunished, and let the legislature provide against the commission of future crimes of the same sort. The escape of one delinquent can never produce so much harm as may arise from the infraction of a rule upon which public justice, and civil liberty, depend.

Q. What is the next security for the impartial administration of justice, especially in decisions to which government is a party?

A. The independency of the judges. As they become not unfrequently arbitrators between the king and the people, they ought to be independent of either; or, what is the same, equally dependent upon both; that is, if they be appointed by the one, they should be removable only by the other. Hence [illegible] tution, by which the judges, who before the Revolution held their offices during the pleasure of the king, can now be deprived of them only by an address from both houses of parliament. To make this independency complete, the public salaries of their office ought not only to be certain but so liberal as to secure their integrity from the temptation of secret bribes, preserve their jurisdiction from contempt, and their characters from suspicion.

Q. What third precaution is to be observed?

A. That the number of the judges be small. For, beside that the violence and tumult of large assemblies are inconsistent with patience, method, and attention; beside that all passions and prejudices act with augmented force upon a multitude; judges, when they are numerous, *divide* the shame of an unjust determination, and shelter themselves under one another's example: for which reason, they ought to be so few, as that the conduct of each may be conspicuous to public observation, and himself responsible for the decisions in which he concurs. The truth of this has been exemplified in the effects of that wise regulation which transferred the trial of parliamentary elections from the House of Commons at large, to a select committee of thirteen members. This alteration has given to a judicature, long swayed by interest and solicitation, the solemnity and virtue of the most upright tribunals. An even is preferable to an odd number of judges, and four to almost any other number: for in this, beside that it consults the idea of separate responsibility, nothing can be decided but by a majority of three to one; which ought to be so, when we consider that every decision establishes a perpetual precedent.

Q. What is a fourth requisite in the constitution of a court of justice?

A. That its proceedings be carried on in public, *apertis foribus*; not only before a promiscuous concourse, but in the audience of the whole profession of the Law. The opinion of the Bar will be impartial, and commonly guide that of the public. The most corrupt judge will fear to indulge his dishonest wishes in the presence of such an assembly.

Something is also gained by appointing two or three courts of concurrent jurisdiction, that it may be in the option of the suitor to which he will resort. By this means, a tribunal occupied by ignorant or suspected judges, will be deserted for others that possess more of the confidence of the nation.

Q. But lastly, if several courts, co-ordinate to and independent of each other, subsist together in the country, what seems necessary?

A. That the appeals from all should terminate in the same judicature; in order that one supreme and final tribunal may superintend and preside over the rest. This is necessary to preserve an uniformity in the decisions of inferior courts, and to maintain to each the proper limits of its jurisdiction. Without it, different courts might establish contradictory rules, and the contradiction be without remedy; the same question might receive opposite determinations, as it was brought before one court or another, and the determination in each be irreversible. Moreover, if questions arise between independent courts, concerning the extent of their respective jurisdiction, as each will be desirous of enlarging its own, an authority which both acknowledge can alone adjust the controversy.

Q. What are the two kinds of judicature, one of which may be called *fixed* and the other *casual*?

A. The first is where the office of the judge is permanent in the same person, and consequently the judge is known long before the trial; the other, where the judge is determined by lot at the time of the trial, and for that turn only.

Q. What are the advantages and disadvantages of the former kind?

A. Those qualifications may be expected which are sought for in the choice of judges, and that knowledge and readiness which result from experience. But the judge being known beforehand, he is accessible to the parties; there exists a possibility of secret management and undue practices; or, in contests between the crown and the subject, the judge appointed by the crown may be suspected of partiality to his patron.

Q. What is the advantage and defect of the latter kind?

A. The advantage is, indifferency; the defect, the want of that legal science which produces uniformity and justice in decisions.

Q. What may be said of the construction of

English courts of law, in which causes are tried by a jury, with the assistance of a judge?

A. It combines the two species with peculiar success; unites the wisdom of a fixed with the integrity of a casual judicature; and avoids in a great measure the inconveniencies of both: for the judge imparts to the jury the benefit of his erudition and experience; the jury, by their disinterestedness, check any corrupt partialities which previous application may have produced in the judge.

Q. In proportion to the acknowledged excellency of this mode of trial, what ought to be guarded against with vigilance?

A. Every deviation from it; as summary convictions before justices of the peace; courts of conscience; extending the jurisdiction of courts of equity; urging too far the distinction between questions of law and matters of fact.

Q. Yet the trial by jury is sometimes inadequate to the administration of equal justice: when does this imperfection take place?

A. Chiefly in disputes in which some popular passion or prejudice intervenes; as where a particular order of men advance claims upon the community, which is the case of the clergy contending for tithes; or where an order of men are obnoxious by their profession, as are officers of the revenue, &c.; or where one of the parties has an interest in common with the general interest of the jurors, and that of the other is opposed to it; or, where minds are inflamed by political dissen-

tional and religious hatred. The force and danger of which prejudices are also increased by carrying juries out of the county in which the subject of dispute arises; when the cause is often prejudged more upon sentiments of favour or hatred, or upon some opinion of the sect, family, profession, character, or circumstances, of the parties, than upon any knowledge of the merits of the question. More exact justice would often be rendered, if the determination were left entirely to the judges; provided we could depend upon the same purity of conduct, when their power was enlarged, which they have long manifested in the exercise of a restrained authority. But this is an experiment too big with public danger to be hazarded. The effects of some local prejudices might be obviated by a law empowering the court to send the cause to trial in a distant county; the expenses always falling upon the party who applied for this change.

Q. There is a second division of courts of justice, which presents a new alternative of difficulties: what is this?

A. Either one, two, or a few sovereign courts might be erected in the metropolis, for the whole kingdom; or courts of local jurisdiction might be fixed in various districts of the empire.

Q. What are the great, though opposite, inconveniences which attend each arrangement?

A. If the court be remote and solemn, it thus becomes expensive and dilatory; when witnesses, and parties, must be brought to attend from distant parts: and, where the whole judicial business of a large nation is collected into a few courts, it will be found impossible to give a prompt hearing to every complaint, or an immediate answer to any. On the other hand, if distinct and summary tribunals be erected in each neighbourhood, their advantages will be accompanied with all the dangers of ignorance and partiality, as well as of confusion and contrariety in decision.

Q. How does the law of England contain a provision much relieved from both these objections?

A. By its circuits, or itinerary courts. As the presiding magistrate comes into the county a stranger to its prejudices and rivalships, he brings none of those attachments and regards which are there apt to pervert the course of justice. Again, as he is usually one of the supreme judges, and has passed his life in the study and administration of the laws, he possesses those professional qualifications which befit his dignity and station. Lastly, as both he, and the advocates who accompany him, are employed in the business of those superior courts (to which also their proceedings are amenable), they will conduct themselves by the rules they have applied or learned there; and thus maintain a principal perfection of civil government, one law of the land in every part of the empire.

Q. Next to the constitution of courts of justice, we are naturally led to consider the maxims which ought to guide their proceedings: upon this subject, what will the chief inquiry be?

A. How far, and for what reasons, it is expe-

tions to adhere to former determinations; or whether it be necessary for judges to attend to any other consideration than the apparent and particular equity of the case before them.

Q. Now although it would be wrong to attribute to precedents or the sentences of judges, all the authority we ascribe to the most solemn acts of the legislature; yet the general security of private rights, and of civil life, requires that such, especially if confirmed by repeated adjudications, should not be overthrown, without a detection of manifest error, or imputation of dishonesty. Upon what reasons is this deference to prior decisions founded?

A. Upon two; first, that the discretion of judges may be bound down by positive rules; and secondly, that the subject, upon every occasion, may know beforehand how to act, and what to expect. To set judges free from any obligation to conform themselves to the decisions of their predecessors, would be to lay open a latitude of judging with which no description of men can safely be intrusted. It is in vain to allege, that parliament is always at hand to control and punish abuses. By what rules can parliament proceed? How shall they pronounce a decision to be wrong, where there exists no acknowledged standard of what is right? which would often be the case, if prior determinations were not to be appealed to.

Q. Diminishing the danger of partiality, is one thing gained by adhering to precedents; but what is the principal thing?

A. The subject of every system of laws must expect that decision in his own case, which he knows others have received in similar cases. If he expect not this, he can expect nothing. To deprive him therefore of this expectation, by rejecting the authority of precedents, is to entail upon him the worst property of slavery,—to have no assurance of his rights, or knowledge of his duty. The confidence also and satisfaction of each man's mind, requires uniformity in judicial proceedings. Nothing quells a spirit of litigation, like despair of success: therefore nothing so completely puts an end to law-suits, as a rigid adherence to known rules of adjudication. When justice is rendered to the parties, only half the business is done; the more important part remains,—to put an end, for the future, to every fear, and quarrel, and expense, upon the same point; and in effect that the whole train of law-suits which issue from one uncertainty, may die with the parent question. Now, this can be attained only by making each decision a direction to succeeding judges. Moreover, every departure from former determinations, especially those often repeated or long submitted to, shakes the stability of all legal title.

Q. From an adherence however to precedents, by which so much is gained to the public, what two consequences arise which are often lamented?

A. The hardship of particular determinations, and the intricacy of the law as a science.

Q. What must be replied to these complaints?

A. To the first, we must apply this reflection:

—"That uniformity is of more importance than equity, in proportion as a general uncertainty would be a greater evil than particular injustice." The second is attended with no greater inconveniency than that of erecting the practice of the law into a separate profession: which this reason makes necessary.

Q. To a mind considering the subject of human jurisprudence, what question frequently occurs?

A. How comes it to pass, that although the principles of the law of nature be simple, and for the most part sufficiently obvious, there should exist in every system of municipal laws, and administration of relative justice, numerous uncertainties and acknowledged difficulty? Whence, it may be asked, so much room for litigation, and so many disputes, if the rules of duty be neither obscure nor dubious? If a system of morality, containing both the precepts of revelation and the deductions of reason, may be comprised within the compass of one moderate volume; what need of those codes of positive and particular institutions, which require a long life even to peruse? for, unless there be found some greater uncertainty in the law of nature, or what may be called natural equity, when it comes to be applied to real cases and to actual adjudication, than what appears in the written rules and principles of the science, it were better that the determination of every cause should be left to the conscience of the judge, unfettered by precedents and authorities; since the very purpose for which these are introduced, is to give a certainty to judicial proceedings.

Q. How to account for so many sources of litigation, notwithstanding the clearness and perfection of natural justice, what should be observed?

A. First, that treatises of morality always suppose facts to be ascertained; and not only so, but the intention likewise of the parties to be known and laid bare. Wherefore the discussion of facts, which the moralist supposes to be settled, the discovery of intentions which he presumes to be known, still remain to exercise the inquiry of courts of justice. And as these are often to be inferred from obscure indications, from suspicious testimony, or from a comparison of opposite probabilities, they afford a never-failing supply of doubt and litigation. For this reason the science of morality is to be considered rather as a direction to the parties, who are conscious of their own thoughts, and motives; than as a guide to the judge whose arbitration must proceed upon rules of evidence, and maxims of credibility, with which the moralist has no concern.

Secondly: there exist many cases, in which the law of nature, that is, the law of public expediency, prescribes nothing, except that some certain rule be adhered to, and that the rule actually established be preserved. In all such cases, it sends us to the law of the land. It directs that either some fixed rule be introduced, by the legislature, or that the rule which accident, or custom, hath established, be steadily maintained. Thus; whether the degrees of consanguinity shall be computed through the common ancestor, or from him; whether the widow shall take a third or a moiety of her husband's fortune; whether sons shall be preferred to daughters, or the elder to the younger, &c. &c.; in these, and in a great variety of questions which the same subject supplies, the law of nature determines nothing. The only answer it returns to our inquiries is, that some certain rule be laid down by public authority; be obeyed when laid down; and that the quiet of the country be not disturbed, nor just expectations frustrated, by capricious innovations. This silence or neutrality of the law of nature, holds concerning most questions relating to the right or acquisition of property. Recourse, therefore, must be had to statutes, or precedents, or usage, to fix what the law of nature has left loose. The interpretation of these statutes, the search after precedents, the investigation of customs, compose a large and intricate portion of forensic business. Positive constitutions or judicial authorities are also wanted to give precision to many things which are in their nature *indeterminate*. The age of legal discretion; whether at twenty, or twenty-one, or earlier or later; can only be ascertained by a rule of the society to which the party belongs. The line has not been drawn by nature. Yet it is necessary, for the sake of mutual security, that a precise age be fixed, and that what is fixed be known to all. Again, there are other things perfectly arbitrary, and capable of no certainty but what is given to them by positive regulation. It is fit that a limited time should be assigned to defendants, to plead to the complaints alleged against them; but to how many days or months that term should be extended, though necessary to be known with certainty, cannot by any information from the law of nature. And the same remark seems applicable to almost all those rules of proceeding, which constitute what is called the practice of the court.

Thirdly; in contracts, whether express or implied, which involve a great number of conditions; as in those which are entered into between masters and servants, principals and agents, &c.; the original expectation of the parties was, that both sides should be guided by the course and custom of the country. Consequently, when these contracts come to be disputed, natural justice can only refer to that custom. But as such customs are not always sufficiently uniform or notorious, and such custom being only that which amongst a variety of usages seems to predominate; we have here also ample room for doubt and contest.

Fourthly; as the law of nature, founded in the very construction of human society, formed to endure through a series of generations, requires that a man's just engagements should continue in force beyond his life; the private rights of persons frequently depend upon what has been transacted in remote times, by their predecessors, under whom they claim, or to whose obligations they have succeeded. Thus every dispute concerning tithes, in which an exemption or composition is pleaded, depends upon the agreement between the predecessor of the claimant and the ancient owner of the land. The appeal to these grants or agreements is dictated by natural equity; but concerning the existence, or the conditions, of such old covenants, doubts will occur, to which it affords no solution. What therefore cannot be produced or proved, must be left to loose and fallible presumption. Under the same head may be included another topic of altercation;—the tracing out of boundaries, which time, or neglect, or mixture of occupation, has confounded or obliterated, &c. &c.

Fifthly; the quantity or extent of an injury, even when the cause and author of it are known, is often dubious and undefined. Thus what a man may have suffered in his person, from an assault; in his reputation, by slander; or what shall be deemed a reparation for such damages, cannot be ascertained by any rules from the law of nature. It commands, that reparation be made; and adds to the command, that, when the aggressor and the sufferer disagree, the damage be assessed by authorised and indifferent arbitrators. Here then recourse must be had to courts of law, with the permission, and in some measure by the direction, of natural justice.

Sixthly; when controversies arise in the interpretation of written laws, they generally arise upon some contingency which the composer of the law did not foresee. In the adjudication of such cases is this dilemma: if the laws are to operate only upon the cases actually contemplated by the law-makers, they will always be found defective: if they be extended to every case to which the spirit, and expediency, of the provision seem to belong, we shall allow to the judges a liberty of applying the law, which will fall very little short of the power of making it. In a literal construction, the law will often fail of its end; in a loose and vague exposition, it might as well have never been enacted; for this licence will bring back all the discretion and uncertainty which it was the design of the legislature to take away. As it never can be known before hand, in what degree either consideration may prevail in the mind of the judge, there remains an unavoidable cause of doubt and contention.

Seventhly; the deliberations of courts of justice upon every *new* question, are rendered difficult, by the authority which the judgment of the court possesses as a precedent; which authority appertains not only to the conclusions it delivers, but to the principles and arguments upon which they are built. The view of this effect makes it necessary for a judge to look beyond the case before him; and to reflect whether the principles and reasoning, which he adopts, can be applied with safety to all cases which admit of a comparison. The consequence of establishing the principle which such a decision assumes, may be difficult, though of the utmost importance, to be foreseen and regulated.

Finally, after all the certainty that can be given to points of law, one principal source of disputation, and into which the greater part of legal controversies may be resolved, will remain, namely, "the competition of opposite analogies." When a point of law has been once adjudged, neither that question, nor any which in all circumstances corresponds with *that*, can be brought a second time into dispute: but questions arise, which resemble this only indirectly, in certain views and circumstances, and which may seem to bear an equal or a greater affinity to other adjudged cases; questions which can be brought within any fixed rule only by analogy, and which hold a relation by analogy to different rules. It is by the urging of the different analogies that the contention of the bar is carried on: and it is in their comparison, adjustment, and reconciliation; in the discerning of such distinctions; and in the framing of such a determination, as may either save the various rules alleged in the cause, or if that be impossible, may give up the weaker analogy to the stronger; that the sagacity and wisdom of the court are seen and exercised.

Doubtful and obscure points of law are not, however, nearly so numerous as they are apprehended to be. Out of the many causes which occur each year in the metropolis, or upon the circuits, there are few in which any point is reserved for the judgment of superior courts. Yet these few contain all the doubts with which the law is changeable: for as to the rest, the uncertainty is not in the law, but in the means of human information.

Q. There are two peculiarities in the judicial constitution of this country, which do not carry with them that evidence of their propriety which recommends almost every other part of the system. What are these?—and what may be remarked upon them?

A. The first is the rule which requires that juries be *unanimous* in their verdicts. To expect that twelve men, taken by lot out of a promiscuous multitude, should agree in their opinion upon points confessedly dubious, even to the wisest judgments; or to suppose that any real *unanimity*, in the dissenting jurors, could be procured by confining them until they all consented to the same verdict; bespeaks something of the conceit of a barbarous age. Nevertheless, the effects are not so detrimental as the rule is unreasonable;—in criminal cases, it operates in favour of the prisoner: for if a juror find it necessary to surrender to the obstinacy of others, he will more readily incline to the side of mercy than of condemnation: in civil suits, it adds weight to the direction of the judge; for when a conference does not seem likely to produce the agreement that is necessary, they will naturally close their disputes by a common submission to the opinion of the bench. However there seems to be less concurrence, and consequently less assurance that the conclusion is founded in reasons of apparent truth and justice, than if the decision were left to a plurality, or to some certain majority.

The second circumstance which, however it may succeed in practice, does not seem to have been suggested by any intelligible fitness in the nature of the thing, is the choice that is made of the *House of Lords*, as a last court of appeal to which the subject can resort. There appears to be nothing in the constitution of that assembly; in the education, habits, character, professions, or mode of appointment, of the members who compose it; that should qualify them for this arduous office: except, perhaps, that the elevation of their rank and fortune affords a security against the offer and influence of small bribes. The greater part of the assembly born to their station, that is, placed in it by chance; most of the rest advanced for services, and from motives, utterly unconnected with legal erudition; these men compose the tribunal, to which the constitution entrusts the interpretation of her laws, and the ultimate decision of every dispute between her subjects. The effect only proves the truth of this maxim;—"That when a single institution is extremely dissonant from other parts of the system to which it belongs, it will always find some way of reconciling itself to the analogy which governs and pervades the rest." By constantly placing in the House of Lords some of the most eminent and experienced lawyers; by calling in the aid of the judges upon any abstract question of law; by the almost implicit deference, which the uninformed part of the house pay to the learning of their colleagues; the appeal to the House of Lords becomes, in fact, a solemn and dignified appeal to the collected wisdom of our supreme courts of justice.

These, however, even if real, are minute imperfections. A politician who should delineate a plan for the dispensation of public justice, guarded against all access to influence and corruption, and bringing together the separate advantages of knowledge and impartiality, would find, when he had done, that he had been transcribing the judicial constitution of England. And it may make the most discontented acquiesce in the government of his country, to reflect, that the pure, wise, and equal administration of the laws, forms the first end and blessing of social union; and that this is enjoyed by him in a perfection which he will seek in vain in any other nation.

CHAP. IX.

OF CRIMES AND PUNISHMENTS.

Q. What is the proper end of human punishment?

A. Not the satisfaction of justice, but the prevention of crime.

Q. What is meant by the satisfaction of justice?

A. The retribution of so much pain for so much guilt; which is the dispensation we expect at the hand of God. This however is not the motive or occasion of human punishment. What would it be to the magistrate, that offences went unpunished, if impunity were followed by no danger to the commonwealth? The fear lest the escape of the criminal should encourage him, or others, to repeat his enormities, alone authorises the infliction of punishment by human laws.

Q. Now that which is the cause and end of the punishment, ought undoubtedly to regulate the measure of its severity. But in what does this cause appear to be founded?

A. Not in the guilt of the offender, but in the necessity of preventing the repetition of the offence.

Q. And what results from hence?

A. That crimes are not by any government punished in proportion to their guilt, but in proportion to the difficulty and necessity of preventing them. Hence the stealing of goods privately out of a shop, though not, in its moral quality, more criminal than stealing of them out of a house; is more severely punished; for crime must be prevented by some means or other; and severe ones are adopted rightly, because they are adopted upon the principle which alone justifies the infliction of punishment at all.

Q. What else follows from this consideration?

A. That punishment ought not to be employed,

much less rendered severe, when the crime can be prevented by any other means; it being an evil resorted to only for the prevention of a greater; and the necessity for it does not exist where the public may be defended from the effects of the crime, by any other expedient.

Q. What other circumstance, which has often been thought an absurdity in the penal law, does this principle account for?

A. That breaches of trust, where violation of confidence encreases the guilt, are either not punished at all, or with less rigour than other frauds.

Q. In what reasonable distinction is this lenity, or rather forbearance, of the laws, founded?

A. A due circumspection in the choice of the persons whom they trust, caution in limiting the extent of that trust, or the requiring security for its faithful discharge, will commonly guard men from injuries of this description; and the law will not interpose its sanctions to protect negligence and credulity.

Q. What observation will shew us that the law proceeds solely upon this consideration?

A. Where the confidence is unavoidable,—where no practicable vigilance could watch the offender, as in the case of theft by a servant in the shop or dwelling-house of his master,—the law is not less severe, and its execution commonly more certain, than if no trust had intervened.

Q. What else takes place in pursuance of the

same principle, which pervades the whole penal jurisprudence?

A. That the facility with which any species of crimes is perpetrated is deemed a reason for aggravating the punishment. Thus, sheep-stealing, horse-stealing, the stealing of cloth from tenters or bleaching-grounds, subject the offender to sentence of death: not that these crimes are more heinous than many other simple felonies, but because the property, being more exposed, requires greater protection. This severity would be absurd, if the guilt were its immediate cause and measure; but is consistent with the supposition, that the right of punishment results from the necessity of preventing the crime: for then the severity of the punishment must be increased in proportion to the expediency and difficulty of attaining this end.

Q. What else is a circumstance to be included in the same consideration?

A. The difficulty of discovery, which constitutes with respect to the crime, the facility of which we speak. By how much therefore the detection of an offender is more rare and uncertain, by so much the more severe must be the punishment when he is detected?

Q. From the justice of God, we look for a gradation of punishment exactly proportioned to guilt; when, therefore, in human punishment, we introduce considerations distinct from that guilt, so that equal crimes frequently undergo unequal punishments, or the less crime the greater; it is natural to demand the reason why that rule, which befits the perfect justice of the Deity, should not be again imitated by human laws. Where must the solution of this difficulty be sought?

A. In those attributes of the Divine nature, which distinguish Supreme Wisdom from human judicature. An omniscient Being, from whose will no act or flight can escape, and in whose hands punishment is sure, may conduct the moral government of his creation, in the best and wisest manner, by pronouncing a law that every crime shall finally receive a punishment proportioned to the guilt which it contains; and may testify his veracity, by carrying this law into strict execution. But when the care of the public safety is intrusted to men, whose authority is limited by defects of power and knowledge; from whose utmost sagacity the greatest offenders often lie hid; whose precautions and pursuit may be eluded by artifice or concealment; a new rule of proceeding results from the very imperfection of their faculties. In their hands, the facility of crime must be counteracted and the uncertainty of punishment must be compensated by increased severity. For the very end of human government requires that its regulations be adapted to the suppression of crimes.

Q. There are two methods of administering penal justice: what are these?

A. The first method assigns capital punishment to few offences, and inflicts it invariably.

The second method assigns capital punishment to many kinds of offences, but inflicts it only upon a few examples of each kind.

Q. Which method has been long adopted in this country?

A. The latter: for of those who receive sentence of death, scarcely one in ten is executed.

Q. In what does this preference seem to be founded?

A. In the consideration, that the selection of proper objects for capital punishment depends upon circumstances, which, however easy to perceive in each particular case after the crime, it is impossible to enumerate or define beforehand; or to ascertain with that exactness requisite in legal descriptions. Hence, although it be necessary to fix by precise rules of law the limit to which the punishment may be extended; and also that nothing less than the authority of the whole legislature determine that boundary; yet the mitigation of punishment may, without danger be intrusted to the executive magistrate, whose discretion will operate upon those circumstances, which constitute or qualify the malignity of each offence. Without such power of relaxation in a living authority, either some would escape whom the public safety required to suffer; or some would suffer when it was neither deserved nor necessary. For if judgment of death were reserved for one or two species only, crimes might occur of the most dangerous example, and might escape capital punishment, because they did not fall within *any* description that the laws had made capital; and what is worse, it would be known beforehand that such crimes might be committed without danger to the offend-

their lives. But if, to reach these, the whole class to which they belong be subjected to death, without a power of remission, the execution of the laws would become more sanguinary than is necessary, or than the public compassion would endure.

Q. Upon what different and better policy is the law of England constructed?

A. By the number of statutes creating capital offences, it sweeps into the net every crime which can possibly merit the punishment of death; but when the execution comes to be deliberated upon, a small proportion of each class are singled out, the general character of whose crimes render them fit examples of public justice. By this expedient, few suffer death, whilst the dread and danger of it hang over many. The life of the subject is spared as far as the necessity of restraint and intimidation permits; yet no one will venture to commit any enormous crime, from a knowledge that the laws have not provided for its punishment. The wisdom and humanity of this design furnish a just excuse for the multiplicity of capital offences, created by the laws of England. As to the charge of cruelty, these laws were never meant to be carried into indiscriminate execution; and the legislature, when it establishes its last and highest sanctions, trusts to the benignity of the crown to relax their severity, as circumstances require. This vindicates the lenity of the laws, that *some* instances are to be found in each class of capital crimes, which require the restraint of capital punishment, which restraint could not be applied without subjecting the whole class to the same condemnation.

Q. There is, however, one species of crimes, the making of which capital can hardly, as Paley thinks, be defended, even upon this comprehensive principle: what is that?

A. Privately stealing from the person. As every degree of force is excluded by the description of the crime, and without gross and culpable negligence on the part of the sufferer, such examples can ever become frequent.

Q. Why is the prerogative of pardon properly assigned to the chief magistrate?

A. The power of suspending the laws is too high a privilege to be committed to many hands, or to those of any inferior officer. The king can best collect the advice by which his resolutions should be governed; and is removed at the greatest distance from the influence of private motives.

Q. But let this power be deposited where it will, what ought the exercise of it to be regarded?

A. Not as a favour to be yielded to solicitation or friendship, and least of all, made subservient to political attachments, but as a judicial act; as a deliberation to be conducted with the same impartiality, and attention to the merits of the case, as the judge was expected to maintain in the trial. Whether the prisoner be guilty, and whether, being guilty, he ought to be executed, are equally questions of public justice, and of the latter functions of magistracy. The public welfare is interested in both. Conviction should depend upon the proof of guilt alone; and the execution of the sentence upon nothing but the quality and circumstances of the crime. This is necessary to the good order of society, and to the reputation and authority of government.

Q. What are the aggravations which ought to guide the magistrate in the selection of objects of condign punishment?

A. Principally these three,—repetition, cruelty, combination. The first two, manifestly add to every reason upon which the justice or necessity of rigour can be founded: with respect to the last, when thieves and robbers are once collected into gangs, their violence becomes more formidable and desperate, and the difficulty of defence much greater, than in the case of solitary adventurers.

Q. In crimes, however, which are perpetrated by a multitude, or by a gang, what is proper?

A. To separate, in punishment, the ringleader from his followers, the principal from his accomplices, and even the person who struck the blow, or first entered the house, from those who joined him; not so much on account of any distinction in their guilt, as for the sake of casting an obstacle in the way of such confederacies. Here also the punishment which expediency directs, does not pursue the exact proportion of the crime.

Q. Injuries effected by terror and violence, are those which it is the chief concern of legal government to repress: why so?

A. Because their extent is unlimited; no private precaution can protect us against them; they endanger life as well as property; and render society wretched, by a sense of personal insecurity. These reasons apply not to frauds which circumspection may prevent; which must wait for opportunity; and by the apprehension of which, although business be incommoded, life is not made miserable.

Q. What has the appearance of this distinction led some humane writers to express?

A. A wish, that capital punishments might be confined to crimes of violence.

Q. In estimating the comparative malignancy of crimes of violence, to what must regard be had?

A. Not only to the proper and intended mischief, but to the fright occasioned by the attack, the general alarm excited by it in others, and the consequences which may attend similar attempts in future. Thus, in affixing the punishment of burglary, we are to consider not only the peril to which valuable property is exposed by this crime, but the danger of murder in case of resistance, or to prevent discovery; the universal dread with which the defenceless hours of rest must be disturbed, were attempts of this sort to become frequent; which dread alone, is almost of all evils the most insupportable.

Q. Of frauds, or of injuries, which are effected without force, what are the most noxious kinds?

A. Forgeries, counterfeiting, or diminishing of the coin, and the stealing of letters in the course of their conveyance; inasmuch as they tend to deprive the public of social accommodations, which are essential to the prosperity, as well as the existence of commerce. Of these crimes, although they seem to affect property alone, the mischief does not terminate there. For suppose the violators of the laws which refer to offences of this sort to grow into such a frequency, as to render the use of money, the circulation of bills, or the public conveyance of letters, no longer safe or practicable; what would follow, but that every species of trade and of activity must decline; the sources of subsistence fail; the country itself, where the intercourse of civil life was so defective, be deserted; and that, beside distress and poverty, a rapid depopulation must take place, till solitude and barrenness overspread the land, like that which obtains in many countries of Asia, once the most civilized and frequented parts of the world?

Q. When, therefore, we carry forwards our views to the more distant, but not less certain consequences of these crimes, what do we perceive?

A. That although no living creature be destroyed by them, yet human life is diminished: that an offence which seems to deprive only an individual of a small portion of his property, and obstruct the enjoyment of certain public conveniences, may, by its ultimate effects, conclude in the laying waste of human existence. This observation will be an answer to those who regard the divine rule of "life for life, and blood for blood," as the only authorized and justifiable measure of capital punishment.

Q. In the case of forgeries, how does there appear a substantial difference between the forging of bills of exchange, or of securities which are circulated to serve and facilitate valuable purposes of commerce, and the forging of bonds, leases, mortgages, or instruments which are not commonly transferred from one hand to another?

A. Because, in the former case, credit is necessarily given to the signature, without which the negotiation of such property could not be carried on, nor the public utility sought from it, be attained: in the other case, all possibility of deceit might be precluded, by communication or due care in the choice of agents, without interrupting business, or destroying the uses for which these instruments are calculated. This distinction is precise enough to afford a line of division between forgeries, which, as the law now stands, are almost universally capital, and punished with undistinguishing severity.

Q. Why is perjury another crime of the same class and magnitude?

A. When we consider what reliance is necessarily placed upon oaths; that all judicial decisions proceed upon testimony; that consequently there is not a right that a man possesses, of which false witnesses may not deprive him; that perjury may often be committed without a possibility of contradiction or discovery; that its success and prevalency tend to introduce the most fatal injustice, distrust, and embarrassment, into the administration of human affairs:—when we reflect upon these

another, we shall probably agree with those who contend that perjury, in its punishment, should be placed upon a level with the most flagitious frauds.

Q. What else deserves to be classed with the worst species of robbery?

A. The obtaining of money by secret threats, whether we regard the difficulty with which the crime is traced out, or the odious imputations and profligate conspiracies to which it may lead.

Q. To what three causes does the frequency of capital punishments owe its necessity in this country?

A. Much liberty, great cities, and the want of a punishment short of death, possessing a sufficient degree of terror. The liberties and jealousy of a free people, permit not those precautions and restraints, that inspection and control, which are exercised in arbitrary governments. For example, neither the spirit of the laws, nor of the people, will suffer the confinement of suspected persons, without proofs of guilt, which it is often impossible to obtain; nor will they allow that masters of families be obliged to render up a description of the inmates whom they entertain; nor men to be confined to certain districts; nor the inhabitants of each district to be made responsible for one another's behaviour, &c. &c.; least of all will they tolerate an armed force, or military law; or intrust the police with such discretionary powers, as may make sure of the guilty, however they involve the innocent. These expedients, although arbitrary and rigorous, being effectual in rendering the commission or concealment of crimes more difficult, subtract from the necessity of severe punishment.—*Great cities* multiply crimes, by presenting easier opportunities, and more incentives to libertinism; by collecting thieves and robbers into confederacies, which increase their art, courage, strength, and wickedness; but principally by the refuge they afford to villany, in the means of concealment and secrecy. These facilities can only be counteracted by adding to the number of capital punishments.—But a *third* cause is a defect of the laws, in not being provided with any other punishment sufficiently terrible to keep offenders in awe. Transportation appears to answer the purpose of example very imperfectly; not only because it is a slight punishment to those who have no property, friends, reputation, or regular means of subsistence, at home; and because their situation becomes little worse by their crime; but because the punishment, being unobserved and unknown, strikes no terror into those for whose warning and admonition it was intended. This chasm in the scale of punishment produces also two farther imperfections:—the first is, that the same punishment is extended to crimes of very different character; the second, that punishments separated by a great interval, are assigned to crimes hardly distinguishable in their guilt and mischief.

Q. What is the end of punishment?

A. It is two-fold,—*amendment*, and *example*. In the first of these, little has ever been effected.

and little probably is practicable. From every species of punishment that has hitherto been devised, malefactors return more hardened in their crimes, and more instructed. If any thing shakes the soul of a confirmed villain, it is the expectation of approaching death: and it is probable, that many of those who are executed, would, if they were delivered at the point of death, retain such a remembrance of their sensations, as might preserve them, unless urged by extreme want, from relapsing into their former crimes. But this is an experiment that cannot be repeated often.

Q. Of the *reforming* punishments which promises most success?

A. *Solitary* imprisonment, or the confinement of criminals in separate apartments. This augments the terror of the punishment; secludes the criminal from a society in which the worse are sure to corrupt the better; weans him from his companions, and his turbulent, precarious mode of life: is calculated to raise up in him sober reflection, and to dispose his mind to bitter and continued penitence.

Q. As aversion to labour is the cause from which half of the vices of low life deduce their origin, punishments ought to be contrived with a view to the conquering of this disposition. What two opposite expedients have been recommended for this purpose?

A. The one, solitary confinement with hard labour; and the other, solitary confinement with nothing to do. Both expedients seek the same end, to reconcile the idle to a life of industry; the former, by making labour habitual; the latter, by making idleness insupportable: and the preference of one method to the other depends upon the question, whether a man is more likely to work, of his own accord, who has been accustomed to employment, or who has been distressed by the want of it. When gaols are provided for the separate confinement of prisoners, which both proposals require, the choice may soon be determined by experience.

Q. If labour be exacted, what does Paley propose?

A. To leave the whole, or a portion, of the earnings to the prisoner's use, and to debar him from any other provision or supply; that his subsistence may be proportioned to his diligence, and that he may taste the advantage of industry together with the toil. Also to measure the confinement, not by the duration of time, but by the quantity of work, both to excite industry and to render it more voluntary.

Q. What, however, is the principal difficulty which still remains?

A. How to dispose of criminals after their enlargement. By a rule which is, perhaps, too invariably adhered to, no one will receive a man or woman out of a gaol into any service or employment. It seems incumbent upon the state to secure a maintenance to those who are willing to work for it; and yet it is necessary to divide criminals as far from one another as possible. Whe-

[illegible]

Q. What does Paley remark upon the subject of *torture*?

A. *Torture* is applied either to obtain confessions of guilt, or to exasperate or prolong the pains of death. No bodily punishment receives the name of torture, unless it be designed to kill the criminal by a more lingering death, or to extort from him the discovery of some secret. The question by *torture* is equivocal in its effects: for since extremity of pain, and not any remorse, produces them, an innocent man may sink under the torment, as well as he who is guilty. The innocent and almost irresistible desire of relief may draw from one sufferer false accusations, as it may sometimes extract the truth out of another. This ambiguity renders the use of torture liable to the risk of grievous and irreparable injustice. For which reason, though recommended by ancient and general example, it has been properly exploded in this country.

[illegible]

[illegible] their [illegible] design [illegible] [illegible] of the [illegible] tution of the criminals. But if a mode of execution could be devised, which would augment the horror of the punishment, without impairing the public sensibility by cruel exhibitions, it might add something to the efficacy of the example, especially if it were reserved for a few atrocious crimes: for now we hang a malefactor for a simple robbery, and can do no more to the villain who has poisoned his father.

Q. How are *infamous* punishments to be managed in this country, with respect both to the crimes and the criminals?

A. First, they ought to be confined to offences undisputedly and universally detested. To condemn to the pillory the author of a publication, who has thereby rendered himself the favourite of a party, or of the people, is to gratify the offender and to expose the laws to mockery. Secondly, they who receive this sentence, are for the most part such as have long ceased to value reputation, or to fear shame; of whose happiness, character makes no part. Thus, the low ministers of libertinism are [illegible] in vain with a punishment that affects a sense of shame which they have not. The pillory, or any other infamous distinction, might be employed rightly, and with effect, in the punishment of some offences of higher life; [illegible] frauds and peculation in offices of [illegible] [illegible], of perjury; of the [illegible] of places; of [illegible] in the exercise of confidential engage-

[illegible] effects, [illegible] which, the only [illegible] would be the triumph of justice.

Q. Is not the certainty of punishment of more consequence than the severity, and criminals do not so much flatter themselves with the lenity of the sentence, as with the hope of escaping; what best contributes to the suppression of crimes?

A. A vigilant magistracy, an accurate police, together with due rewards for the discovery and apprehension of malefactors, and an undeviating impartiality in carrying the laws into execution. And so of all contrivances directed to this end, those are most effectual which facilitate the conviction of criminals. The statute which made possession of the implements of coining capital, that is, which constituted that possession complete evidence of the offender's guilt, was the first thing which gave efficacy to the denunciations of law upon this subject. The statute of James the First, relative to the murder of bastard children, which makes concealment of the birth a proof of the charge, though a harsh law, was well calculated to put a stop to the crime.

Q. From the principle of this observation, what remarks does Paley draw respecting juries?

A. He apprehends that much harm has been done by their overstrained scrupulousness, or timidity, which often demands such proof of guilt, as the nature and secrecy of the crime scarcely admit of; and which holds it the part of a safe conscience not to condemn any man, whilst there [illegible].

[illegible] in the perplexity of the [illegible] any story told or [illegible] in [illegible] have been misled by presumptions of guilt, they hold an acquittal, where positive proof is wanting. I do not mean that juries should indulge conjectures, or magnify suspicions into proofs; but when the preponderation of evidence is so manifest as to persuade every private understanding of the prisoner's guilt; when it furnishes the degree of credibility upon which men decide and act in all other doubts; to reject such proof, from an insinuation of uncertainty that belongs to all human affairs, and from a general dread of the charge of innocent blood, is authorised by no considerations of rectitude or utility. It counteracts the care and activity of government, and holds out encouragement to villany, by confessing the impossibility of bringing villains to justice.

Q. What two popular maxims, seem to have a considerable influence in producing these injudicious acquittals?

A. One is:—"That circumstantial evidence falls short of positive proof." The other is,—"That it is better that ten guilty persons should escape than that one innocent man should suffer."

Q. What does Paley observe upon the first of these assertions?

A. In the unqualified sense in which it is applied, it is not true. A concurrence of well authenticated circumstances is a stronger ground of assurance than positive testimony, unconfirmed by circumstances. Circumstances cannot lie. The concursion also which results from them is commonly more to be relied upon than the veracity of an unsupported witness. The danger of being deceived is less, and deception is rarer in the one case than the other. What is called positive proof, as where a man swears to the person of the prisoner, and that he actually saw him commit the crime, may be founded in the mistake or perjury of a single witness; of which there are not wanting examples. Whereas, to impose upon a court of justice a fabricated chain of *circumstantial* evidence, requires so many false witnesses as seldom meet together; an union also of skill and wickedness which is still more rare; moreover, this species of proof lies much more open to discussion, and is more likely, if false, to be contradicted or betrayed by unforeseen inconsistencies, than that direct proof, which, being confined within the knowledge of a single person, is incapable, by its very simplicity, of being confronted with opposite probabilities.

Q. What does he observe upon the second maxim?

A. If by saying it is *better*, be meant that it is more for the public advantage, the proposition cannot be maintained. The security of civil life, which is essential to the enjoyment of all its blessings, and the interruption of which is followed by universal misery and confusion, is protected chiefly by the dread of punishment. The misfortune of an individual cannot be placed in competition with this object. The life or safety of the meanest sub-

just ought not, indeed in any case, to be knowingly sacrificed: no principle of judicature, no end of punishment, can ever require that.

But when certain rules must be pursued, and certain degrees of credibility accepted, in order to reach the crimes with which the public are infested; men should not be deterred from the application of these rules, by the mere possibility of confounding the innocent with the guilty. He who falls by a mistaken sentence, may be considered as falling for his country; whilst he suffers under those rules, by the general effect of which the welfare of the community is maintained.

CHAP. X.

OF RELIGIOUS ESTABLISHMENTS, AND OF TOLERATION.

Q. What previous remarks does Paley make concerning a *religious establishment?*

A. "That it is no part of Christianity; it is only the means of inculcating it." Amongst the Jews, the rights, offices, order, family, and succession of the priesthood, were marked out by divine authority and were *parts* of the religion. But it cannot be proved that any form of church-government was laid down in the Christian Scriptures with a view of fixing a constitution for succeeding ages, and which, consequently, the disciples of Christianity would at all times be obliged to adopt. No command for this purpose was delivered by Christ; and if the apostles ordained bishops and presbyters, be it remembered that deacons also and deaconesses were appointed by them, with functions very dissimilar to any which now obtain in the church. Such offices in truth were at first erected in the Christian church, as its good order, instruction, and exigencies, at that time, required; without any intention, at least without any declared design, of regulating Christian ministers under future circumstances. This reserve in the Christian Legislator, is accounted for by two considerations; first, that no constitution could be framed, suitable to the primitive state of Christianity, and with that it was to assume when advanced into a national religion: Secondly, that a designation of office or authority amongst the ministers of the new religion, might have so interfered with the arrangements of civil policy, as to have formed a considerable obstacle to its progress and reception.

Q. In what then is the authority of a church establishment founded?

A. In its utility; and whenever we deliberate on the form, propriety, or comparative excellency of establishments, the single view under which we ought to consider any of them is, that of "a scheme of instruction;" the single end we ought to propose by them is, "the preservation and communication of religious knowledge."

every other idea, or end, as the making of the church an engine, or even an ally of the state; converting it into the means of strengthening or diffusing influence, &c. has served only to debase the institution.

Q. What does the notion of a religious establishment comprehend?

A. Three things:—a clergy, or order of men secluded from other professions to attend upon the offices of religion; a legal provision for their maintenance; and the confining of that provision to the teachers of a particular sect. If any one of these three things be wanting, there exists no national religion or established church. He, therefore, who would defend ecclesiastical establishments, must shew the separate utility of these three essential parts of their constitution.

Q. What is the question first in order upon the subject, as well as the most fundamental in its importance?

A. Whether the knowledge and profession of Christianity can be maintained, without a class of men set apart by public authority to the study and teaching of religion, and to the conducting of public worship, and secluded from other employments. This last circumstance is added, because in it consists the substance of the controversy.

Q. What must here be remembered?

A. That Christianity is an historical religion, founded in facts which are related to have passed, upon discourses which were holden, and letters which were written, in a remote age and country as will

a ruder state of life, and manners, and opinions, and institutions, very unlike any found among mankind at present. This religion having been first published in Judea, and being built upon the more ancient religion of the Jews, is intimately connected with the sacred writings, history, and polity of that singular people: also the records of both revelations are preserved in languages which have long ceased to be spoken. Books which come down from times so remote, and under so many causes of obscurity, cannot be understood without study and preparation, in the learning and investigation of languages, writings, &c. in order to interpret doubtful forms of speech, and to explain allusions which refer to objects, or usages that no longer exist. Above all, the modes of expression and habits of reasoning then in use, and to which the discourses even of inspired teachers were necessarily adapted, can only be known by a due acquaintance with ancient literature. Lastly, to establish the genuineness and integrity of the canonical SS., a series of testimony must be deduced from times near to their first publication, down the succession of ages. The qualifications necessary for such researches demand a degree of leisure, and a kind of education, inconsistent with the exercise of any other profession.

Q. But how few amongst the clergy, from whom any thing of this sort can be expected! how small a proportion, who seem likely to augment the fund of sacred literature, or even to collect what is already known? To the objection what may be replied?

[illegible]. That we see many seem to take the answer. In order to produce a few capable of improving and continuing the stock of Christian erudition, leisure and opportunity must be afforded to great numbers. Original knowledge of this kind can never be universal; some should always be found qualified for such enquiries, in whose concurring independent conclusions, the rest of the Christian community may safely confide: whereas, without an order of clergy educated for that purpose, it may be questioned whether the learning itself would not have been lost, by which the records of our faith are interpreted and defended.

[illegible]. But passing this, what else calls for qualifications incompatible with the common employments of civil life?

[illegible]. The more ordinary offices of public teaching, and of conducting public worship. "It has been acknowledged by some, who cannot be suspected of making unnecessary concessions in favour of establishments, to be barely possible, that a person who was never educated for the office should acquit himself with decency as a public teacher of religion." And that must be a very defective policy which trusts to possibilities for success, when provision is to be made for regular and general instruction.

[illegible]. If [illegible] an order of clergy be necessary, it it be necessary also to exclude therefrom the employments and profits of other professions, what follows?

A. That they ought to be enabled to derive a maintenance from their own; which must either depend upon the voluntary contributions of their hearers, or arise from revenues assigned by law.

Q. To the scheme of voluntary contributions what insurmountable objection exists?

A. That few would ultimately contribute any thing. However zeal or novelty might support such an experiment for a while, no reliance could be placed upon it as a permanent provision. It is a bad constitution, which opposes temptations of interest to the duties of religion; makes the offices of religion expensive to those who attend them; allows pretences of conscience to be an excuse for not sharing in a public burthen.

Is there not reason to fear, that, if it were referred to the discretion of each neighbourhood, whether they would maintain a teacher of religion or not, many districts would remain unprovided with any? The devout and pious might lament the want or distance of a religious assembly; they could not form or maintain one, without the concurrence of neighbours who felt neither their zeal nor liberality.

Q. From the difficulty with which congregations would be upheld upon the *voluntary* plan, if we carry our thoughts to the condition of those who are to officiate in them; what, then, would become of preaching?

ple. It would be a mode of begging. With what decency or dignity, can a preacher dispense the truths of Christianity, whose thoughts are ever solicited to the reflection how he may increase his subscription? His eloquence resembles rather that of a player computing the profits of his theatre, than the simplicity of a man who, feeling the awful expectations of religion, is seeking to bring others to such a sense of their duty as may save their souls. He too whose success and subsistence depends upon collecting and pleasing a crowd, must resort to other arts than the acquirement and communication of sober and profitable instruction. For a preacher to be thus at the mercy of his hearers; to be obliged to adapt his doctrine to the pleasure of a capricious multitude; to live in constant bondage to tyrannical and insolent directors; are circumstances so mortifying to the virtuous love of independency, that they are rarely submitted to without a sacrifice of principle, and a depravation of character; and it may be pronounced, that a ministry so degraded would soon fall into the lowest hands.

Q. If then it be admitted, that a legal provision for the clergy, compulsory upon those who contribute to it, is expedient; what will the next question be?

A. Whether this provision should be confined to one sect of Christianity, or extended indifferently to all?

Q. Now what may be observed upon this?

A. This last question seldom can offer itself where the people are agreed in their religious opinions; and that it never ought to arise, when a system may be framed of doctrines and worship wide enough to comprehend their disagreement, in a mode of divine worship that omits every subject of controversy or offence. Where this is practicable, the comprehending religion ought to be made that of the state.

Q. But if this be despaired of; if religious opinions exist so contradictory, as that they cannot be reconciled to any one confession of faith, rule of discipline, or form of worship [illegible] what becomes a subject of discussion and [illegible]?

A. Whether the laws ought to establish any one in preference to the rest, that is whether they ought to confine the provision ordained for the maintenance of religion unto the teachers of one system alone.

Q. And whatsoever we may determine concerning speculative rights and abstract proprieties, when we set about the framing of an ecclesiastical constitution adapted to real life, and to the actual state of religion, to what other question shall we find this very nearly related and principally dependent upon?

A. The following: "In what way, or by whom ought the ministers of religion to be appointed? If the species of private patronage be retained to which we are accustomed in this country, [illegible] utmost discordancy of religious opinions [illegible] arise between the teachers and their [illegible] congregations; a parish priest might [illegible] given to any man to a congregation of protestants; any episcopal clergyman be sent to officiate in a parish of presbyterians, &c.

Q. How then may the requisition of subscription, or any other test by which the national religion is guarded, be considered?

A. Merely as a restriction upon the exercise of private patronage: for the laws speak to the private patron thus:—"Of those whom we have pronounced qualified to teach religion, we allow you to select one; but not to decide what religion shall be established in any particular district; for which decision you are no wise fitted by any qualifications which, as a private patron, you may possess. If it be necessary that this point be determined for the inhabitants, it is better it should be done by a deliberate resolution of the legislature, than by the casual inclination of an individual." Whensoever, therefore, this kind of patronage is adopted, a national religion must almost necessarily accompany it.

Q. But, secondly, let it be supposed that the appointment of the minister of religion was in every parish left to the parishioners; might not this choice be safely exercised without being limited to any particular sect?

A. The effect must be, that a papist, a methodist, a moravian, or an anabaptist, would successively gain the pulpit, according as a majority of the party prevailed at each election. Now, with what violence the conflict would, on every vacancy, be renewed; what bitter animosities [illegible] would be received by the defeated party need scarcely be mentioned.

Q. Or, thirdly, if the state appoint the ministers of religion, will this constitution differ from the establishment of a national religion?

A. Very little; for the state will undoubtedly appoint those alone, whose religious opinions, or rather denominations, agree with its own; unless it be thought that any thing would be gained to religious liberty by transferring the choice of the national religion from the legislature to the magistrate.

Q. Thirdly placed in contrast to the legal establishment of a clergy, particularly with the legal preference of one sect of Christians, is that of an experiment said to be attempted by design in some of the new states of North America. What is the nature of this plan?

A. A tax is levied upon the inhabitants for the general support of religion; the collector goes round with a register, in which are inserted at the head of so many distinct columns, the names of the several religious sects professed in the country. The person called upon for the assessment, as soon as he has paid his quota, subscribes his name and sum in which of the columns he pleases; and the amount of what is collected in each column is paid over to the minister of that denomination. It is not left to the option of the subject, whether he will contribute, or how much, to the religion

pence of a Christian ministry; he may only determine by what sect his contribution shall be employed.

Q. The above arrangement bears the appearance of liberality and justice, and it may contain some solid advantages; nevertheless it labours under inconveniencies which will be found, upon trial, to overbalance all its recommendations: what are these?

A. It is scarcely compatible with the first requisite of an ecclesiastical establishment, the division of the country into commodious parishes. If they be small, and ministers of every denomination be stationed in each, the expense of their maintenance will become too burdensome a charge. If, to secure their support, the districts be enlarged, the place of assembling will often be too far removed from the persons who ought to resort to it. Again, the making the pecuniary success of the different teachers to depend on the number and wealth of their followers, would generate strife and indecent jealousies; as well as a pecuniary proselyting spirit, with views of private gain, which would both deprave the principles of the clergy, and distract the country with endless contentions.

Q. By what steps then does the argument by which ecclesiastical establishments are founded, proceed?

A. The knowledge and profession of Christianity cannot be upholden without a clergy; a clergy cannot be supported without a legal provision;

a larger portion for those who cannot, by contributing without the preference of one sect to the rest; and the conclusion will be satisfactory in the degree in which the truth of these several propositions can be made out.

Q. Now if it be deemed expedient to establish a national religion, what does the very notion of it include?

A. Some test, by which its teachers may be distinguished from those of [illegible].

Q. But when [illegible] this [illegible], which is [illegible] done according to the [illegible] of [illegible]?

A. It has furnished [illegible] to [illegible] pretences for [illegible] more [illegible] than the occasion justified. For though some [illegible] order and [illegible] may be [illegible] and [illegible], yet they are [illegible] inconveniencies: they check inquiry, violate liberty, and ensnare the consciences of the clergy; however they may be accommodated to the controversies or fears of the age in which they were composed, in process of time, and changes in the judgment of mankind, they come at length to contradict the opinions of the church, whose doctrines they profess to contain; and often perpetuate the proscription of sects, and tenets from which any danger has long ceased.

Q. Though it may not follow from these objections, that tests and subscriptions ought to be abolished; yet what does follow?

A. That they ought to be made as simple and

easy as possible; that they should be adapted, from time to time, to the varying sentiments and circumstances of the church in which they are received; and that they should at no time advance one step farther than some subsisting necessity requires.

Q. What forms the substantial part of every church establishment?

A. The division of the country into districts, and the stationing in each a teacher of religion. The varieties introduced into the government of different churches, are of inferior importance, when compared with this, in which they all agree.

Q. Of these œconomical questions, which seems most material?

A. Whether a parity amongst the clergy, or a distinction of orders in the ministry, be more conducive to the general ends of the institution.

Q. In favour of that system which the laws of this country have preferred, what reasons may we allege?

A. That it secures tranquillity and subordination amongst the clergy; that it corresponds with the gradations of rank in civil life, and provides for the edification of each rank, by stationing in each an order of clergy of their own class and quality; and, lastly, that the same fund produces more effect, both as an allurement to men of talents, and as a stimulus to industry, when distributed into prizes of different value, than when divided into equal shares.

Q. After the state has once established a particular system of faith as a national religion, what question will soon occur?

A. One concerning the treatment and toleration of those who dissent from it.

Q. But by what other question is this properly preceded?

A. By one concerning the right of the civil magistrate to interfere in matters of religion at all: for, although this be acknowledged whilst employed solely in providing means of public instruction, it will ever be disputed when he proceeds to inflict penalties, and to impose restraints on account of religious distinctions.

Q. What are they, who admit no other just origin of civil government, than some stipulation with its subjects, at liberty to contend?

A. That the concerns of religion were excluded out of the social compact; that, in an affair between God and a man's own conscience, no authority was ever delegated to the magistrate, or could indeed be from the person himself to any other.

Q. Can we, however, who have rejected this theory, make this distinction?

A. No; the reasoning which deduces civil government from the will of God, and collects that will from public expediency, binds us to the conclusion, that the jurisdiction of the magistrate is limited by no consideration but that of general utility. There is nothing in the nature of religion, as such, which exempts it from the authority of the legislator, when the safety or welfare of the community requires his interposition.

Q. It has been said, that religion, pertaining to a life to come, lies beyond the province of civil government, the office of which is confined to this life; what may be replied to this objection?

A. That when the laws interfere, even in religion, it is only with temporals, upon those rights and interests which belong to their disposal. The acts of the legislature, the edicts of the prince, the sentence of the judge, cannot affect my salvation, though they may deprive me of liberty, property, and even life, on account of my religion; and however I may complain of injustice, I cannot allege, that the magistrate has transgressed his jurisdiction; because the property, liberty, and life of the subject, may be taken away by the authority of the laws, for any reason which, in the judgment of the legislature, renders it necessary to the common welfare. Moreover, as the precepts of religion may regulate all the offices of life, or may be so construed as to extend to all, its exemption from the control of human laws might afford a plea to exclude civil government from all authority. Religious, like civil liberty, is not an immunity from restraint, but the being restrained by no law, which does not in a greater degree conduce to the public welfare.

Q. Does any thing that has been said, encroach upon the truth of that sacred and undisputed maxim; that it is right "to obey God rather than man?"

A. Yes. The rights of the magistrate, and the obligation of the subject, in matters of religion, may be very different, and will be so, as often as they flow from opposite apprehensions of the Divine will. In affairs properly of a civil nature, this difference seldom happens. The law authorizes the act which it enjoins; Revelation being either silent, or referring to the laws, or requiring only that men act by some fixed and authorized rule. But when human laws interpose in matters of religion, by dictating the object or mode of worship, by prohibiting the profession of some articles of faith, and exacting others; they are liable to clash with what persons believe to be already settled by precepts of Revelation, or to contradict what God himself, they think, hath declared to be true. In this case, whatever plea the magistrate may allege to justify its edict, the subject can have none to excuse his compliance. According to the same distinction, the magistrate is not to be obeyed in temporals more than in spirituals, where a repugnancy is perceived between his commands and any credited manifestations of the Divine will; but such is much less likely to arise in one case than the other.

Q. When we grant that interference of the magistrate in religion is lawful, as often as it appears to him to conduce, in its general tendency, to the public happiness, what may be argued from this concession?

A. That since salvation is the highest interest of mankind, and, consequently, to advance that is to promote public happiness in the greatest degree, it is not only the right, but the duty of every supreme magistrate to enforce upon his subjects that religion which he deems most acceptable to God. A popish king, for example, would derive a right from, and be bound by, these principles to employ his power over the lives and fortunes of his subjects, in reducing them within that communion.

Q. Does Paley confess that this consequence is inferred from the principles laid down concerning the foundation of civil authority, and not without the resemblance of a regular deduction?

A. Yes; he confesses also that it is a conclusion which ought to be disposed of; because, if it really follows from this theory of government, the theory itself ought to be given up.

Q. But what must it be considered are the terms of his proposition?

A. "That it is lawful for the magistrate to interfere in the affairs of religion, whenever his interference appears to him to conduce, by its general tendency, to the public happiness."

Q. When this rule comes to be applied, what will be found a very significant part of the direction?

A. The clause "of general tendency"—this obliges the magistrate to reflect, not only whether the religion he wishes to propagate be that which will best secure their eternal welfare, and whether the methods he employs be likely to effectuate its establishment; but also whether the kind of [illegible] if it were adopted as a common maxim, or received as a general rule of government in matters of religion, would upon the whole conduce to the furtherance of human salvation. If, for example, he should think, that although the application of his power might, in this instance, advance the true religion and happiness of his people, yet that the same engine, in other hands, who might assume the same right, would more frequently obstruct truth and the means of salvation; he would be bound, by submitting public utility to be the rule of his conduct, to refrain from expedients which, whatever particular effects he may expect from them, are, in their general operation, dangerous or hurtful.

Q. Is there any difficulty in this inquiry; whence does it arise?

A. From that which is the source of every difficulty in morals;—the competition of particular and general consequences; or the subordination of one general rule to another rule which is still more general.

Q. Bearing then in mind, that it is the general tendency of the measure, or the effects which would arise from its being *generally* adopted, that fixes upon it the character of rectitude or injustice; what do we proceed to inquire?

A. What is the degree and the sort of interference of secular laws in matters of religion, which are likely to be beneficial to the public happiness?

Q. What two maxims will in a great measure regulate our conclusions upon this head?

A. First, that any form of Christianity is better than no religion: secondly, that, of different systems of faith, that is the best which is the truest.

Q. What does Paley remark upon these two positions?

A. The first will hardly be disputed, when we reflect that every modification of Christianity holds out future happiness and misery, as depending upon the practice of virtue or of vice; and that the distinctions of virtue and vice are nearly the same in all. A person who acts under these impressions, though combined with many errors, is more likely to advance both the public happiness and his own, than one who is destitute of all such expectation. The latter proposition is founded in the consideration, that the principal importance of religion consists in its influence upon the fate and condition of a future existence. This influence belongs only to that religion which comes from God. A political religion may be framed, which shall embrace the purposes and duties of society perfectly well; but if it be not delivered by God, what assurance does it afford, that the Divine judgment will have any regard to its rules? With a man who acts with a view to future judgment, a religion which wants authority, wants every thing; and since this appertains, not to the religion which is most commodious, sublime, and efficacious, or which suits best with the form, power, and stability of civil government,—but only to that which comes from God; we are justified in pronouncing the *true* religion by its *very truth*, and that alone to be universally the best.

Q. From the first proposition, what inference follows?

A. That when the state enables its subjects to learn *some* form of Christianity, by distributing teachers of a religious system throughout the country, and by providing for their maintenance; that is, when the laws *establish* a national religion; they exercise an interference, likely, in its general tendency, to promote the interest of mankind: for, even supposing this system erroneous and corrupt, yet when the option lies between this religion and none at all, our proposition teaches us that the former alternative is constantly to be preferred.

Q. But after the right of the magistrate to establish a particular religion has been, upon this principle, admitted, what doubt sometimes presents itself?

A. Whether the religion which he ought to establish, be that which he himself professes, or that which he observes to prevail amongst the majority of the people.

Q. Now when we consider this question with a view to the formation of a general rule upon this subject, which must be assumed to be an equal chance?

A. Whether of the two religions contains most of truth,—that of the magistrate, or that of the people.

Q. The chance, then, that is left for truth being

equal upon both suppositions, what will be the remaining consideration?

A. From which arrangement more efficacy can be expected;—from an order of men appointed to teach the people their own religion, or to convert them to another?

Q. What is Paley's opinion upon this?

A. That the advantage lies on the side of the former scheme: and this, if it be assented to, makes it the duty of the magistrate to consult the faith of the nation, rather than his own.

Q. How must the case also of dissenters be determined?

A. By the principles just now stated.

Q. What are the two kinds of toleration?

A. The allowing to dissenters the unmolested profession and exercise of their religion, but with an exclusion from civil offices; which is a *partial* toleration: and the admitting them, without distinction, to all civil privileges; which is a *complete* toleration.

Q. From what is the expediency of toleration, and consequently the right of all to demand it, as far as relates to liberty of conscience, and the claim of protection in the free profession of his religion, deducible?

A. From the *second* of the foregoing propositions, which asserts that truth, and truth in the abstract, is the supreme perfection of every religion; to the advancement of which all regulations ought principally to be adapted. Now, every species of intolerance which enjoins and enforces suppression and silence, is adverse to the progress of truth; as it causes that to be fixed by one set of men, at one time, which with much more probability of success, is left to the independent and progressive inquiry of individuals. Truth results from discussion, controversy, and research. Whatever, therefore, prohibits these, obstructs that industry and liberty, which it is the interest of mankind to promote. In religion, as in other subjects, truth, if left to itself, will always obtain the ascendancy. If different religions be professed in the same country, and the minds of men remain unfettered and unawed, that religion which is founded in maxims of reason and credibility, will gradually gain over the other.

Q. The principal argument for the justice and expediency of toleration is in its conduciveness to truth, and in the superior value of truth to that of any other quality which a religion can possess; but what other auxiliary and important considerations exist?

A. The confining of the subject to the religion of the state, is a needless violation of natural liberty, and one in which constraint is always grievous. Persecution produces no real change of opinion; but vitiates the public morals, by driving men to prevarication; and commonly ends in a general though secret infidelity; whilst it disgraces the character, and wounds the reputation of Christianity itself.

Q. Under the idea of a religious toleration, Paley includes the toleration of all books of serious argumentation: but what does he deem it no infringement of religious liberty, to restrain?

A. The circulation of ridicule, invective, and mockery, upon religious subjects; because this applies solely to the passions, and has no tendency whatever to assist either the investigation or the impression of truth: on the contrary, it destroys alike the influence of all religions.

Q. Concerning the admission of dissenters to offices and employments in the public service, what doubts have been entertained, with some appearance of reason?

A. It is possible that religious opinions may be holden, which are incompatible with the functions of civil government; and which consequently disqualify those who maintain them from any share in its administration. Thus it would be absurd to entrust a military command to a Quaker, who believes it to be contrary to the Gospel to take up arms. This is possible; therefore it cannot be laid down as an universal truth, that religion is not, in its nature, a cause which will justify exclusion from public employments.

Q. When we examine, however, the sects of Christianity which actually prevail what must we confess?

A. That, with the single exception of refusing to bear arms, we find no tenet in any which incapacitates men for the service of the state. There is no reason why men of different religious persuasions may not sit upon the same bench, deliberate in the same council, or fight in the same ranks, as well as men of various or opposite opinions upon any controverted topic of philosophy, or history.

Q. What are the two cases in which test-laws are wont to be applied, and in which, if in any, they may be defended?

A. One is, where two or more religions are contending for establishment; and where there appears no way of putting an end to the contest, but by giving to one such a decided superiority as to secure it against danger from any other.

Q. Does Paley assert that he should entertain any scruples in assenting to this precaution?

A. Yes: he says if the dissenters from the establishment become a majority of the people; it ought to be altered or qualified. If there exist amongst the different sects such a parity of numbers, and power, as to render the preference of one to the rest, a matter of hazardous success and doubtful election, some plan similar to that meditated in North America, and which has been described in a preceding part of the chapter, may perhaps suit better with this divided state of public opinion, than any constitution of a national church. In all other cases the establishment will be strong enough to maintain itself. However, if a test be applicable with justice upon this principle at all, it ought to be applied in regal governments to the chief magistrate himself, whose power might otherwise change the established religion in opposition to the will of the people.

Q. What is the second case of *exclusion*, and in which the measure is more easily vindicated?

A. That of a country in which some disaffection to the government is connected with certain religious distinctions: for the state has a right to refuse its power and confidence to those who seek its destruction.

Q. But even *here* what should be observed?

A. That government shuts its doors, not against the religion, but against those political principles, which the members of that communion are found in fact to hold. Nor would religious tenets be made the test of men's inclinations, if any other could be discovered equally certain.

Q. After all, why should not the legislator direct his test against the political principles themselves, rather than through the medium of religious tenets, the only crime and danger of which is in their presumed alliance? What two answers only can be given to this question?

A. First, that it is not opinions which the laws fear, so much as inclinations; and political ones are not so easily detected by the affirmation or denial of any abstract proposition in politics, as by the discovery of the religious creed with which they are wont to be united;—secondly, that particular persons might insinuate themselves into offices of trust and authority, by subscribing political assertions, and yet retain their predilection for the interests of the religious sect to which they continued to belong. By which means, government would sometimes find, though it could not accuse the individual of disaffection to the civil establishment, yet that, through him, it had communicated the influence of a powerful station to a party hostile to the constitution.

Q. What does Paley however observe upon these answers?

A. They are proposed rather than defended. The measure cannot be defended at all, except where the suspected obnoxious union is nearly universal; in which case, it makes little difference to the subscriber, whether the test be religious or political; and the state is somewhat better secured by the one than the other.

Q. What is the result of this examination of those general tendencies, by which every interference of civil government in matters of religion ought to be tried?

A. "That a comprehensive national religion, guarded by a few articles of peace and conformity, together with a legal provision for the clergy of that religion; and with a *complete* toleration of all dissenters, without any other limitation than what arises from the conjunction of dangerous political dispositions with certain religious tenets; appears to be the most liberal, just, and safe system: inasmuch as it unites the several perfections which a religious constitution ought to aim at,—liberty of conscience, with the means of instruction; the progress of truth, with the peace of society; the right of public judgment, with the care of the public safety.

CHAP. XI.

OF POPULATION AND PROVISION; AND OF AGRICULTURE AND COMMERCE, AS SUBSERVIENT THERETO.

Q. What is the final view of all rational politics?

A. To produce the greatest quantity of happiness in a given tract of country. The riches, strength, and glory of nations, those topics which history celebrates, have no value farther than as they contribute to this end. When they interfere with it, they are evils, and not the less real for the splendor that surrounds them.

Secondly: although we speak of communities as of sentient beings, and ascribe to them happiness and misery, &c. nothing really exists or feels but *individuals*. The happiness of a people is made up of that of single persons; and the quantity can only be augmented by increasing the number of the percipients, or the pleasure of their perceptions.

Thirdly: notwithstanding that a diversity of condition, greatly varies the quantity of happiness enjoyed by the same number of individuals; and that extreme cases may be found, of human beings so galled by the rigours of slavery, that the increase of numbers is only the amplification of misery: yet, within certain limits, and within those to which civil life is diversified under [illegible] governments, it may be affirmed, that the quantity of happiness produced in any given district, so far depends upon the number of inhabitants, that, in comparing adjoining periods in the same country, the collective happiness will be nearly in the exact proportion of the numbers; that is, a larger portion of happiness will be enjoyed amongst ten persons possessing the means of healthy subsistence, than can be produced by five [illegible] every advantage of power and affluence.

Q. What follows from these principles?

A. That the quantity of happiness in a given district, although possible it may be increased, the number of inhabitants remaining the same, is chiefly affected by alteration of the numbers: consequently, the decay of population is the greatest evil of a state, and the improvement of it the object to be aimed at in preference to every other.

Q. Why is the importance of population, and the superiority of it to every other object, so necessary to be inculcated and understood?

A. Because false estimates of national good are perpetually drawing the attention of statesmen from the care of this, at all times the foundation [illegible] of prosperity.

Q. What lesson we may be enabled [illegible]?

A. That [illegible] the advancement of [illegible] of [illegible]

[illegible]

make a people happier, tends to render them more numerous.

In the fecundity of the human, as of every other species of animals, nature has provided for an indefinite multiplication.

Q. What therefore becomes a question?

A. What are the causes which confine or check its natural progress?

Q. And what answer first presents itself?

A. That the population of a country must stop when the inhabitants are so numerous as to exhaust all the provision which the soil can produce.

Q. Why however will this, though an insuperable bar, seldom be found to be that which actually checks the progress of population?

A. Because the number of the people have seldom, in any country, arrived at this limit, or even approached to it. The two principles upon which population seems primarily to depend, the fecundity of the species, and the capacity of the soil, would in most, perhaps in all countries, enable it to proceed much further than it has yet advanced.

Q. What is the fundamental proposition upon the subject of *population*, which must guide every endeavour to improve it, and from which every conclusion concerning it may be deduced?

A. Wherever the commerce between the sexes is regulated by marriage, and a provision for that mode of subsistence, to which each class is accustomed, can be procured with ease and certainty, there the people will increase; whilst the rapidity and extent of the increase, will be proportioned to the degree in which these causes exist."

Q. How does Paley draw out this proposition into the several principles which it contains?

A. First, the proposition asserts the "necessity of confining the intercourse of the sexes to the marriage-union." It is only in the marriage-union that this intercourse is sufficiently prolific. Beside which, family establishments alone are fitted to perpetuate a succession of generations. Now, nature, in the constitution of the sexes, has provided a stimulus which will infallibly secure the frequency of marriages, provided the male part of the species be prohibited from irregular gratifications, by difficulty, danger, infamy, sense of guilt, or fear of punishment. Wherefore, in countries in which subsistence is scarce, the state must watch over public morals; for nothing but the instinct of nature, under the restraint of chastity, will induce men to make that sacrifice of personal liberty and indulgence, which the support of a family requires.

The second requisite of the proposition is, "the ease and certainty with which a provision can be procured for that mode of subsistence to which each class of the community is accustomed." It is not enough that men's natural wants and real exigencies be supplied; habitual superfluities become actual wants. And it must not be expected from men in general, at least in the present relaxed state of morals and discipline, that they will enter into marriages which degrade their condition, and deprive them of the accommodations to which they have been accustomed, and which they have been taught to regard as belonging to their birth, class, or place in society. This view to their *accustomed* mode of life, has the same influence upon those ranks which compose the mass of the community. It is in vain to allege, that a more simple diet, ruder habitations, or coarser apparel, would be sufficient for the purposes of life and health, or even of physical ease and pleasure; for men will not marry with this encouragement.

The ease, then, and certainty with which the means can be procured, not barely of subsistence, but of that mode of subsisting which custom hath in each country established, form the point upon which the state and progress of population chiefly depend.

Q. Now, what are the three causes which evidently regulate this point?

A. The mode itself of subsisting which prevails in the country; the quantity of provision suited to that mode of subsistence, which is either raised in the country or imported into it; and, lastly, the distribution of that provision.

Q. 1. What does Paley remark upon the first of these causes?

A. In China, where the inhabitants frequent the sea-shore, or the banks of large rivers, and subsist in a great measure upon fish, the population is described to be excessive; not from any good policy, but simply because the species of food to which custom hath reconciled the desires of the inhabitants is procured in the greatest abundance, and stands in need of the least preparation. The natives of Indostan, requiring little except rice, which the country produces in plentiful crops; and food, in warm climates, composing the only want of life; these countries are populous, under all the injuries of a despotic and unsettled government. In Ireland, the simplicity of living alone, maintains a considerable degree of population, under great defects of police, industry, and commerce.

Q. From a view of these considerations, may be understood the true evil and proper danger of luxury. What does Paley remark upon this?

A. LUXURY, as it supplies employment and promotes industry, assists population. But then there is another consequence which often counteracts these advantages. When, by introducing more superfluities into general reception, it has rendered the usual accommodations of life more expensive and artificial, the difficulty of maintaining a family in the established mode, becomes greater, and marriages grow less frequent; as men will not marry, to *sink* their place in society, or *change* their habits. This principle is applicable to every article of diet and dress, to houses, furniture, attendance; and this effect will be felt in every class of the community.

Q. Luxury then, considered with a view to population, acts by two opposite effects; and probably there exists a point in the scale to which it may ascend, or to which the wants of mankind may be multiplied usefully, and beyond which its evils begin to preponderate. The determination of this point, depends upon circumstances too numerous and intricate, to admit of a precise solution. However, from what has been observed, what general conclusions may be established?

A. 1st. That of different kinds of luxury, those are the most innocent, which afford employment to the greatest number of artists; or in which the price of work bears the greatest proportion to that of the raw material.

2ndly. That it is the *diffusion*, rather than the *degree* of luxury, which is to be dreaded. The mischief of luxury consists, in the obstruction it forms to marriage. Now it is only a small part of the people that compose the higher ranks in any country; for which reason, the facility or the difficulty of supporting the expense of *their* station, and the consequent increase or diminution of marriages among *them*, will influence the state of population but little. But when the imitation of the same manners descends, as it always will do, into the mass of people; then it checks the formation of families, in an alarming degree.

3dly. That the condition most favourable to population is that of a laborious, frugal people ministering to the demands of an opulent, luxurious nation; because this situation, whilst it leaves

[illegible] example [illegible]

[illegible]

Q. 11. Next to the mode of living, is to be considered "the quantity of provision, suited to that mode, which is either raised in the country, or imported into it;" for this is the order in which we assigned the causes of population. What does Paley say on this head?

If we measure the quantity of provision by the number of human bodies it will support in due health, this quantity, the extent and quality of the soil being given, will depend greatly upon the *kind*. Thus a piece of ground capable of supplying animal food for the subsistence of ten persons, would sustain twice that number with grain, roots, and milk. The first resource of savage life is in the flesh of wild animals; hence their numbers, compared with the tract of country which they occupy, are universally small. The next step was the invention of pasturage, or the rearing of tame animals: this added to the stock of provision much. But the last and principal improvement was tillage, or the artificial production of corn, esculent plants, and roots; which, whilst it changed the quality of food, augmented the quantity in a vast proportion. So far as population is governed and limited by the quantity of provision, perhaps there is no single cause that affects it so powerfully, as the kind and quality of food which chance or usage hath introduced into a country. Tillage, as an object of national care and encouragement, is preferable to pasturage, because the provision it yields, goes much farther in the sustentation of life. It is also recommended by its affording employment to a much more numerous peasantry.

The kind and quality of provision, together with the extent and capacity of the soil, being the same; the quantity will principally depend upon two circumstances,—the *ability* of the occupier, and the *encouragement* he receives. The greatest misfortune of a country is an indigent tenantry. Whatever be the advantages of the soil, or the skill and industry of the occupier, the want of a sufficient capital confines every plan, and cripples every operation of husbandry. This evil is felt, where agriculture is accounted a mean employment; where farms are extremely subdivided, and badly furnished with habitations; where leases are unknown, or are of short or precarious duration. With respect to the *encouragement* of husbandry; in this, as in every other employment, the true reward and stimulus of industry is in the price and sale of the produce. All therefore that the laws can do, is to secure this right to the occupier of the ground; that is, to constitute such a system of tenure, that the full advantage of every improvement go to the benefit of the improver; and that no one share in the profit who does not assist in the production. By the *occupier* is here meant, not so much the person who performs the work, as him who procures the labour and directs the management: and the whole profit is received by the occupier, when he is benefited by the whole value of what is produced, which is the case with the tenant who pays a fixed rent for the use of land, no less than with the proprietor who occupies it as his own. Likewise the proprietor, though he grant out his estate to farm, may be considered as the occupier, since he regulates the occupation by the choice, superintendency, and encouragement of his tenants, by the disposition of his lands, by erecting buildings, &c. or supplying implements of improvement; and is entitled, by the rule of public expediency, to receive in the advance of his rent, a share of the benefit. The violation of this fundamental maxim of agrarian policy is the chief objection to the holding of lands by the state, by the king, by corporate bodies, by private persons in right of their offices. The inconveniency arises not so much from the unalienable quality of lands thus holden in perpetuity, as from hence; that such proprietors seldom contribute much attention or expense to their cultivation, yet claim, by the rent, a share in the profit of every improvement. This complaint can only be obviated by "long leases at a fixed rent," which convey a large portion of the interest to those who actually conduct the cultivation.

Q. III. Beside the production of provisions, there remains to be considered the distribution. —What does Paley say upon this head?

A. It is in vain that provisions abound in the country, unless I be able to obtain a share of them. This reflection belongs to every individual. The plenty of provisions produced, affords nothing

tence to individuals, and encouragement to the formation of families, only in proportion as it is *distributed*, or as these individuals are allowed to draw from it a supply of their own wants. The *distribution*, therefore, becomes of equal consequence to population with the *production*.

Q. Now there is but one principle of distribution that can ever become universal; What is this?

A. The principle of "exchange;" that every man have something to give in return for what he wants; for men will not work to give the produce of their labour away.

Q. What are the only equivalents that can be offered in exchange for provision?

A. *Power* and *labour*. All property is power. Property in land, is the power to use it, and to exclude others from the use. Money is the representative of power, because it is convertible into power; it procures power over things and persons. But power which results from civil conventions is necessarily confined to a few, and soon exhausted; whereas the capacity of *labour* is every man's natural and constant possession. The hire, therefore, or produce of personal industry, is what the bulk of every community must bring to market, in exchange for the means of subsistence; employment must be the medium of distribution, and the source of supply to individuals.

Q. But when we consider the *production* and *distribution* of provision, as independent of each other; when, supposing the same quantity to be produced, we inquire in what way, or according to what rule, it may be distributed; to what conclusions of the subject are we led?

A. To one not at all agreeable to truth and reality; for, the production of provision depends, in a great measure, upon the distribution. The quantity raised out of the ground, so far as the raising of it requires human art or labour, will evidently be regulated by the demand, the price and sale being that which alone rewards the care and diligence of the inhabitants. But the sale depends upon the number of those who have something to offer in return for what they want; that is, upon the number of those who have the fruits of some other kind of industry to tender in exchange for what they stand in need of from the production of the soil.

Q. What connection then do we perceive here?

A. That between population and employment. Employment affects population "directly," as it affords the only medium of distribution by which individuals can obtain from the common stock a supply for the wants of their families; "indirectly," as it augments the stock of provision, in the only way by which the production of it can be effectually encouraged,—by furnishing purchasers.

Q. And upon this basis what is founded?

A. The public benefit of trade, or its subserviency to population. Of those arts and branches of trade employed in the production, conveyance, and preparation, of any principal species of human food, or of the business of the husbandman, the butcher, baker, &c. we acknowledge the necessity ty. Likewise of those manufactures which furnish us with warm clothing, convenient habitations, domestic utensils, as of the weaver, tailor, carpenter, &c. we perceive the conduciveness to population, by their rendering human life more healthy and comfortable. But not one half of the occupations which compose the trade of Europe, fall within either of these descriptions, being employed upon articles of confessed luxury, ornament, or splendour. What can be less necessary to the sustentation of life, than the produce of the silk, lace, and glass manufactory? yet what multitudes labour in the different branches of these arts! What can be more capricious than the fondness for tobacco and snuff? yet how many thousands are set at work in administering to this frivolous gratification! Concerning trades of this kind it may fairly be asked, "How, since they add nothing to the stock of provision, do they tend to increase the number of the people?" In like manner, with respect to foreign commerce, of that merchandise which brings the necessaries of life into a country we allow the tendency to advance population, because it increases the stock of provision by which the people are subsisted; but how does that, which brings into the country no one article of human subsistence, promote the multiplication of human life?

Q. In what will the answer to this inquiry be contained?

A. In the discussion of another point: since the soil will maintain many more than it can employ, what must be done, supposing the country to be fed, with the remainder of the inhabitants? They who, by the rules of partition, are entitled to the land, and they who, by their labour upon the soil, acquire a right in its produce, will not part with their property for nothing; or, rather, they will not raise from the soil what they can neither use nor exchange. Or, lastly, if these were willing to distribute what they could spare, to others who had no share or concern in the property or cultivation of it, yet still the most enormous mischiefs would ensue from great numbers remaining unemployed. One only way presents itself of removing the difficulty; that they, whose work is not wanted, nor can be employed, in the raising of provision out of the ground, convert their hands and ingenuity to the fabrication of articles which may gratify and requite those who are so employed, or who are entitled to the exclusive possession of certain parts of them. By this contrivance, all things proceed well, and the community is kept quiet, while both sides are engaged in their respective occupations.

Q. What appears, then, the business of one half of mankind to do?

A. To set the other half at work; that is, to provide articles which, by tempting the desires, may stimulate the industry of those upon the exertion of whose industry, and faculties, the production of human provision depends. A certain portion only of human labour is, or can be, *productive*; the rest is *instrumental*;—both equally necessary, though the one have no other object than to excite the other. It signifies nothing, as to the main purpose of trade, how superfluous its articles are; whether the want of them be real or imaginary; whether it be founded in nature, opinion, or fashion; it is enough that they be actually desired. Flourishing cities are raised and supported by trading in tobacco or by the manufactory of ribands. A watch may be very unnecessary to a peasant; yet if he will till the ground to obtain a watch, the design of trade is answered: and the watch-maker is contributing to the production of corn as effectually as if he handled the spade or held the plough. The use of tobacco affords a remarkable example of the caprice of human appetite; yet, if the fisherman will ply his nets, or the mariner fetch rice to procure this indulgence, two important articles are supplied by a merchandise which has no other apparent use than the gatification of a vitiated palate.

Q. But it may come to pass that the husbandman, or land-owner, will no longer exchange its produce for what the manufacturer has to offer. For instance, he wants no more cloth; he will no longer therefore give the weaver corn in return for the produce of his looms: but he would readily give it for tea, or for wine. When the weaver finds this to be the case, what has he to do?

A. Nothing but to send his cloth abroad, in exchange for tea or for wine, which he may barter for that provision. The circulation is thus revived: and whereas the number of weavers, who could find subsistence from their employment, was before limited by the consumption of cloth in the country, that number is now augmented, in proportion to the demand for tea and wine.

Q. Of what is this the principle?

A. Of *foreign* commerce. In the magnitude and complexity of the machine, the principle of motion is sometimes lost or unobserved; but it is always simple and the same, to whatever extent it may be diversified and enlarged.

Q. Where is that effect of trade upon agriculture, the process of which has been described, visible?

A. In the neighbourhood of trading towns, and in those districts which carry on a communication with the markets of trading towns. The husbandmen are busy and skilful; the peasantry laborious; the land is managed to the best advantage; and double the quantity of corn or herbage raised from it, of what the same soil yields in remoter and more neglected parts of the country.

Q. What then must we remember concerning agriculture?

A. That it is the immediate source of human provision; that trade conduces to the production of provision only as it promotes agriculture; that the whole system of commerce, hath no other public importance than its subserviency to this end.

Q. Paley now returns to the proposition "that employment universally promotes population." What follows from this proposition?

A. That the comparative utility of different

branches of national commerce is measured by the number which each branch *employs*; so that a scale may easily be constructed, which shall assign to the several kinds and divisions of foreign trade their degrees of public importance.

Q. In this scale, what does the first place belong to?

A. The exchange of wrought goods for raw materials, as of broad-cloth for raw silk; cutlery for wool, &c.; because this traffic provides a market for the labour that has already been expended, whilst it supplies materials for new industry. Population always flourishes where this species of commerce obtains. As it takes off the manufactures of the country, it promotes employment; as it brings in raw materials, it supposes the existence of manufactories in the country, and a demand for the article when manufactured.

Q. To what is the second place due?

A. To that commerce, which barters one species of wrought goods for another, as stuffs for callicoes, fustians for cambrics, &c. or wrought goods for articles which require no farther preparation, as for wine, oil, tea, &c. This also assists employment; because, when the country is stocked with one kind of manufacture, it renews the demand by converting it into another; but it promotes this end by one side only of the bargain,—by what it carries out.

Q. What is the *last*, the lowest, and most disadvantageous species of commerce?

A. The exportation of raw materials for wrought

goods: as when wool is sent abroad to purchase velvets, &c. This trade is unfavourable to population, because it leaves no room or demand for employment, either in what it takes out, or in what it brings in. On both sides it is noxious. By its exports, it diminishes the very subject upon which industry ought to be exercised; by its imports, it lessens the encouragement of that industry, by the produce of foreign labour.

Q. Of different branches of *manufactory*, which are, in their nature, the most beneficial?

A. Those in which the price of the wrought article exceeds in the highest proportion that of the raw material: for this excess measures the quantity of employment. The produce of the ground is never the most advantageous article of foreign commerce. The soil should be applied solely to the raising of provision for its inhabitants, and its trade be supplied by their industry. A nation will never reach its proper population, so long as its principal commerce consists in the exportation of corn and cattle, or even of wine, oil, tobacco, timber, &c. because these last articles take up that surface which ought to be covered with the materials of human subsistence.

Q. What, however, must be noticed here?

A. That we have all along considered the inhabitants of a country as maintained by its produce, and that what has been said is applicable with strictness to this supposition alone.

Q. May the reasoning, easily be adapted to a different case?

A. Yes; for when provision is not produced but imported, what has been affirmed concerning provision, will be, in a great measure, true of that article, whether it be money, produce, or labour, which is exchanged for provision. Thus, when the people of America plant tobacco, and send it to Europe for cloth; the cultivation of tobacco becomes as necessary to the subsistence of the inhabitants, and will affect the state of population in that country as sensibly, as the actual production of food, or the manufactory of raiment. So when the inhabitants of Holland earn money by the carriage of the produce of one country to another, and with that purchase the provision which their own land is not extensive enough to supply, the increase or decline of this carrying trade will influence the numbers of the people like similar changes in the cultivation of the soil.

Q. The few principles already established will enable us to describe the effects upon population, which may be expected from some important articles of national conduct and œconomy: what is the first of these?

A. Emigration—which may be either the overflowing of a country, or the desertion. As the increase of the species is indefinite; and the number which any given tract can support, finite; great numbers may be constantly leaving a country, and yet the country remain full. Or whatever be the cause which invincibly limits the population of a country; when the number has arrived at that limit, the progress of generation, beside con-

limiting the consumption, will supply multitudes for emigration. In these cases, emigration neither indicates any political decay, nor diminishes the numbers of the people; nor ought to be discouraged. But emigrants may relinquish their country, from a sense of insecurity, oppression, and inconveniency. Neither, again, *here* is it emigration which wastes the people, but the evils that occasion it. It would be in vain, if it were practicable, to confine the inhabitants at home; for the same causes which drive them out would prevent their multiplication if they remained. Lastly; men may emigrate by the allurement of a better climate, of a more luxurious manner of living; by the prospect of wealth; or of higher wages and prices. This class, with whom alone the laws can interfere with effect, will never be numerous. With the generality of a people, the attachment to their homes and country, and the irksomeness of living among strangers, will outweigh, so long as men possess the necessaries of life in safety, all the inducements that the advantages of a foreign land can offer. There appear, therefore, to be few cases in which emigration can be prohibited, with advantage to the state; it appears also that emigration is but an equivocal symptom of decline.

Q. What is the second article, as considered by Paley?

A. COLONIZATION.—The only view under which we need consider *colonization*, is in its tendency to augment the population of the parent state.—Suppose a fertile, but empty, island to lie within the reach of a civilised country; suppose a colony sent out to take possession of the island, and to live there under the protection of their native government: the settlers will convert their labour to the cultivation of the vacant soil, and with its produce draw a supply of manufactures from their countrymen at home. Whilst they continue few, and lands cheap and fresh, the colonists will find it easier and more profitable to raise corn, or rear cattle, and with them to purchase woollen cloth or linen, than to spin or weave for themselves. The mother-country derives from this connexion an increase both of provision and employment; the two great requisites upon which the facility of subsistence, and by consequence the state of population, depend,—*production* and *distribution;* and this in a manner the most direct and beneficial: for as, in a genial climate, and from a fresh soil, the labour of one man will raise provision enough for ten, it is manifest that, where all are employed in agriculture, the greater part of the produce will be spared from the consumption; and that three out of four of those who are maintained by it, will reside in the country which receives the redundancy. When the new country does not remit *provision* to the old one, the advantage is still less; but still the exportation of wrought goods, by whatever return they are paid for, advances population in a secondary way. Thus the system of colonisation is founded in apparent national utility, as well as upon principles favourable to the common interest of human nature: for it does not appear by what other method newly-discovered countries can be peopled, or during their infancy be protected or supplied. Errors are committed not so much in the original formation of colonies, as in the subsequent management; in imposing restrictions too rigorous, or in confining them too long.

Q. What is the third article?

A. MONEY.—Where it abounds, the people are generally numerous: yet gold and silver neither feed nor clothe mankind; nor are they in all countries converted into provision by purchasing the necessaries of life at foreign markets; nor do they compose those articles of personal or domestic ornament without which certain orders will not enter into family-establishments;—at least, this property obtains in a very small degree. The effect of money upon the number of the people, though visible to observation, is not explained without some difficulty. To understand it properly, we must return to the proposition, "that population is chiefly promoted by employment." Now of employment, money is partly the indication, and partly the cause. The only way in which money regularly *flows into* a country, is in return for goods sent out of it, or work performed by it; and the only way in which money is *retained in* a country, is by its supplying, in a great measure, its own consumption of manufactures. Consequently, the quantity of money denotes the amount of labour and employment: but still, employment, not money, is the cause of population; the accumulation of money is merely a collateral effect of the same cause, and measures its operation. And this is true of money, only whilst it is acquired by industry. The treasures which belong to a country by the possession of mines, or foreign dependencies, afford no conclusion concerning the state of population; of this, we see an egregious example in Spain, since the acquisition of its South American dominions.

But money may become also a real and operative *cause* of population, by acting as a stimulus to industry, and facilitating the means of subsistence. The ease of subsistence, and the encouragement of industry, depend neither upon the price of labour, nor upon that of provision, but upon the proportion which one bears to the other. Now, an influx of money tends to advance this proportion; that is, every accession of money raises the price of labour before it raises that of provision. When money is brought from abroad, provision is not bought up first with it, but it is applied to the purchase and payment of labour. The state dispenses what it receives amongst soldiers, sailors, artificers, shipwrights, workmen, &c.;—if private persons bring home treasures, they usually expend them in building houses, in the improvement of estates, in the purchase of furniture, dress, equipage, &c.:—the merchant applies his increased capital to the enlargement of his business at home. The money, ere long, comes to market for provision; but it comes through the hands of the manufacturer, the artist, the husbandman, &c. Its effect upon the price of art and labour, will *precede* its effect upon the price of provision; and during this interval, the means of subsistence will be multiplied, as well as industry excited by new rewards. When the greater plenty of money has produced an advance in the price of provision, corresponding to the advanced price of labour, its effect ceases. It is not, therefore, the quantity of specie collected into a country, but the continual increase of that quantity, from which the advantage arises to employment and population. Now, whatever consequence arises from an influx of money, the contrary may be expected to follow from its diminution: accordingly we find, that whatever drains off the specie of a country, faster than it can be supplied by the streams which feed it, impoverishes and depopulates it. The knowledge and experience of this effect have given occasion to a phrase which often occurs. The *balance of trade* with any nation is said to be against or in favour of a country, as it tends to carry money out, or bring it in; that is, as the price of the imports exceeds or falls short of that of the exports: so invariably is the increase or diminution of the specie regarded as a test of advantage or detriment arising from any branch of commerce.

Q. What is the fourth article considered?

A. IV. TAXATION.—As *taxes* take nothing out of a country, nor diminish the public stock, but only vary its distribution; they are not necessarily prejudicial to population. If the state exact money from some members of the community, she dispenses it amongst others; which they who contribute to the revenue, and they who are supported by the expenses of government, are placed one against the other, the common fund of the society is not lessened. It must however be observed, that although the sum distributed be always *equal* to the sum collected, yet the gain and loss to the means of subsistence may be very *unequal*, according as the money passes from the industrious to the idle, from the many to the few, from those who want to those who abound, or the contrary. Thus, a tax upon wine or tea distributed in bounties to fishermen or husbandmen, would augment the provision of a country; a tax upon fisheries and husbandry, however indirect, to be converted to the procuring of wine or tea for the idle and opulent, would naturally impair the public stock. The effect, therefore, of taxes, upon the means of subsistence, depends not so much upon the amount levied, as upon the object of the tax and the application. Taxes likewise may conduce to the restraint of luxury, and the correction of vice; to the encouragement of industry, trade, agriculture, and marriage. Thus contrived, they become rewards and penalties; not only sources of revenue, but instruments of police.

Yet although taxes cannot be pronounced to be detrimental to population, by any absolute necessity in their nature; and though, under some modifications they may even operate in favour of it;

and, in a great plurality of instances, their tendency is noxious. Suppose that nine families inhabit a neighbourhood, each possessing barely the means of subsistence; let a tenth family be quartered upon them; or rather, let one of the nine have his income augmented by deduction from the incomes of the rest; in either case, it is evident that the district would be broken up, since the entire income of each is supposed to be barely sufficient for its maintenance. Now, it is no answer to this objection to say, that nothing is taken out of the neighbourhood; or that the stock is not diminished: the mischief is done by deranging the distribution. Nor, again, will the luxury or maintenance of an additional family, compensate the country for the ruin of nine others. Nor will it alter the effect, that the contribution, instead of being levied directly, is mixed up in the price of some article of constant use and consumption. This illustrates the tendency of taxes to obstruct subsistence; and the minutest degree of this obstruction will be felt. The evil may be magnified, in order to render its operation distinct and visible; but though, in real life, families may not be broken up, houses quitted, or countries suddenly deserted, in consequence of any new imposition; marriages will become less frequent.

It seems necessary, however, to distinguish between the operation of a new tax, and the effect of taxes long established. In the course of circulation, the money may flow back to the hands from which it was taken. The proportion which a

the supply and the expense of subsistence, disturbed by the tax, may at length recover itself. In the instance just now stated, the addition of a tenth family, or the enlarged expenses of one of the nine, may, in some shape or other, so advance the profits, or increase the employment, of the rest, as to make full compensation; or a reduction may take place in their mode of living, suited to the abridgment of their incomes. Yet still the ultimate effect of taxation, though distinguishable from the impression of a new tax, is adverse to population. The above *proportion*, can only be restored by one side or other of this alternative; by the people contracting their wants, which diminishes consumption and employment; or by raising the price of labour, which adding to the price of productions and manufactures checks their sale at foreign markets. A nation burthened with taxes, must be undersold by one which is free from them, unless the difference be made up by some singular advantage of climate, soil, skill, or industry. This quality belongs to all taxes which affect the mass of the community, even when most properly imposed. But as governments are usually administered, the produce of taxes is expended in the maintaining of pomp, or in the purchase of influence. The conversion of property through taxes, employed in this manner, is attended with obvious evils. It takes from the industrious, to give to the idle; it increases the number of the latter; it sacrifices the conveniency of many to the luxury of a few; it makes no satisfactory return to the people; it encourages no activity which is useful or productive.

A wise statesman will contrive his taxes principally with a view to their effect upon *population*. We are accustomed to think that a tax, to be just, ought to be accurately proportioned to the circumstances of the persons who pay it. But upon what is this opinion founded; unless it could be shown that such a proportion interferes the least with the general conveniency of subsistence? Whereas a tax, constructed with a view to that conveniency, ought to rise upon the different classes of the community, in a higher ratio than the simple proportion of their incomes. The point to be regarded is, not what men have, but what they can spare; and a man who possesses a thousand pounds a year, can more easily give up a hundred, than a man with a hundred pounds a year can part with ten; it is still more evident, that a man of a hundred pounds a year would not be so much distressed by a demand of ten pounds, as a man of ten pounds a year would be by the loss of one: to which add, that population being replenished by the marriages of the lowest ranks, their accommodation becomes of more importance than the conveniency of any less numerous order of its citizens. But whatever be the proportion which public expediency directs, it can never be attained by any *single* tax; as no single object of taxation can be found, which measures the ability of the subject with sufficient exactness. It is only by a variety of taxes mutually balancing each other, that a due proportion can be preserved. For instance; a tax upon lands may be properly counterpoised by a tax upon the rent of houses. Distinctions may also be framed in some taxes, which shall allow abatements or exemptions to married persons, or parents; to improvers of the soil; to particular modes of cultivation; and in general to that industry which is immediately *productive*; but above all, which may leave the heaviest burthens upon the methods of acquiring wealth without industry.

Q. What is the fifth article?

A. V. Exportation of Bread-corn.—Nothing seems to have a greater tendency to reduce the number of the people, than the sending abroad part of the provision by which they are maintained; yet this has been the policy of legislators very studious of improvement. In order to reconcile ourselves to such a practice, we must be reminded of a maxim which belongs to the productions both of nature and art, "that it is impossible to have enough without a superfluity." The point of sufficiency cannot be exactly hit upon, especially in an article of which the annual increase is so variable. As it is necessary that the crop be adequate to the consumption in a year of scarcity, it must greatly exceed it in a year of plenty. A redundancy therefore will occasionally arise from the very care taken against the danger of want; and the exportation of this subtracts nothing from the number that can regularly be maintained by the produce of the soil. Moreover, the benefits which indirectly arise to population from foreign commerce, belong to the exportation of corn, together with the peculiar advantage of presenting a constant incitement to the skill and industry of the husbandman, by the promise of a certain sale and price, under every contingency. Corn also not only may be exported, but must be so when a country is newly inhabited, with a fertile soil. The exportation of a large proportion of corn, proves that the inhabitants have not yet attained to the number which the country is capable of maintaining; but it does not prove but that they may be hastening to this limit with the utmost practicable celerity. In all cases except those two, and in the former to any greater degree than is necessary to take off occasional redundancies, the exportation of corn is either itself noxious to population, or argues a defect of population, arising from some other cause.

Q. What is the sixth article?

A. Abridgment of labour.—It has long been a question, whether mechanical contrivances which *abridge labour* be detrimental or not to the population of a country. From what has been already delivered, it will be evident that this question is equivalent to another,—whether they diminish or not the quantity of employment. Their first and obvious effect is this; because, if one man be made to do what three men did, two are discharged: but if, by some remote consequence, they increase the demand for work, in a greater proportion than they contract the number of workmen, the quantity of employment will gain an addition. It may be observed, therefore, that whenever a mechanical invention succeeds in one place, it must be imitated where the same manufacture is carried on: for he who has the benefit of a conciser operation will soon undersell a competitor who uses a more circuitous labour. It is also true, that whoever *first* adopt a mechanical improvement will, for some time, gain an increase of employment; which may continue even after it has become general; for, in every trade, it is a great and permanent advantage to have pre-occupied public reputation. Thirdly, after every superiority derived from a secret has ceased, it may be questioned whether any loss can accrue to employment. In proportion as an article can be afforded at a lower price, by reason of an easier process in the manufacture, it will either grow into more general use, or its improvement will demand a proportionable addition of hands. The number employed in the manufactory of stockings has not decreased since the invention of stocking-mills. The amount expended upon the article, after subtracting the price of the raw material, is not less than it was before. Goods of a finer texture are worn in the place of coarser; and this compensates to the manufactory for every other inconveniency. Also, an improvement which conduces to the recommendation of a manufactory, either by the cheapness or quality of the goods, generally draws after it many dependent employments, in which no abbreviation has taken place.

Q. What remarks does Paley make upon the reasoning and considerations in this chapter?

A. A judgment may, in some sort, be formed, how far regulations of law are capable of contributing to the support and advancement of population. He says here, as in many subjects relating to commerce, plenty, number of people, &c. more is expected from laws than they can do. Laws can only imperfectly restrain that dissoluteness which, by diminishing marriages, impairs the source of population. Laws cannot regulate the wants of mankind, their mode of living, or desire of superfluities, &c. Laws cannot induce men to enter into marriages, when the expenses of a family must deprive them of their customary indulgences. Laws, by their protection, may help to make a people industrious; but without industry, they cannot provide subsistence or employment; cannot make corn grow, or trade flourish. In spite of all laws, the expert, laborious, honest workman will be *employed*, in preference to the lazy, the unskilful, and the fraudulent; and this is true also of the people of two different countries, which communicate with the rest of the world. The natural basis of trade is rivalship of quality and price; *i. e.* of skill and industry. Every attempt to *force* trade, by operation of law, is sure to be eluded by the quick-sightedness and activity of private interest, or to be frustrated by retaliation. Perhaps the only way in which the interposition of law is salutary in trade, is in the prevention of frauds.

A great advantage derived to population from the interference of law, consists in the encouragement of *agriculture*. This is the direct way of increasing the number of the people; every other mode being effectual only by its influence upon this. Its office here is to adjust the laws of property, as nearly as possible, to the following rules: first, "to give to the occupier all power over the soil necessary for its perfect cultivation;"—secondly, "to assign the whole profit of improvement to those by whom it is carried on." Property in land is power over it. Now it is indifferent to the public in whose hands this power resides, if it be rightly used; to whom the land belongs, if it be well cultivated. The owner of ten thousand pounds a year, *consumes* little more of the produce than the owner of ten. If the cultivation be equal, the estate in the hands of one great proprietor, affords subsistence and employment to the same number of persons as if it were divided amongst a hundred. The same may be said of lands holden by the king, or by the subject; by private persons, or by corporations; by laymen, or ecclesiastics; in fee, or for life; &c. not that these varieties make no difference, but all the difference they do make respects the cultivation of the lands so holden.

There exist in this country, conditions of tenure which condemn the land itself to perpetual sterility. Such is the right of *common*, which precludes each proprietor from any improvement of his estate, without the consent of many others,

By [illegible], but inasmuch as it often happens that the estate belongs to many owners, and the [illegible] that neither can stir at all without the concurrence of his partners. In many manors, the tenant cannot grant leases beyond a short term of years, which renders all solid improvement impracticable. In these cases, the owner wants sufficient power over the soil for its perfect cultivation. This ought to be given him by some easy and general law of enfranchisement and partition, which, though compulsory upon the lord, or the rest of the tenants, tenders an equitable compensation for every right, and is not more arbitrary or dangerous to property, than that which is done in the construction of roads, navigable canals, &c. in which private owners of land must accept that price for their property, which a jury may award. It may, however, be observed, that although the enclosure of wastes, &c. be generally beneficial to population, yet the enclosure of lands in tillage, in order to convert them into pastures, is as generally hurtful.

But, secondly, agriculture is discouraged by every coustitution of landed property which lets in those, who have no concern in the improvement, to a participation of the profit. This is applicable to all such customs of manors as subject the proprietor, upon the death of the lord or tenant, or the alienation of the estate, to a fine apportioned to the improved value of the land. But of all institutions thus adverse to cultivation and improvement, none is so noxious as that of tithes. When years of care and toil have matured an improvement; when the husbandman sees new crops ripening to his skill and industry; the moment he is ready to put his sickle to the grain, he finds himself compelled to divide his harvest with a stranger. Tithes are a tax not only upon industry, but upon that industry which feeds mankind; to uphold and excite which, composes the main benefit that the community receives from the whole system of trade, and the success of commerce. And, together with their more general inconveniency there is this additional evil, that they operate as a bounty upon pasturage. The burthen of the tax falls with its chief weight, upon tillage; that mode of cultivation which it is the business of the state to relieve and remunerate, in preference to every other. No single alteration appears so beneficial, as the conversion of tithes into corn-rents. This commutation might be so adjusted, as to secure to the tithe-holder a complete equivalent for his interest, and leave to industry its full operation, and reward.

CHAP. XII.

OF WAR, AND OF MILITARY ESTABLISHMENTS.

Q. Because the Christian Scriptures describe wars, as what they are, as crimes or judgments, what have some been led to believe?

A. That it is unlawful for a Christian to bear arms.

Q. But what should be remembered?

A. That it may be necessary for individuals to unite their force, and for this end to resign themselves to the direction of a common will; and yet that will is often actuated by criminal motives, and determined to destructive purposes. Hence, although the origin of wars be ascribed, in the gospel, to the operation of lawless and malignant passions; and though war itself be enumerated among the direst calamities, the profession of a soldier is no where forbidden or condemned. When the soldiers demanded of John the Baptist what they should do, he said unto them, "Do violence to no man, neither accuse any falsely, and be content with your wages." In which answer we only find that is was required of soldiers to beware of the vices of which this profession was accused. The precept, "Be content with your wages," supposing them to continue in their situation. The first Gentile convert who was received into the Christian Church, held the same station; and we discover not the smallest intimation, that Cornelius, upon becoming a Christian, quitted the service of the Roman legion; or that his profession was objected to.

Q. In applying the principles of morality to the affairs of nations, whence does the difficulty which meets us, arise?

A. From hence; "that the particular consequence sometimes appears to exceed the value of the general rule." "In private transactions, no advantage that results from the breach of a general law of justice, can compensate the public for the violation of the law; in the concerns of empire, this may sometimes be doubted. Thus, that the faith of promises ought to be maintained, whatever inconveniency either party may suffer by his fidelity, in the intercourse of private life, is seldom disputed; because the common happiness gains more by the preservation of the rule, than it could do by the removal of the inconveniency. But when the adherence to a public treaty would enslave a whole people; would block up seas, depopulate cities, &c. the magnitude of the particular evil calls in question the obligation of the general rule.

Q. Does Moral Philosophy furnish any precise solution to these doubts?

A. No: she cannot pronounce any rule of morality so rigid as to bend to no exceptions; nor can she comprise these exceptions within any previous description. She confesses that the obligation of every law depends upon its ultimate utility; that, this having a finite and determinate value, situations may possibly arise, in which the general tendency is outweighed by the particular mischief: but she recalls to our consideration the vast importance, as of other general rules of relative justice, so especially of national and personal fidelity; the extent of mischief which must follow from the want of it; the danger of leaving it to the sufferer to decide upon the comparison of particular [illegible] and the [illegible] being drawn into [illegible], we no longer [illegible] them while they are convenient; or if such [illegible] by examples, come to [illegible] the only method of averting or [illegible] the calamities of war, is lost to the world [illegible]. It is not said that no evil can [illegible] any possible advantage compensate [illegible] will scarcely be [illegible] of human happiness by [illegible] that can be preferred to a single [illegible] a proportion [illegible].

Q. As in [illegible] it is found [illegible] to ascertain every duty by an immediate [illegible] to public [illegible] and as certain [illegible] constitutions are wont to be established in every society, which become as [illegible] as the original principles of natural justice; so, likewise, it is between independent communities. Together with those maxims of universal equity common to states and to individuals, and by which the rights and conduct of the one as well as the other ought to be adjusted, what also exists amongst [illegible]?

A. A system of artificial jurisprudence, under the name of the *law of nations*.

Q. In this code what are found?

A. The rules which determine the right to newly discovered countries; those which relate to the protection of fugitives, the condition and duties of neutrality, the immunities of neutral ships and ports, the distinction between free and contraband goods, and a variety of subjects of the same kind.

Q. Concerning which examples, and the principal part of what is called the *jus gentium*, what may be observed?

A. That the rules derive their moral force, not from their internal reasonableness or justice, for many are arbitrary, nor yet from any authority; for the greater part have grown insensibly into usage, without any public compact, or known original; but simply from the fact of their being established, and the general duty of conforming to established rules, where nothing else can prevent disputes, and these dangerous ones. When we reflect that the claims to newly-discovered countries can hardly be settled without some positive rule or other; that such claims, if left unsettled, would prove sources of fatal contentions; that the rule already proposed, however arbitrary, possesses one principal quality of a rule,—determination and certainty; above all, that it is acquiesced in, and that no one has power to substitute, though he might contrive a better: when we reflect upon these properties of the rule, or rather upon these consequences of rejecting its authority, we ascribe to it the virtue and obligation of a precept of natural justice, perceiving in it that which is the foundation of justice itself,—public importance and utility. And a prince who should dispute this rule, for the want of regularity in its formation, or of in-

overplus justice in its principle, would be little less criminal than he who breaks the public peace by a violation of engagements to which he had himself consented, or by an attack upon those national rights which are founded immediately in the law of nature, and in the first perceptions of equity.

Q. How may war be considered?

A. With a view to its causes and to its conduct.

Q. What are the *justifying* causes of war?

A. Deliberate invasions of right, and the necessity of maintaining such a balance of power, as that no single state, or confederacy of states, be strong enough to overwhelm the rest. The objects of just war are, precaution, defence, or reparation. In a larger sense, every just war is a defensive war, as it supposes an injury perpetrated, attempted, or feared.

Q. What are the insufficient causes or unjustifiable motives of war?

A. The family alliances, personal friendships, or personal quarrels, of princes; internal disputes carried on in other nations; the justice of other wars; the extension of territory, or of trade; the misfortunes or accidental weakness of a neighbouring or rival nation.

Q. There are two lessons of rational and sober policy, which, if inculcated into the councils of princes, would exclude many of the motives of war, and allay restless ambition. What are the [illegible] of these [illegible] princes?

A. To place their glory and emulation, not in

extent of territory; but in raising the greatest quantity of happiness out of a given territory. Enlargement of territory by conquest is not only not a just object of war, but generally not even desirable. It is certainly not so, where it adds nothing to the numbers, enjoyments, or security, of the conquerors. What commonly is gained to a nation, by the subjugation of other countries, but a wider frontier to defend; more quarrels, enemies and rebellions to encounter; a greater force to keep up by sea and land; and more establishments to keep up? Thus the provinces are oppressed, in order to pay for being ill-governed; and the original state is exhausted in maintaining a feeble authority over discontented subjects. Or if the grandeur of the prince were magnified by these exploits; the glory which is purchased, and the ambition which is gratified, by the distress of one country without adding to the happiness of another, ought to be an object of universal execration; and oftentimes not more so to the vanquished, than to the very people who have achieved the victory.

Q. There are, indeed, two cases in which the extension of territory may be of real advantage, and to both parties. What are these?

A. The first is, where an empire thereby reaches to the natural boundaries which divide it from the rest of the world. Thus we account the British Channel the natural boundary which separates England and France; and if France possessed any cities or provinces on this, or England on that side [illegible] [illegible] [illegible] to what way [illegible] [illegible] [illegible], though it may [illegible] [illegible] [illegible] [illegible], whilst the people are drunk with victory. The other case included is, where neighbouring states, being severally too small and weak to defend themselves against the dangers that surround them, can only be safe by a strict and constant junction of their strength: here conquest will effect the purposes of confederation and alliance; and the union which it produces is often more close and permanent than that which results from voluntary association.

Q. What is the second rule of prudence recommended to those who conduct the affairs of nations?

A. "Never to pursue national *honour* as distinct from national *interest*." This rule acknowledges that it is often necessary to assert the honour of a nation for the sake of its interest. The spirit and courage of a people are supported by flattering their pride. Concessions which betray a consciousness of fear or weakness, though in points of mere ceremony, invite demands and attacks of more serious importance. The rule allows all this; and only directs that, when points of honour become subjects of contention, or are likely to be made occasions of war, they be estimated with a reference to utility, and not by *themselves*. "The dignity of his crown, the honour of his flag, the glory of his arms," in the mouth of a prince are imposing terms; but the ideas they inspire are insatiable. The pursuit of honour, when set loose from [illegible] [illegible] [illegible] justified, because it is simple, a wild and romantic passion, eager to engage, and gathering fury in its progress; it forgets or despises those considerations of safety, ease, and plenty, which, in the eye of true public wisdom, compose the objects to which the renown of arms, and fame of victory, are only instrumental and subordinate. The pursuit of interest, on the other hand, is a sober principle; computes costs and consequences; and is cautious of entering into war; when regulated by the universal maxims of relative justice, it is the right principle for nations to proceed by; even when it trespasses upon these regulations, it is much less dangerous, because much more temperate, than the other.

Q. II. What does Paley observe on the conduct of war?

A. If the cause and end of war be justifiable; all the means that appear necessary to the end, are justifiable also. This is the principle which defends those extremities to which the violence of war usually proceeds: for since war is a contest by force between the parties who acknowledge no common superior, and includes not the supposition of any convention which should place limits to the operations of force, it has naturally no boundary but the destruction of the life against which the force is directed.

Q. What however must be remembered here?

A. That the licence of war authorises no acts of hostility but what are necessary or conducive to the end and object of the war. Gratuitous bar-

but it is bound to no extremities from this plea, such as appear plainly inadequate to the sufferings, nor tending [illegible] of an enemy, without weakening his strength, or tending to procure his submission; such as the slaughter of captives, the subjecting them to indignities or torture, the violation of women, &c. &c.; which enormities are prohibited by the law of nature itself; as having no proper tendency to accomplish the object of the war; and as containing that which in peace and war is equally unjustifiable,—ultimate and gratuitous mischief.

Q. What may be observed with regard to other restrictions imposed upon the conduct of war, not by the law of nature primarily, but by the laws of war first, and by the law of nature as seconding and ratifying them?

A. The laws of war are part of the law of nations, and founded, as to their authority, upon the same principle; namely, upon the fact of their being established, upon the expectation of their being mutually observed in consequence, and upon the general utility which results from such observance. The binding force of these rules is the greater, because the regard that is paid to them must be universal or none. The breach of the rule can only be punished by the subversion of the rule itself: on which account, the whole mischief that ensues is justly chargeable upon the first aggressor. To this, may be referred the duty of refraining in war from poison and assassination. If the laws of nature simply be consulted, it may be difficult to distinguish between these different methods of destruction, practised without scruple. That if it be lawful to kill an enemy at all, it seems lawful to do so by one way as well as by another; by a dose of poison, as by the point of a sword; for if it be said that one species of assault leaves him the power of defending himself against it, and that the other does not; it may be answered, that we possess at least the same right to cut off an enemy's defence, as to seek his destruction. Thus might the question be debated, if there existed no rule or law of war upon the subject. But when we observe that such practices are at present excluded by the usage of civilized nations; that the first recourse to them would be followed by instant retaliation; which example would fill both sides with the misery of continual dread, without adding to the strength or success of either; that when the example came to be more general, it would probably aggravate the horrors and calamities of war, yet procure no superiority to any engaged in it; when we view these effects, we join in the public reprobation of such fatal expedients, as of the admission of new and enormous evils without necessity or advantage. The law of nature, we see at length, forbids these innovations, as so many transgressions of a beneficial general rule actually subsisting.

[illegible]

[illegible]

Mr. Wyndham [illegible] remark concerning the appointment of a standing army [illegible] experience seems to have [illegible]

[illegible] by [illegible] and [illegible] is augmented by novelty and [illegible] possible that [illegible] with a great [illegible] it is also true that any [illegible] little and little to the habits of [illegible]

[illegible] produce [illegible] to repel [illegible] [illegible] [illegible] country. [illegible] acknowledged superiority [illegible] among [illegible]

4. Not only that it is [illegible] troops, while [illegible] also the regular [illegible] public service [illegible] [illegible] [illegible] the principal [illegible] soldier [illegible] and for the business of regular occupation. Of [illegible] capable [illegible] himself entirely [illegible] [illegible] constantly at home; [illegible] those should quit the avocations of the camp with the business of husbandry. By the former arrangement, the country gains one complete soldier, and two industrious husbandmen; from the latter, it receives three raw militia-men, who are at the same [illegible] and profligate peasants. [illegible] it may be [illegible] from the fields [illegible] [illegible]

[illegible] in [illegible] of [illegible] of a nation,—its stock of productive industry.

Q. What other [illegible]?

A. When the state relies [illegible] [illegible] Now it appears doubtful whether [illegible] can be long secure, where the people [illegible] with the use of arms, and [illegible] to them. Every faction will find [illegible] of an army, any degree, will [illegible] and become a civil war. Nothing [illegible] an army, a despotism. Not that a regular government would become despotic, by [illegible] subjects to the [illegible] of arms, [illegible] ere long be forced [illegible] in some other shape; and that the people [illegible] liable [illegible] constitutional [illegible] and revolutions; to short and violent usurpations; to the successive tyranny of governors, rendered cruel and jealous by the danger and instability of their situation.

Q. What do the same purposes of strength and efficiency which make a standing army necessary at all, make it necessary, in mixed governments?

A. That this army be under the management and direction of the prince: for however well a popular council may be qualified for the offices of legislation, it is unfit for the conduct of war: in which success usually depends upon vigour, enterprize, secrecy, unanimity, &c. also the government of an army should be as prompt and active as possible; for which reason it ought to be under an obedience of will and emulation. Hence the expediency of leaving to the prince not only the government of the army, but the appointment and promotion of its officers: because a design is then alone likely to be executed with zeal and fidelity, when the person who issues the order, chooses the instruments, and rewards the service. Besides in a constitution like ours, if the direction and officering of the army were in the hands of the democratic part, this power, added to what they already possess, would so overbalance all that would be left of regal prerogative, that little would remain of monarchy but the name and expense; nor would these probably remain long.

Q. Whilst we describe, however, the advantages of standing armies, we must not conceal the danger. Whence does this arise?

A. From these properties of their constitution, —the soldiery being separated from the rest of the community, their being closely linked amongst themselves by habits of society and subordination, and the dependency of the whole chain upon the will and favour of the prince; which give them an aspect in no wise favourable to public liberty.

Q. How is the danger, however, diminished?

A. By maintaining on all occasions, as much alliance of interest, and as much intercourse of sentiment, between the military part of the nation and the other orders, as are consistent with the union and discipline of an army. For which purpose, officers should be taken from the principal families of the country, as well as be admitted to seats in the senate, to hereditary distinctions, and to all civil honours and privileges compatible with their profession: which circumstances of connexion and situation will give them such a share in the general rights of the people, and so engage their inclinations on the side of public liberty, as to afford a reasonable security that they cannot be brought, by any promises of personal aggrandisement, to assist in any measures which might enslave their posterity, their kindred and country.

THE END.

Printed by T. C. Newby, Bury St. Edmunds.

www.ingramcontent.com/pod-product-compliance
Lightning Source LLC
Chambersburg PA
CBHW080328170426
43194CB00014B/2494

* 9 7 8 1 5 3 5 8 0 0 6 9 3 *